Essential
Finance

OTHER ECONOMIST BOOKS

Guide to Analysing Companies
Guide to Business Modelling
Guide to Economic Indicators
Guide to the European Union
Guide to Financial Markets
Guide to Management Ideas
Numbers Guide
Style Guide

Business Ethics
China's Stockmarket
Economics
E-Commerce
E-Trends
Globalisation
Measuring Business Performance
Successful Innovation
Successful Mergers
Wall Street

Dictionary of Business
Dictionary of Economics
International Dictionary of Finance

Essential Director
Essential Internet
Essential Investment

Pocket Asia
Pocket Europe in Figures
Pocket World in Figures

Essential

Finance

Nigel Gibson

THE ECONOMIST IN ASSOCIATION WITH
PROFILE BOOKS LTD

Published by Profile Books Ltd
58A Hatton Garden, London EC1N 8LX

Developed from a title previously published as *Pocket Finance*

Designed and typeset in EcoType by MacGuru Ltd
info@macguru.org.uk

Printed in Italy by Legoprint – S.p.a. – Lavis (TN)

A CIP catalogue record for this book is available
from the British Library

ISBN 1 86197 530 9

Contents

Introduction

Essential Finance is one of a series of *Economist* books that brings clarity to complicated areas of business, finance and management. It is a guide to the increasingly complex world of money, financial markets and the things that revolve around them. It owes much to the entertaining and often irreverent guides to banks, bankers and international finance written over the years by Tim Hindle, a former finance editor and currently business features editor of *The Economist*.

An introductory essay examines the changing face of markets: how stocks and bonds have become more important as sources of finance for companies, how financial institutions have expanded not just in size but also across borders and in the kinds of business they do. The complexity of corporate deals and the speed with which huge amounts of money are moved today have undoubtedly increased the volatility of markets and the risks for investors, risks that are at the same time made worse and spread by the use of derivatives (futures, options and the like).

Following the essay is an extensive A to Z of terms widely used by those in finance and banking. Often the terms have different meanings even for those within the same arcane world. In this section words in SMALL CAPITALS usually indicate a separate and sometimes related entry (although abbreviations such as EU also appear in the same form).

Nigel Gibson
March 2003

The changing face of markets

If Rip Van Winkle had gone to sleep in the early 1970s and woken up 30 years later, he would recognise little of today's financial landscape. True, there are companies with shareholders, and banks and stock exchanges; and there are still plenty of lawyers and bankers who help to transfer money from one pocket to another so that companies can raise the finance they need and business may be done. But the way the money is raised and the speed with which it is done have changed virtually beyond recognition. Thirty years ago, banks were still the main source of finance for most big companies, especially in Japan and continental Europe.

Today, for the most part, banks play second fiddle to the equity and bond markets for big companies; even in Germany and Japan, the part played by banks has diminished. Equity and bond markets have become more international and have extended their influence in ways that would have been unimaginable 30 years ago.

Compared with their counterparts of even a decade ago, today's financial institutions are not only more diverse, both geographically and in terms of their businesses, they are also better capitalised. In 1990, the biggest financial firms were commercial banks, most of them Japanese, whose main function was the taking of deposits and the making of loans. At that time, banks in continental Europe were typically engaged in a broader range of activities than their US counterparts which, under the Glass-Steagall Act, since repealed, had to choose between commercial banking, investment banking and specialist financial services such as insurance.

Nowadays, by far the largest firms are financial-services conglomerates. These combine commercial banking with a range of other financial services, such as underwriting bond and equity issues and advising on mergers and acquisitions. They also provide consumer finance and sell on loans to other investors, for example, by arranging syndicates, buying and selling derivatives, and issuing securities backed by mortgages, credit-card receivables and the like. In 1990, the list of the top 15 financial firms by market capitalisation (as compiled by Morgan Stanley Capital International) was dominated by Japanese banks, the largest of which had a stockmarket capitalisation of $57 billion. A decade later, partly because of a spate of mergers among such firms, international financial-services groups took up most of the places; and the biggest (Citigroup) was then capitalised at more than $250 billion.

The sheer size of the conglomerates has undoubtedly helped them to withstand the shocks that have beset the banking system since the dotcom boom turned to bust and stockmarkets began to slide. Between 1998 and 2001, according to the Federal Reserve, America's central bank, telecommunications firms worldwide alone borrowed around $1 trillion. Many of these loans have since had to be written off because their borrowers went bankrupt. In quick succession in the United States, Enron, WorldCom, Global Crossing and others collapsed. Yet in contrast to previous setbacks following similar bouts of overexuberance and overinvestment, banks were able to continue lending to companies that needed money. The growth of sophisticated debt markets also helped to reduce companies' reliance on bank credit and equity to finance their operations. As a result, the US economy in particular was able to maintain a faster pace of growth than many had feared.

That J.P. Morgan Chase was able to absorb the billions of dollars in losses that resulted from the collapse at the end of 2001 of Enron, an energy-trading company, speaks volumes not just about the size of J.P. Morgan Chase's balance sheet, but also about its ability to spread the risk by selling derivatives to other investors. In the 1980s, a loss on the scale of Enron, then one of the world's biggest companies, might have toppled Texas's banking system. In the event, Texas was spared by the deregulation of state banking laws that subsequently took place, which allowed J.P. Morgan Chase (itself an amalgam of two big banking groups) to buy Texas Commerce Bank, one of Enron's biggest lenders.

It is true that banks have successfully shifted a large proportion of their risk on to others, and this has helped them to withstand a welter of shocks internationally. But are banks really as adept at diversifying this risk as they like to think? Are those to whom they are passing the risk capable of managing it, particularly if markets remain volatile? In short, could the shift from a system reliant on banks to one based largely on markets contain dangers of its own?

Insurers at risk

One worry is that insurance companies – not always the most sophisticated of investors – have taken on part of the risk that banks and other intermediaries in the financial markets are shedding. Swiss Re and Munich Re, two of the world's biggest insurers, between them account for a large proportion of credit derivatives outstanding. Credit derivatives are securities that allow banks to pass on to other investors the risk that some of their borrowers will default. Insurance companies have also been big buyers of asset-backed securities, financial instruments backed by pools of loans and other forms of debt. If insurance companies were unable to meet their liabilities and went bust, there is a danger that the problems would rebound on the banks.

Another worry is that, with fewer and larger international banks, the pressure to succeed on even the best-managed banks may reach a point where they make mistakes on a colossal scale. Consolidation also brings dangers of its own. Take the foreign-exchange markets. In 1995, 20 banks in the United States accounted for 75% of foreign exchange traded; six years later, the number was down to 13. Liquidity, argue some, is a function not just of the size of the market but also of the diversity of opinion of those trading within it. Moreover, financial institutions increasingly use the same models for assessing and managing risk. So when one decides to move, generally they all move. As the deals become bigger and the stakes higher, observers worry that a sudden loss of liquidity or a shock on the scale of the terrorist attacks of September 11th 2001 could cause a black hole to open up. If it does, the risk is that even sound companies could be sucked into it.

There have already been a few close calls. From 1997, commercial banks have been permitted to use so-called value-at-risk (VAR) models to calculate the amount of capital they are required to hold under the Basel rules on liquidity, so-called because they were devised by the Bank for International Settlements, which has its headquarters in Basel. Drawn up by the Basel Committee on Banking Supervision, a body that includes representatives from the world's main central banks, the new rules were designed to make banks more sensitive to market risk while at the same time giving them greater flexibility in running their businesses.

The new system did not have to wait long for its first test. In 1998, the financial markets were jolted first by Russia's decision to default on its external debt, and then by the near collapse of Long Term Capital Management (LTCM), a US hedge fund which included two Nobel Prize winners among its directors as well as heavyweights on Wall Street. Hedge funds are largely unregulated investment funds that take big (and risky) positions in the financial markets, often on exchange or interest rates. In this case, LTCM bet wrongly that the prices of certain securities would move closer together; instead, they drifted apart. Required to put up more money by the institutions with which it had contracts, the fund became overstretched and eventually had to be bailed out by a group of banks gathered together by the Federal Reserve.

Some observers fret that regulations based on VAR models contribute to the volatility of financial markets by leading to a vicious circle, in which traders are forced to reduce their positions in the market in order to put up fresh money, which puts renewed pressure on prices, and so on. In other words, the VAR rules make an old problem worse by forcing participants to get out of the market when they can least afford to, and by forcing banks to reduce their lending when borrowers most need it.

Two recent studies suggest that these fears may be exaggerated. The first, by Philippe Jorion, a professor of finance at the University of California, found that financial markets have been no more volatile since the introduction of derivatives. Moreover, says Jorion, VAR rules should not be viewed as a panacea for market ills. "They provide no guarantee that market losses will not occur," he says. Indeed, there is evidence that, far from exacerbating a fall in prices, derivatives help to stabilise markets by spreading risk. The second study, by Alain Chaboud and Steven Weinberg of the US Federal Reserve, looked at the foreign-exchange markets. It found no evidence that electronic trading and the growing use of derivatives had made the markets more volatile, or that liquidity had been drained away from them because of the growing use of electronic trading. So far, so good. The study did concede, however, that the use of trading platforms that connect the ultimate customer more directly with the dealer in foreign exchange, reducing still further the role of intermediaries, may bring more volatility.

If so, the stakes are high. Until the Bretton Woods agreement, a post-war attempt to stabilise international finance, was dismantled in the early 1970s, fixed exchange rates were the norm. Today it is hard to think of a developed country that does not allow its exchange rate to float or, as with the euro, is linked to one that does. At the touch of a keypad, trillions of dollars-worth of foreign currencies routinely change hands every day, much of it in the form of obligations traded as derivatives.

Thirty years ago, markets of this size and scope would have been unimaginable. In the days of fixed exchange rates, the market for foreign exchange was a servant of trade, easing the exchange of goods across borders. Today, as services become more important in international trade, the value of foreign currencies changing hands each day far exceeds the value of the goods being shipped from producer to user.

The first truly electronic services for dealing in foreign exchange were launched by Reuters in the early 1980s. The first systems allowed brokers to communicate directly, but did not simultaneously match different counterparties, as had been done over the telephone. That came in the early 1990s, when Reuters launched a version which automatically matched buy and sell orders from anonymous dealers. Nowadays, dealers exchange over $4 trillion-worth of foreign currency a day, the bulk of it over two electronic systems. One concentrates on transactions in dollars and Japanese yen, the other on sterling, the euro and the currencies of emerging markets.

International equity

Stockmarkets have also been undergoing dramatic change, most of which has involved becoming more international. In 1999, at least one out of every six deals done on stockmarkets involved a foreign buyer or seller – a far cry from the situation not much more than a decade ago. In the mid-1980s, Salomon Brothers, an investment bank, estimated that 99% of the world's trading in equities was done on the exchange where the shares had their primary listing. Of course, a proportion of those who bought and sold shares then were foreign investors, but the number has since grown substantially.

The New York Stock Exchange (NYSE), still the world's biggest, led the way towards a more international world. It did this through the introduction of American Depositary Receipts (ADRs), which enabled domestic investors to buy the shares of foreign companies with US dollars, and later by attracting a growing number of foreign companies to list their shares on the exchange. But the prize for internationalism must go to the London Stock Exchange. According to figures compiled by the World Federation of Exchanges, London accounted for more than half of the worldwide trade in foreign equities in 2002, compared with a combined share of 25% for the NYSE and NASDAQ, America's main exchange for trading in the shares of technology companies.

London is also the international centre for another market that has mushroomed over the years: the derivatives market. Derivatives are financial instruments that are "derived" from another, for example, an option to buy a Treasury bond. The value of the option depends on the performance of the under-lying instrument, in this case a Treasury bond. This can be taken a stage further: for example, an option on a futures con-tract. The value of the option depends on the price of the futures contract, which, in turn, will vary with the value of the underlying instrument.

Although the term derivative was little used until the 1980s, the practice of trading forward (which is what a derivative does) to mitigate the effects of risk has been a part of dealing in physical commodities for centuries. It has been claimed that forward trading began in Roman times, that Japanese rice traders first exchanged contracts for future delivery in the 17th century and that its origins can be traced back to Amsterdam and London's Royal Exchange a century earlier. Whatever the truth, it is beyond dispute that, in 1865, the Chicago Board of Trade shaped the first grain futures contract. Thirteen years later, the London Metal Exchange and the London Corn Trade Association followed with their own futures contracts. Such contracts were developed to protect traders from unknown but expected risks in the future: in the case of grain, the vagaries of the weather and an uncertain transport system.

During the past decade or so, the growth of trading in derivatives on organised exchanges has been brisk. Fastest growing have been derivatives of financial instruments tied to currencies and exchange rates, interest rates and equities. Since 1995 alone, the number of contracts of this kind traded on exchanges worldwide has increased two and a half times. Despite increases in other markets, particularly in South Korea, US exchanges still account for the lion's share of the business, around 35% of all contracts traded. Together, European exchanges are not far behind.

Over the counter

Yet even growth on this scale is dwarfed by the speed with which trading of financial instruments over the counter (OTC), that is, directly between institutions, has galloped ahead. According to the Bank for International Settlements, which tracks such things, in 2001 the average daily turnover of OTC trading in derivatives worldwide was more than $760 billion, five times the level of trading on recognised exchanges throughout the world. Of this, about one-third was centred on London, the leader by far in OTC trading of this kind.

One reason for the growth in OTC trading is the surge in demand for interest-rate products of one sort or another. The repayment of US government debt during the Clinton administration reduced the liquidity of long-term government bonds, forcing banks and other financial institutions to look for other ways of hedging their risks in the financial markets. Interest-rate derivatives, in particular swaps traded directly between banks and other institutions, seemed to fit the bill. Swaps are transactions in which two parties (say, a bank and a securities house) exchange financial assets and the interest payments due on them, the idea being, of course, that both parties should benefit from the transaction. In the case of an interest-rate swap, a borrower who has raised, say, Swiss francs will exchange the interest payments on the loan with those of another borrower who may have raised, for example, dollars.

Another influence on OTC trading was the introduction of the euro, the new currency that came into circulation in 12 European countries at the beginning of 2002, replacing old stalwarts such as the Deutschemark, French franc, Italian lira and Spanish peseta. Financial institutions began trading in notional euros in 1999, and euro-denominated swaps quickly became a new benchmark for buyers and sellers of fixed-income instruments throughout Europe as the market for corporate debt in euros developed.

With much of their currency and interest-rate risk eliminated by the introduction of the euro, financial institutions needed a tool with which to reduce the remaining credit risk (the chance that borrowers might renege on their debts). Credit derivatives – a way of laying off risk to other investors until the loan matures – became just such an instrument. Turnover in credit derivatives remains small compared with that of interest-rate contracts, but it is growing fast. The British Bankers' Association reckons that in early 2002 London accounted for around half the expanding activity in credit derivatives, and that the market had increased no less than eight times since 1997.

At the heart of any market is the free flow of information, which is why, according to Alan Greenspan, veteran chairman of the Federal Reserve, credit derivatives have proved so successful. They not only allow bank treasurers to lay off part of their risk, by reflecting the probability of default in the price; they also make the jobs of banks' loan officers a lot easier. In the past, banks relied largely on their own credit analysis (together with what market information they could glean) to tell them whether a borrower was likely to default. Since the advent of credit derivatives, they have been able to judge from the price of a derivative the probability of a net loss in the underlying loan.

But what about the dangers to those, such as insurance companies, which pick up the risks? Some insurers promised guaranteed returns to their customers during the boom years of the 1990s, only to find that, because falling stockmarkets had reduced the value of their assets and depleted their reserves, they were unable to fulfil their promises. To make up the income they have lost, insurers have been big buyers of credit derivatives and asset-backed securities, which have a higher yield and so are often riskier than other investments.

Observers fret that the banking system may be storing up problems for itself through the wholesale transfer of risk to insurers and other investors. Indeed, some insurance companies are owned by banks. A number of Japanese insurers have gone bust in recent years because they were unable to meet guaranteed payments to their policyholders, and others have not been allowed to go bust because of the threat it would pose to the banking system. Because of falling stockmarkets, many more insurers around the world have been forced to increase penalties to savers for withdrawing their money, thus helping to shore up their own balance sheets.

Insurance companies are carrying another burden too. During the boom years of the 1990s many insurers, particularly life companies, relied too heavily on equities. Many UK insurers held as much as four-fifths of their assets in shares, or at one point about 20% of all domestic equities traded on the London stockmarket. When the markets began to slide, the companies were forced to sell. After a while, the sales become self-fulfilling. The more equities tumble in value, the more the insurance companies have to sell in order to meet the levels of free capital demanded by regulators. Regulators have already had to be lenient in the way they apply their rules.

Back-scratching

It is not surprising that greater internationalisation has encouraged demands for closer co-operation between regulators in different countries and in different industries. It is an irony that a country with one of the most sophisticated financial systems, the United States, also has one of the most fragmented systems of regulation. While other countries moved during the late

1990s to reduce the number of regulatory bodies – the UK, for example, has a single omnipotent Financial Services Authority – the United States has been reluctant to tamper with the jurisdictions held by such bodies as the Federal Reserve, the Securities and Exchange Commission (SEC) and the Commodity Futures Trading Commission. As a result, duplication among agencies abounds.

Nevertheless, there is little doubt that regulators, particularly those that preside over the world's most sophisticated financial centres, are now co-operating much more than they used to even a decade ago. Although no single regulator oversees the giants of international finance (nor perhaps is one ever likely to), such firms are watched closely wherever they trade in the developed world. The key to effective regulation and smooth-running financial markets is transparency as well as the free flow of information.

One hope is that the improved regulation of banks will provide early warning of dangers. Under the Basel rules of the 1980s, banks have had to link the amount of capital they must hold to the level of risk carried by the loans they make. This sounds fine in principle but does not always work in practice. Critics claim that the system is too crude: banks have to set aside as much capital for a loan to General Electric as they do to a hotelier in Poland. Basel 2, a more sophisticated version of the rules, is being drawn up by the central banks of the developed world. It would cover many more banks worldwide. Yet central bankers have found it difficult to agree on the scope of the new rules and how they should be applied. For example, some want more leeway for banks lending mainly to small businesses because, in theory, the risks are fewer. Originally planned for 2004, the introduction of Basel 2, as the new rules are known, has been delayed until 2006, and even that may be in doubt.

Better regulation of banks may reduce the chances of a collapse in the financial system, but should regulators also be thinking about ways of preventing the investment bubbles that lead to capital being misallocated in the first place? Until the dotcom bubble burst, the answer was invariably no. Advocates of efficient market theory argued that the system was inherently self-correcting. In efficient markets, prices are assumed to

reflect fundamental values and to price in all available information. If ill-informed investors move prices away from their true
value, informed ones will simply arbitrage them back again.

Purists believe that if share prices rise to a level for which
there is no obvious explanation, then investors will conclude
that there is another less obvious explanation, such as the dawn
of a new age of productivity or, as dotcom enthusiasts believed
at the time, a "new economic paradigm". What believers will
not conclude, at least until after it has burst, is that a bubble
exists – which, of course, is both irrational and inefficient.

Many observers would like to see the Federal Reserve and
other central banks attempt to control not just the level of inflation, their main preoccupation, but asset prices too. They argue
that the costs of pricking an inflating bubble – possibly recession, deflation or sometimes a combination of the two – out-
weigh the risks of raising interest rates pre-emptively to prevent
a bubble forming. After all, argue interventionists, history is lit-
tered with examples of the results of inaction on the part of
central banks that have resulted in problems of a comparable
magnitude; for example, Japan's prolonged period of economic
stagnation and occasional deflation following the bursting of its
own asset-price bubble in the early 1990s.

The danger, of course, is that when a bubble does burst, its
impact can be far-reaching, not just on the financial markets but
also on the underlying economy. The wealth effect, which helps
to boost consumers' confidence and so propel share prices ever
higher when markets are rising, also works in reverse. Equally
damaging can be the sudden loss of confidence produced by a
realisation on the part of investors, particularly private ones,
that they have been duped.

Revelations in 2002 by Eliot Spitzer, the crusading attorney-
general of New York State, that investment banks on Wall Street
had routinely touted shares in public which they privately believed to have been "junk" had a predictable result. Aggrieved
that they had been misled when they bought the shares of companies seeking initial public offerings during the heady days of
the technology boom, investors called their lawyers and sued. It
was not so much the knowledge that investment banks suffered
from conflicts of interest – Wall Street has long had to balance

its own interests with those of its clients – but the blatant way in which the abuses had occurred.

The revelations cast doubt not just on the legitimacy of Chinese walls, the ability of investment banks to separate one function from another and therefore the interests of different clients, but also on the role of the securities analyst, the individual whose job it is to analyse the businesses of individual companies and to put a value on their shares. For years investors had taken what analysts write with a pinch of salt because, after all, they are often part of investment-banking teams that advise companies on (lucrative) acquisitions, mergers and the like. But the degree to which investment research had become the handmaiden of investment banking shocked many of them. Investors were also surprised by the extent to which the directors of big companies had been handed perks (often by giving them priority in share issues that they could later sell at a hefty profit) in return for investment-banking mandates and other advisory work.

Litigation between the banks, investors and bodies such as the National Association of Securities Dealers, the regulator of NASDAQ, is likely to rumble on for years. However, the combined fine of nearly $1 billion that Spitzer levied on a group of Wall Street's largest investment banks, together with $500m or so to sponsor independent research and to educate investors, should encourage higher standards of integrity and professionalism among investment bankers.

Some investment banks have taken the precaution of casting off their research staff into separate companies with their own management. But research on its own rarely pays, at least not well enough to cover the multimillion-dollar bonuses that star analysts came to expect during the boom years. Many observers believe that what is needed is a change of culture, not just a change in the rules. This will be hard to bring about. There are dangers, too, in trying to reverse the deregulation that has occurred, particularly the separation again of trading in equities, bonds and derivatives from the advisory work that, during good years, accounts for the lion's share of investment banks' profits.

That could change the nature of financial markets and, possibly, make them less liquid. Trading volumes could decline and, perversely, the banks' customers could also suffer because companies and investment firms might find it more expensive to hedge their risks and to react quickly enough to changes in the markets.

Credit where it is due

If nothing else, the greater degree of transparency that has been forced on companies, banks and the markets on which they both rely will provide additional safeguards for investors. Many were surprised by the failure of credit-rating agencies to spot the problems at Enron, WorldCom and others before they went bust. Such lapses raised questions about the agencies' roles in the credit markets. Their main business is rating the creditworthiness of bonds issued in the debt markets, but in the 1990s, like auditors before them, they started to stray into other, more lucrative forms of consultancy. Where did the rating agencies get their information from, how was it analysed, and are their opinions worth the paper they were then written on, asked Congress.

The loss of confidence resulting from the slew of corporate failures not only contributed to the demise of Andersen, then one of the world's oldest accounting firms. It also led to the passing of the Sarbanes-Oxley Act by Congress in 2002, an attempt to bolster standards of corporate governance in the United States and one of the toughest pieces of securities legislation to be enacted since the Great Depression of the 1930s. Wisely, Congress let the SEC, the main US regulator of securities markets, enforce the rules. Among other things, the act imposed an independent regulator on the auditing profession, in the form of the Public Company Accounting Oversight Board. It also banned auditors from doing some non-audit work for audit clients, thus preventing them from accepting certain types of lucrative consultancy work that might conflict with their responsibilities as auditors.

Enron was brought down by the shifting of liabilities to off-balance-sheet "special-purpose vehicles", whose existence was not disclosed to shareholders. To guard against similar abuses in future, the act requires public companies to provide details of all such entities above a certain threshold. It also tightened up the rules governing when senior executives of public companies may buy and sell shares (many directors had cashed in their options ahead of bad news, which depressed the share price); and it curtailed the use of pro-forma accounts, which exclude several inconvenient things, such as the cost of mergers, and so massage profits.

To curb the power of chief executives, who until then had reigned supreme over most public companies in the United States (partly because they invariably combine their role with that of chairman), the NYSE followed up with several measures of its own, aimed at giving shareholders more control over the companies they own. For example, all boards of companies quoted on the NYSE have to have a majority of independent members. This excludes almost anyone who has a business link with the company, from suppliers to lawyers, bankers and consultants. A better answer in the long run might be to adopt the practice long favoured by most big companies in the UK: to split the roles of chief executive and chairman.

Suspending disbelief

Will such measures restore faith in a system seen as damaged by many investors? To a degree. If shareholders (not to mention analysts and commentators) are ready to suspend disbelief when confronted by companies with inflated numbers and implausible business plans, as many did during the dotcom boom, then no amount of regulation is likely to save them. However, there is a chance that, for a time at least, the abuses that had become endemic during the 1990s will be squeezed out of the system.

For investors, the costs of failure are likely to rise, not fall, as financial institutions increase in size and the bets they make in markets become bigger. Greenspan, for one, believes that the pace of change in worldwide financial markets is accelerating, not slowing down. He thinks that the implied rewards for the risk associated with many investments all over the world suggest that global finance could yet grow to become even larger in terms of its contribution to gross domestic product than it is today. If so, central banks such as the Federal Reserve will have to keep a firmer hand on the tiller and watch out for storms.

As lenders of last resort, if no longer regulators, central bankers have to strike a delicate balance between intervening and not intervening in financial markets. In Greenspan's words: "The question is not whether our actions are seen to have been necessary in retrospect; the absence of a fire does not mean that we should not have paid the fire insurance. Rather, the question is whether, *ex ante*,[1] the possibility of a systemic collapse was sufficient to warrant an intervention. Often we cannot wait to see whether, in hindsight, the problem will be judged to have been an isolated event and largely benign."

Having encouraged the deregulation of financial markets during the heady days of the 1990s, both regulators and investors are now living with the consequences. While stockmarkets remain flat or worse and the world economy is unstable, regulators will refrain from tightening controls on investment banks to the point that they threaten their profitability. However, it is likely that such institutions and the markets from which they draw their business will continue to change, perhaps at an even faster pace than before. If so, they are likely to appear to somebody who wakens from a long, deep sleep at the end of the present decade as different as they did to our Rip Van Winkle wakening today after 30 years asleep.

---

1 As a result of something done before.

A to Z

Acceptance

A BILL OF EXCHANGE that has been endorsed by a BANK; that is, a bank has given its GUARANTEE that it will pay the bill should the buyer fail to do so. This is a time-honoured way of financing trade. An exporter whose bill is accepted by a top-rank bank can then sell the bill at a DISCOUNT in the financial markets, so improving the exporter's CASH FLOW. Or the exporter can wait until the importer's bank has remitted the funds or until the bill has matured.

Account

The balance of a customer's borrowing and lending with a BANK. This type of account can take several forms, as follows.

- **Current account.** An account on which CHEQUES can be drawn and an OVERDRAFT arranged. Current accounts do not usually pay significant amounts of INTEREST on positive balances. CHARGES are usually related to the volume of transactions, the size of the balance on the account and the type of service provided.
- **DEPOSIT account.** An account which is always kept in credit, and on which interest is paid.
- **Savings account.** An account designed specifically to assist customers to accumulate large sums by means of small, regular payments.
- **Budget account.** An account designed to help individuals make bulky, bothersome payments (like telephone or electricity bills) more smoothly. Regular payments into the account allow the account holder to borrow several times the value of each payment. Sometimes such an account is in credit; sometimes it is overdrawn. The aim, however, is that it should have the same balance at the end of the year as it has at the beginning.
- **Term account.** An account designed for savers who have spare cash and do not mind tying it up for several months or years at a time. In return, they receive a higher

A

interest rate; generally, the longer the period it is on deposit, the higher the rate is. A snag is that usually a minimum amount has to be deposited and there are often penalties for withdrawing part or all of the money early.

Although bank accounts follow a similar pattern in most developed countries, there are important variations. In France, for example, it is illegal to write a cheque without sufficient funds in an account to cover it. Those flouting the law may be banned from holding a bank account and reported to the country's CENTRAL BANK. By contrast, German banks will continue to provide cash through AUTOMATIC TELLER MACHINES even if there is not enough money in the account to cover the withdrawal. However, the interest rate charged on the amount withdrawn can be high and the account holder may suffer other penalties.

Accrual rate

The rate at which INTEREST is charged on a LOAN or MORT-GAGE. Most such rates are set directly by the market or by reference to a market INDEX, plus a margin for the lender. In the UK, the term usually applies to the rate at which a PENSION increases each year, usually expressed as a fraction. Most people are part of a one-eighth or one-sixteenth pension scheme. This means that for each year that they are in the scheme they receive one-eighth or one-sixteenth of their pensionable EARN-INGS on retirement.

Accrued interest

The INTEREST that has been earned, but not yet paid, on a BOND or LOAN. Interest on bonds is paid half yearly or sometimes quarterly. When a bond is sold, the buyer pays the seller the market price, plus the accrued interest that the buyer will receive at the end of the relevant period. Accrued interest is usually calculated on the basis of a 30-day month for CORPOR-

ATE BONDS and MUNICIPAL BONDS, but on the actual number of days in the month for government bonds.

ACH

See AUTOMATED CLEARING HOUSE.

Actual

The physical COMMODITY or SECURITY underlying a FUTURES contract. What, in other words, is delivered to the holder when the contract is completed or matures – be it a bar of GOLD or an INTEREST rate contract on a government BOND.

Actuarial surplus

See OVERFUNDING.

Actuary

A mathematician employed to calculate how much an INSURANCE company should charge to cover all sorts of RISKS, including life ASSURANCE, and how much to set aside as RESERVES just in case. Most actuaries rely on tables that set out the probability of death occurring within prescribed periods of time. This helps them to assess an insurer's potential LIABILITIES and the PREMIUMS needed to cover certain types of risk.

Adjustable-rate mortgage

A MORTGAGE with a RATE OF INTEREST that varies over time and in line with market rates. In the UK, most mortgages are adjustable-rate mortgages (ARMS) and move up or down with base rates set by the BANK OF ENGLAND. During periods of

A

low interest rates, this leads to lower costs for borrowers, but it often pushes up house prices in places where the supply is limited. House buyers in countries within the EURO zone, though fewer proportionately than in the UK, have benefited because interest rates set by the EUROPEAN CENTRAL BANK have been lower than many experienced when borrowing in their former domestic currencies. Historically, the bulk of mortgages in the United States have been at a fixed rate.

When interest rates are volatile, financial institutions sometimes get into trouble because they are unable to match their FLOATING-RATE LIABILITIES against their FIXED-RATE ASSETS. To guard against such risks, most BANKS and mortgage companies try to issue long-term BONDS that mature at the same time as the LOANS that they are granting.

Adjustable-rate note

See FLOATING-RATE NOTE.

ADR

See AMERICAN DEPOSITARY RECEIPT.

Advance/decline ratio

A measure of the difference between the number of stocks whose price is rising on a market during a given day or trading session and the number whose price is falling. In the United States, when this difference or ratio itself starts to decline, it is often taken as a sign that the market has peaked.

Afloats

COMMODITIES that are on board a ship, shipshape and ready to sail.

After-hours

SHARES that are bought and sold after an official STOCK EXCHANGE has closed. After-hours trades are usually treated by the exchange as having been executed on the following day. Such trades not only influence the direction of trading the following day by setting the tone for future trading; they also help to boost LIQUIDITY at the outset of trading.

Agent

An individual or firm authorised to act on behalf of another (called the PRINCIPAL) in, say, buying a house, selling a SECURITY or executing any transaction. An important distinction between agent and principal is that, unlike a DEALER, the former assumes no RISK in the transaction.

> It is well known what a middle man is:
> he is a man who bamboozles one party and plunders the other.
> Benjamin Disraeli

AIM

Short for Alternative Investment Market, the junior arm of the LONDON STOCK EXCHANGE (LSE). Launched in June 1995, the aim of the AIM was to offer small companies a cheap and less onerous path to raising CAPITAL. In that it has succeeded better than its predecessor, the Unlisted Securities Market (USM), which failed to distinguish itself sufficiently from the main market of the LSE, with the result that it was disbanded because of a lack of interest. To keep costs to a minimum, companies listed on the AIM are (lightly) regulated by DEALERS licensed to trade in their SHARES, not by the exchange itself. Such companies do not have to provide nearly as much information to investors as those listed on the main exchange.

A   Allfinanz

An Anglo-German neologism for the coming together of banking and INSURANCE services under one institutional umbrella. Many such institutions have been formed by merger or by a joint venture between a BANK and an insurance company. Some (like Deutsche Bank) started what they lacked from scratch (in this case forming an insurance company). The term has since been embraced by many companies from Ireland to New Zealand, offering everything from life ASSURANCE to tax planning.

Allotment

The amount of STOCK allocated to each participant of a SYNDI-CATE formed by an INVESTMENT BANK to underwrite and distribute a new ISSUE of SHARES. It can also be the amount of stock allocated to each subscriber when such an issue is over-subscribed.

Alpha

A mathematical estimate of the RETURN to be expected from a particular STOCK based on such things as the rate of growth of the company's EARNINGS PER SHARE. To measure the performance of a particular stock, it is assumed that the return from the market as a whole is zero. So, for example, a stock with an alpha of 1.25 would be expected to rise by 25% during a year in which the market remained flat. A share whose price is low compared with its alpha may therefore be considered good value. Alpha can also be applied to a PORTFOLIO of investments, to measure how well or badly it has done compared with how much RISK it holds. A stock with a high alpha may or may not also have a high BETA, a measure of its VOLATILITY.

Alpha stocks

The most actively traded SHARES on the London STOCKMAR-KET. All such stocks are traded under the STOCK EXCHANGE AUTOMATED QUOTATIONS (SEAQ) system, and are guaranteed continuous two-way trading by MARKET MAKERS. The number of alpha stocks may change from time to time as fashions and markets dictate. Not to be confused with ALPHA or BETA.

Alternative investment

A less obvious way of retaining value than through SECURITIES or BANK DEPOSITS: for example, works of art, coins, stamps, jewels, porcelain, vintage cars or GOLD. In the past, alternative investments have often outperformed traditional investments when INFLATION is high or rising. This is because, during such times, value is seen to attach to real things, which become a HEDGE against inflation.

American depositary receipt

A certificate issued in the United States in lieu of a foreign SE-CURITY. The underlying securities are lodged with a bank abroad, and the American depositary receipts (ADRs) are traded in the United States as if they are a domestic STOCK. Since most are owned by INSTITUTIONAL INVESTORS, one ADR may represent ten or more of the underlying foreign SHARE. DIVIDENDS are paid in dollars, so ADRs provide an easy way for US investors to hold foreign securities without having to leave their shores and without the headache of dealing in and out of foreign currencies. Sponsored ADRs are offered with the full support of the company whose shares underlie them, so they usually carry the full voting rights of a common share. Unsponsored ADRs are issued opportunistically by a BROKER, DEALER or depository BANK without the backing of the company and may therefore have restricted rights.

A

An increasing number of companies now list their shares directly on US exchanges, but this is expensive. Furthermore, the SECURITIES AND EXCHANGE COMMISSION requires companies to report their EARNINGS quarterly and to disclose more information than most are obliged to at home, so ADRs remain a popular way of attracting US investors. The idea of ADRs has since been extended to global depositary receipts, which are traded OVER THE COUNTER in the United States and the EURO-MARKETS, and European depositary receipts, which are traded on recognised exchanges in Paris and Frankfurt.

American Stock Exchange

The second largest STOCK EXCHANGE in the United States after the NEW YORK STOCK EXCHANGE (NYSE). Also based in New York, the American Stock Exchange concentrates on the SHARES of small and medium-sized companies unable to justify the expense of a LISTING on the NYSE. Amex, as it is commonly known, traces its origins back to the trading of SECURITIES on street corners during the 19th century, from which came its other name, the Kerb Exchange, which was officially dropped in the 1950s. Although it has tried to be innovative – for example, in pioneering EXCHANGE-TRADED FUNDS, for which it is still a big market – Amex has been squeezed in recent years by its main rivals. So much so that in 1998 it was taken over by NASDAQ, a competitor that specialises in technology-company shares. However, Amex continues to be run as an independent exchange and trades in a wide range of OPTIONS, as well as in EQUITIES and structured products.

American-style option

An OPTION that can be exercised at any time between the date it is purchased and the date it expires. It is the opposite of a EUROPEAN-STYLE OPTION, which can only be exercised on the date it expires. Most options in the United States are American-style. Since they offer investors more flexibility than European-style options, the PREMIUM paid for them is at least equal to or higher than the premium for a European-style contract.

Amex

See AMERICAN STOCK EXCHANGE.

Analyst

A person who studies the progress of companies and industries in order to make recommendations about the value of different STOCKS and SHARES, or about the creditworthiness of different DEBT instruments. Such analysts usually work for financial firms like STOCKBROKERS, INVESTMENT BANKS, FUND MANAGERS and INSURANCE companies, but they are also found in independent firms of consultants. The boom and subsequent bust in the shares of companies engaged in technology, media and telecommunications raised questions about the impartiality of the advice given by analysts working in investment banks. Although publicly touting the merits of a particular new ISSUE of shares, for example, some analysts were found privately to be dismissive about its quality and the (inflated) value at which the shares were being offered. This is because analysts' pay is affected by the overall profitability of the investment bank, which relies on a steady diet of new issues and INITIAL PUBLIC OFFERINGS to make money. REGULATION FAIR DISCLOSURE, a rule introduced in the United States in 2000 by the SECURITIES AND EXCHANGE COMMISSION, prohibits listed companies from disclosing price-sensitive information to one analyst ahead of the market as a whole, thus removing the temptation to use privileged information for competitive advantage. Yet the question of conflicts of interest among analysts remains a thorny one.

A piece of s..t.
How one analyst described an internet stock
his firm was recommending people to buy

A Annualised percentage rate

A standard measure of the annual RATE OF INTEREST which enables rates on different instruments to be compared. Before the annualised percentage rate (APR) became established as the yardstick for such calculations, consumers were easily confused. LOAN sharks and unscrupulous salesmen would attempt to gain an advantage by offering what seemed to be a lower rate but which invariably was the rate for a shorter period. The APR is calculated by the formula:

$$APR = [(1 + {}^{x}/_{100})^{y} - 1]$$

where x is the rate of interest quoted for a period of less than a year (for example, 2% a month), and y is the number of such periods during the year.

Annuity

Originally an investment that bought a fixed annual payment for the investor (called an annuitant) until his or her death. Americans usually refer to fixed annuities, which guarantee a minimum regular payment, or variable annuities, which do not but (in theory) can generate even greater RETURNS. Over the years the basic format has also been refined to include the following types.

- **Joint annuity.** The benefit continues throughout the lifetime of two people (usually husband and wife) and continues until both are dead.
- **Tontine annuity.** A joint annuity where the payment increases as the number of annuitants decreases (that is, when the husband dies the wife gets a bigger regular payment, and vice versa). Named after Lorenzo Tonti, an Italian-born banker who lived in France during the 17th century, the aim is to provide for survivors.
- **Deferred annuity.** The regular payments are delayed until after a certain specified period.

☑ **Perpetual annuity.** The payments go on forever (to survivors, that is).

Buy an annuity cheap and make your life interesting to yourself and everybody else that watches the speculation.
Charles Dickens, *Martin Chuzzlewit*

APR

See ANNUALISED PERCENTAGE RATE.

Arbitrage

The buying and selling of FINANCIAL INSTRUMENTS on different markets in order to take advantage of different prices between the markets. Before markets became truly international, the game usually involved dealing in different countries (for example, the FOREIGN-EXCHANGE markets in New York or London). Today, arbitrageurs (the name given to those who practise it) are more likely to trade between baskets of different instruments and between the physical and FUTURES markets. For example, a trader might swap EUROS for dollars and lock in a gain by selling the dollars forward in the futures market. A similar trade could involve buying and selling INTEREST-rate contracts for one or more currencies. An investor could also profit by buying a block of shares in one market and repackaging them for sale in another. In theory, as information travels more quickly, the opportunities for arbitrage should diminish because markets operate more efficiently. In practice, however, the growing diversity of financial instruments (particularly DERIVATIVES of one sort or another) is increasing the opportunity for arbitrage, especially for sophisticated investors.

ARM

See ADJUSTABLE-RATE MORTGAGE.

A | Asset

More or less anything owned by an individual or an organisation that has a monetary value, which is usually recorded at its cost or market worth. An asset can be tangible, such as the title to a property or land, or intangible, like a brand or franchise. LOANS or claims against other financial institutions account for the largest proportion of assets held by BANKS. Otherwise, assets are usually categorised according to their role or form. For example, current assets are CASH and any short-term items that can easily be turned into cash; fixed assets cover plant and machinery owned by a firm; capital assets may include the former and cover long-term assets such as land or buildings which are not bought and sold in the normal course of business. (See also DEPRECIATION.)

Asset allocation

The process of deciding how much CAPITAL to allocate to a particular class or category of investment; for example, CASH and cash equivalent, FIXED-INCOME SECURITIES, EQUITIES, property and so on. The process also applies to individual markets or geographical areas within an ASSET class; for example, government, MUNICIPAL or CORPORATE BONDS and equities listed in North America, Europe, Asia and EMERGING MARKETS. The aim is to balance the potential for RETURN against the possibility of RISK and is as relevant to private investors as it is to the largest institutional ones. A view of the likely returns to be derived from particular asset classes or regions will determine the size of an investor's WEIGHTING of that class or market. Professional investors aiming to beat a particular BENCHMARK need to know whether the investments they choose leave them OVERWEIGHT or UNDERWEIGHT, and thus exposed to more or less risk, in a particular asset class or market. So, for example, a manager whose fund is measured against the FTSE 100 INDEX has to be aware how much of the index is accounted for by, say, food retailers. Holding more food retailers' shares than are represented in the index may help to boost the fund's performance when the economy is down because people have to buy food during good times and bad. Yet if the economy were suddenly to pick up and such retailers went out of favour, their shares would fall in value and drag down the performance of the manager's fund.

Asset-backed securities

BONDS backed by a pool of instruments such as CREDIT-CARD RECEIVABLES, MORTGAGES or, in some cases, the income from intellectual property such as published songs or books. The BANK or finance company that first lent the money sells the receivables, together with the right to receive INTEREST on them, to a new company or SPECIAL-PURPOSE VEHICLE, in which it often retains a shareholding. The new company repackages the receivables as bonds with a minimum face value of, say, $1,000 and a life of five years; an example is certificates of automobile receivables (aptly known as CARS). Like any FIXED-INCOME SECURITY, the price of the bond varies according to demand, the COUPON or interest rate paid each year to the holder, and the period left before it is redeemed or repaid. In 1997, David Bowie, a singer and entertainer, broke new ground by raising $55m through the issue of bonds backed by the income from his past albums. His was the first such issue supported by ASSETS linked to intellectual property. Since then other singers, songwriters and authors have raised money from investors in the same way.

Asset class

See ASSET ALLOCATION.

Asset cover

The number of times that a company's DEBT is covered by its NET ASSETS. This is usually expressed as a ratio and is arrived

A   at by subtracting the value of INTANGIBLE ASSETS, current LIABILITIES and all debt from the BOOK VALUE of its assets. Asset cover is used to determine how large or small a cushion shareholders enjoy if a company gets into trouble or has to be wound up.

Asset management

The art of getting the best RETURN possible from the (largely financial) ASSETS that an individual or institution may own. This involves finding the ideal balance between the return to be gained from income and CAPITAL growth and the RISK of putting too many eggs in one basket. The MATURITY and LIQUIDITY of assets must usually match those of any LIABILITIES. Achieving the best balance has led to the growth of the more recent but equally arcane science of LIABILITY MANAGEMENT.

Asset management account

An account with a BANK or financial institution that combines run-of-the-mill banking services (such as a CURRENT ACCOUNT and CREDIT or DEBIT CARDS) with those usually provided by a STOCKBROKER (such as the ability to buy and sell SECURITIES, sometimes with borrowed money). A boon for users is that such accounts also provide regular statements that give a combined breakdown of all transactions. In the United States, they are also known as central asset accounts.

Asset stripper

A term coined in the 1960s for a corporate raider who acquired a company on the cheap and made a profit by peeling off and selling the various bits (subsidiaries, property, plant and equipment, and the like). The exercise often involved laying off many workers. The opportunity arises most commonly when the STOCKMARKET places a low valuation on the company, either

because its PROFITS have shrunk or because the management
has lost its way. Later refinements of the practice, particularly in
the United States, involved selling off enough bits of the
company to pay off the DEBT and thus place the business on a
more even keel. The remaining ASSETS may then be worth
more than they were when the company, or a controlling interest in it, was acquired. If a company's shares do fall in value but
the underlying business is sound, the existing management may
be able to persuade the shareholders to sell it to them as part of
a MANAGEMENT BUY-OUT. If so, they may seek to raise
finance from banks and from firms specialising in PRIVATE
EQUITY.

Asset value

The value of a company's ASSETS compared with the valuation
placed on them by the company's SHARE price. So a company
is undervalued by the STOCKMARKET when its NET assets
(after deducting any DEBT) are worth more than its stockmarket
CAPITALISATION.

Association of International Bond Dealers

See INTERNATIONAL SECURITIES MARKET ASSOCIATION.

Assurance

A type of INSURANCE taken out against an event that will definitely occur (that is "assured" of happening) but whose timing is
uncertain. The term is applied in particular to life assurance: the
RISK that is being insured is not the event itself (the death of the
assured is not in question) but the timing of it.

At best

An order from a customer to a BROKER to buy or sell a certain SECURITY at the best current price available. In such cases, brokers should use their experience and discretion to secure the best possible deal for the client.

At the money

At or equal to the current price of a SECURITY; most commonly used with OPTIONS. An option is at the money if it is equal to the price of the STOCK or other instrument on which it is written or to the underlying FUTURES contract. Not to be confused with IN THE MONEY, which denotes that the price has moved to the point where it becomes profitable for the holder – that is, above the exercise or STRIKE PRICE of a CALL OPTION or below that of a PUT OPTION.

ATM

See AUTOMATED TELLER MACHINE.

Audit

An examination of a company's accounts and supporting data in order to deliver an opinion as to their fairness and consistency, and whether or not they conform to the accounting rules or principles under which the company operates. The job is done by an auditor, who makes a report to shareholders. The allegations of accounting FRAUD that accompanied the collapse of several high-profile companies in the United States at the start of the 21st century intensified the pressure on auditors to be seen to be acting in shareholders' interests, not those of the directors of the company they were auditing. The SARBANES-OXLEY ACT aimed, among other things, to improve auditing standards in the United States.

Audit trail

A step-by-step record of a transaction which allows the regulator of the market in question to trace the ultimate beneficiary of a transaction (and the price at which it was made). These days such a trail is more likely to be a taped conversation, an e-mail or some other computer record than a piece of paper.

Automated clearing house

An electronic payments system in the United States that handles the bulk of regular payments between individuals, companies and government agencies. Started in the 1970s when the FEDERAL RESERVE worried that the country would drown in a sea of paper, the automated clearing house (ACH) processed more than $12 trillion-worth of payments in 2000. Most are salaries, payments of INTEREST and DIVIDENDS, and social security and other entitlements paid by the government. In recent years, the system has also become popular for paying INSURANCE PREMIUMS, for buying and selling SHARES, and for payments between one company and another.

The ACH acts through a network of associations (composed of BANKS, CREDIT-CARD companies and so on) throughout the country. The system has not only saved companies the cost of processing a growing mound of paper; so far, it has also shown itself able to meet growing demand.

Automated teller machine

A machine that can carry out most of the functions of a BANK teller or cashier. Automated teller machines (ATMs) have come a long way since CASH dispensers were first fitted to the outside walls of banks, allowing customers to withdraw money when the branch was closed. Banks' ATMs are found in supermarkets, restaurants and football stadiums – most places, in fact, where people may want to spend cash. In partnership with retailers,

A

some banks are also using ATMs to get even closer to their customers, by advertising a range of products and services.

Aval

A French word meaning endorsement. A sort of continental European ACCEPTANCE; a GUARANTEE stamped on a BILL OF EXCHANGE. It guarantees that a trusted party (such as a BANK) will meet the LIABILITY if called upon. The bank usually signs or stamps its name under the words *Pour aval* or *Bon pour aval*.

Average cost

See MARGINAL COST.

Averaging

A way of buying more of a certain SECURITY as its price falls, in order to reduce the average cost of the security. It can apply to a simple transaction where, for instance, an investor buys 1,000 SHARES in ABC company at $5 each on one date and a further 1,000 at $4.50 the following week. The average price for the two purchases would therefore be $4.75. Averaging can also apply to a regular savings plan under which an investor puts, say, $100 a month into a UNIT TRUST. When the price of the units is low, that $100 will buy more such units than when the price is higher. Over a year, the cost of the investment is therefore the average price paid for the total number of units. This is called pound, dollar or euro cost averaging.

Back-to-back

COLLATERAL provided by importers to back CREDIT extended to them by exporters. In the case of importers in developing countries, who are buying from developed countries where they are not known, such collateral will be something like a bank DEPOSIT held abroad by the importer.

Backwardation

When a COMMODITY due for delivery today fetches a higher price than the same commodity to be delivered at a future date. Backwardation usually occurs where there are temporary hold-ups in transport or distribution which make the commodity temporarily rare and thus push up its price.

Bad debt

A LOAN or a bill that is not paid within a reasonable time after its due-by date, often because a borrower has gone bankrupt or a customer has CASH FLOW problems. Bad debts are an inevitable part of business; keeping them under control is an art. Banks set aside PROVISIONS out of their regular PROFITS to cover the bad debts that they know they will suffer. Provisions may be general or specific depending on the size and age of the loan and the rules under which the bank operates. Without provisions, all of a bad debt has to be taken out of profits in the year in which it occurs.

If you owe the bank $100 that's your problem.
If you owe the bank $100 million, that's the bank's problem.
J.P. Getty

Balanced (mutual) fund

A UNIT TRUST or MUTUAL FUND holding a mixed PORTFOLIO

B

of EQUITIES, PREFERENCE SHARES and BONDS in order to balance its RISK against the potential for RETURN. A balanced fund usually offers a higher YIELD than a fund composed entirely of equities and generally performs better when the STOCKMARKET is falling, or flat. However, a fund made up of equities, particularly GROWTH STOCKS, usually does better when the stockmarket is rising because such stocks generally increase in value.

Balance sheet

Part of a company's accounts that lists its ASSETS and its LIABILITIES. Fundamental to all such accounts is the idea that assets and liabilities are equal – that they are in balance. The difference between them is called shareholders' funds; so shareholders' funds amount to whatever is needed to put the assets and liabilities in balance. Shifting assets (that is, loans) off a bank's balance sheet, thus giving it more breathing space to meet regulators' requirements over CAPITAL ADEQUACY, has provided a spur for SECURITISATION. For example, a bank may sell MORTGAGES on its books to a SPECIAL PURPOSE VEHICLE (in which it will have a minority stake). The entity will then issue new SECURITIES backed by the loans. Result: the bank raises cash from the mortgages and reduces the number of loans on its balance sheet.

Balloon

A LOAN whose repayments are spread unevenly over its life. As the loan nears MATURITY, the normal number of payments balloon into one or two large ones that finally pay off the DEBT. Such loans or MORTGAGES are popular with borrowers who expect extra CASH FLOW towards the end of a loan's life or where a refinancing is due. In the United States, balloons are sometimes also called partially amortised loans.

Bancassurance

The phenomenon whereby a financial institution combines the **B**
selling of banking products with INSURANCE products through
the same distribution channel or network; it is also called ALL-
FINANZ in Germany. Popular during the early 1990s, especially
in Europe, bancassurance rested on the premise that it is easy to
cross-sell banking and insurance services because customers
feel confident about buying insurance from the same institution
where they keep their savings. The idea has worked best where
borrowers require insurance to help protect them from possible
default on their MORTGAGE. But bancassurance by itself
cannot replace a powerful brand that customers trust. Increasingly, this applies to brands built up outside the world of
finance (for example, the UK's Virgin Group) as well those from
within it. The result is greater competition for suppliers but
more choice for consumers.

Bank

An institution that deals in money and, significantly, makes
some or all of its profits by making LOANS that do not have to
be repaid until some future date. Because of this function, governments have always kept a close eye on banks. There are
many types of banks (see CENTRAL BANK, CLEARING BANK,
CONSORTIUM BANK, INVESTMENT BANK, MERCHANT BANK,
MONEY-CENTRE BANK, MUTUAL SAVINGS BANK, PRIVATE
BANK, SAVINGS BANK, UNIVERSAL BANK). The main difference between them is the amount of emphasis that they place
on various fundamental banking services. These services
include the following.

1 Collecting DEPOSITS from savers and paying INTEREST on
these deposits (the cost of having the use of money over
time).
2 Granting loans to borrowers who seem likely to make good
use of them. This is what banks do to earn enough interest to
pay their depositors.

B

3 Money transmission, enabling customers of one bank to transfer funds directly from their account to somebody else at the same or another bank. This service is provided by means of CHEQUES, STANDING ORDERS, DIRECT DEBITS and so on.

4 Advisory services, in particular, advising companies on how and where to raise new CAPITAL and then arranging for the new capital to be raised.

5 Lending their good name to help customers that they trust. This is fundamental to trade finance. An exporter gives CREDIT to an importer because the importer's bank gives its word to the exporter's bank that payment will be forthcoming. The two banks trust each other; if the importer and exporter did too, they would not need the banks.

6 Providing services to other banks in order, for example, for them to clear funds between themselves. This is a principal function of central banks.

The first three functions are fundamental to the business of commercial banks; the fourth and fifth are fee-earning services that are at the heart of the business of investment banks.

> *A bank is a place that will lend you money*
> *if you can prove you don't need it.*
> Bob Hope

Banker's acceptance

See ACCEPTANCE.

Banker's draft

An order from a buyer or importer to its BANK instructing it to make a payment to the seller or exporter's bank. The draft is sent to the seller, which presents it to its bank for payment. The seller's bank in turn presents it to the buyer's bank for reimbursement.

Bank for International Settlements

A CENTRAL BANK for central bankers, based in Switzerland. It is a meeting place, a multinational regulatory authority and a CLEARING HOUSE for many countries' RESERVES. The Bank for International Settlements (BIS) was set up in 1930 as a private company owned by a number of central banks, one commercial bank (Citibank) and some private individuals. The BIS's headquarters are in Basel, where its main dealing room is situated, and it has an office in Hong Kong covering Asia and Australasia. In a throwback to the days of its incorporation, the bank uses quaintly named gold francs as a unit of account but otherwise keeps abreast of the times. In the international DEBT crisis of the early 1980s, the BIS played a vital role in supplying SHORT-TERM bridging loans that gave dollar-less developing countries time to adjust their economic policies. In the late 1980s, it played a less conspicuous role in setting up an international safety net for rapidly deregulating financial markets.

Bank insurance fund

See FEDERAL DEPOSIT INSURANCE CORPORATION.

Bank of England

The UK's CENTRAL BANK, affectionately known as the Old Lady of Threadneedle Street in the City of London. The nickname comes from a drawing by James Gillray, an 18th-century cartoonist. It depicts William Pitt the Younger, the prime minister of the day, trying to steal the bank's gold from a chest which is being firmly sat upon by an old lady. The Bank of England still holds GOLD and remains chief CUSTODIAN of the country's currency.

Since 1997, the bank's operations have been independent of the government. Its Monetary Policy Committee judges what level of RATES OF INTEREST will best ensure that the economy meets a target for INFLATION set by the government. The bank is also responsible for the stability of the UK's financial system, including THE CITY of London, the world's largest centre for international finance. It does so by working closely with the Treasury, which is a government department, and the FINANCIAL SERVICES AUTHORITY.

> *Bankers are just like anybody else, except richer.*
> Ogden Nash

Bankruptcy

The condition of a bankrupt, that is, a person (or organisation in some jurisdictions) who has been adjudged by a court to be unable to pay his or her debts. A bankrupt is deprived of many powers; for example, he or she cannot be a director of a company for a number of years. A bankrupt's property passes into the hands of a TRUSTEE, who is authorised to divide it among the creditors.

Since the 1970s, legislation in many developed countries has been made more flexible with the aim of giving individuals and companies a chance to recover when they find themselves insolvent and in danger of bankruptcy. A model is the US Bankruptcy Reform Act of 1978 (itself remodelled in 1984). Its Chapter 11 enables insolvent companies to remain in control of their businesses so that they can trade their way out of insolvency. Chapter 11 greatly increases management's room for manoeuvre mainly because it temporarily gives a company protection from its creditors (and thus frees it from the burden of having to pay INTEREST on its DEBT). Continental Airlines found Chapter 11 so appealing that it has entered, and left, twice.

Bargain

A deal done at a good price. Also any transaction in STOCKS and SHARES on the LONDON STOCK EXCHANGE.

B

Here's the rule for bargains: "do other men, for they would do you".
Charles Dickens, *Martin Chuzzlewit*

Barter

Paying for goods or services with other goods or services. Barter is at least as old as the Asian silk road, and often just as tortuous. It enjoyed a renaissance with the opening-up of the former Soviet Union and eastern Europe, regions with a huge demand for imports (particularly of capital goods) but with little FOREIGN EXCHANGE to pay for them. In Argentina, the collapse of the economy in 2001 and the scarcity of currency of any kind forced people to resort to barter.

Financial organisations are not too keen on barter since it threatens to reduce the need for their services. However, recognising that it is here to stay, some institutions have set up specialist barter departments to make money out of complicated trades, which they prefer to call countertrade.

Barter is growing fastest among small businesses, which join exchanges that deal in surplus goods and services. Some 400 such exchanges exist in the United States alone. Some even offer credit: for example, a barterer who owns a roofing company and can work only during the milder summer months draws on CREDIT to get his vehicle repaired during the winter and pays for it in kind when the weather improves. Hotel rooms or unoccupied office space are easily swapped over the internet for other goods and services. At a local level, babysitting may be offered in exchange for other services.

Basis

There are several meanings, as follows.

- ▪ The difference between the forward price of an OPTION or FUTURES contract and the current (or CASH) price of the underlying ASSET; for example, the difference between today's price for a Treasury BOND and the price of an option or futures contract in three months' time.

▱ The relationship between the prices of similar FINANCIAL INSTRUMENTS in two or more related, but not identical, markets (see BASIS RISK).

▱ The YIELD to MATURITY for a bond at a given price; for example, a bond with an interest rate of 10% that sells for $100 has a basis of 10%.

▱ The price established by common consent for odd lots of a SECURITY between two DEALERS on a STOCK EXCHANGE.

Basis point

A unit of measure used to express small movements in the RATE OF INTEREST, FOREIGN-EXCHANGE rates, or BOND yields. One basis point is one-hundredth of a percentage point. So the differential between a bond yield of 5.38% and 5.79% is 41 basis points.

Basis price

See STRIKE PRICE.

Basis risk

The possibility that an investor will lose money because the forward price of an OPTION or FUTURES contract and the current (or CASH) price will drift apart. It also refers to the danger that an investor will fail to offset the RISK from two or more options or futures contracts; for example, if a trader has borrowed Swiss francs to purchase a futures contract but can only protect that investment by selling a contract denominated in euros. The basis risk would be the danger that the two currencies would diverge during the period of the contract. Basis risk also refers to mismatches in the MATURITY of financial instruments; for example, where an investor buys an INTEREST-rate option expiring in three months to HEDGE another CONTRACT that is due to mature in six months.

Basis risk has become increasingly important in recent years as BANKS and other financial institutions attempt to lay off a variety of risks by buying or selling DERIVATIVES. If the basis risk is too great, there may be no point in entering into a transaction because of the danger that it will fail to do what it was designed to do.

Basis trade

A form of ARBITRAGE whereby an investor buys BONDS for cash and sells them to others in the FUTURES market (that is, sells a right to the bonds in the future at a price agreed now). The investor calculates that the cash price plus the cost of "carrying" the investment until the futures CONTRACT matures will be lower than the price paid for the future. Hence the name "cash and carry trade" given to such deals. "Buying the basis" usually refers to buying bonds in the CASH MARKET and selling futures contracts; "selling the basis" means selling cash bonds and buying the futures.

No price is too low for a bear or too high for a bull.
Stock Exchange proverb

Bear

An investor who thinks that the price of an individual SECURITY (or a whole market) is going to fall. A bear, therefore, may sell securities in anticipation of being able to buy them back later at a lower price. Alternatively, bears may buy FUTURES contracts that commit them to selling securities at a fixed price at a future date. They anticipate that the fixed price will be higher than the price they will have to pay for the securities in the cash or SPOT MARKET on that future date. (See also BULL.)

Bearer security

B A BOND or SHARE certificate that is not registered in the name of its owner. Whoever holds (or bears) the certificate can collect the INTEREST or DIVIDEND due, usually by detaching a COUPON. A bearer security can be bought or sold without being endorsed; it is as liquid as CASH and equally vulnerable to theft. A EUROBOND is a bearer bond. Bearer bonds have the great advantage of being more easily kept out of the eye of the tax authorities than bonds that must be registered.

Bear market

A market that is experiencing a sustained fall in the prices of SE-CURITIES; the opposite of a bull market. Markets anticipate events in the real economy, so a bear market usually occurs when investors scent the onset of a prolonged downturn in economic activity. Likewise, SHARE prices may begin to rise again even though the economy remains depressed because the market detects signs of an eventual recovery.

Bellwether

A SECURITY that is seen as an indicator of the direction in which a market is heading, partly because of its significant WEIGHTING in the main STOCKMARKET INDEX. In the UK, Vodafone, a constituent of the FTSE 100 index, is seen as such a share, as are General Electric and Microsoft in the United States, Alcatel in France and DoCoMo in Japan. Long-term government BONDS of varying MATURITY are also seen as bellwethers for national bond markets.

Benchmark

A standard by which other things can be judged. It is usually used to describe a benchmark INTEREST rate, the minimum

COUPON that investors will accept to entice them to buy a non-government BOND; or benchmark RISK, the risk that a UNIT TRUST or MUTUAL FUND will fail to RETURN as much for investors as the benchmark by which it is measured. Such a benchmark might be the MSCI World Index if it is a global fund or, say, the Russell 2000 if it specialises in smaller companies in the United States. The performance of mutual funds may be measured against indices that are broad in scope, such as the FTSE All-Share index or the S&P 500, or narrower ones such as the FTSE Gold Mines index. Indeed, any INDEX which measures economic or financial performance can be a benchmark.

In financial services, as in other industries, companies sometimes also use independent agents to measure their performance against key yardsticks, such as the time taken to answer customers' complaints. The results are aggregated and submitted anonymously to those in the industry. Firms are then able to compare their own performance (which they know) with the average for their peers (the benchmark).

Berne Union

An association of providers of EXPORT CREDIT insurance. Founded in 1834, the Berne Union aims to promote "the international acceptance of sound principles of export credit and insurance". The union's members operate in more than 40 countries worldwide, doing business with individual exporters requiring CREDIT or INSURANCE.

Beta

A measure of the VOLATILITY of a SHARE, UNIT TRUST or PORTFOLIO of investments. The beta coefficient is a relative, not an absolute, measure of RISK. It defines the relationship between the RETURNS from a share and those made from the STOCKMARKET as a whole, as measured by an INDEX such as the S&P 500. Beta is used by investors to assess the price (and therefore relative value) of a particular share or portfolio. The stockmarket's beta is always 1.0, so a share with a beta of 1.5 would be expected to rise by 15% when the market increases by 10%, or to fall in value by 15% when the market falls by 10%. A weakness of beta is that the results can vary markedly depending on the data used and the period taken. For this reason, it is usually used for portfolios of shares over a five-year period.

Beta is often used by investment managers in conjunction with ALPHA, an estimate of the expected return from a STOCK or portfolio of shares. If, say, Microsoft had an alpha of 1.25, it could be expected to rise in value by 25% when the return from the market was zero. But if its beta were 1.5, and the market as a whole stood to rise by 10%, then Microsoft's shares would be expected to increase by a total of 40% (25% plus 15%).

Bid

The highest price that a prospective purchaser is prepared to pay at that moment for something, be it a company, an impressionist painting, or a SECURITY.

Bid costs

The costs incurred by a company in making a TAKEOVER bid for another; not to be confused with the costs of an auction. These include the fees of a panoply of advisers such as investment bankers, lawyers and accountants. Unless a bidder comes to some other arrangement, such costs have to be borne whether a bid is successful or not.

Bid-offer spread

The difference between the lowest price at which a seller will offer goods, services or a FINANCIAL INSTRUMENT and the highest price that a bidder will pay for them. Called bid-asked (on OVER-THE-COUNTER markets) and bid-offered (on STOCK EXCHANGES) in the United States, the two figures together constitute a QUOTATION or quote for a SECURITY. In the FOREIGN-EXCHANGE markets, BANKS quote two prices: the highest price that the bank (as a buyer) will offer for a particular currency; and the lowest price it will accept for it (as a seller). So if a company's shares are bid at $35 each and offered at $37, the spread will be $2. If the shares fall out of favour, the spread could widen to $3 if the bid drops to $33 and the offer is $36.

Big Bang

The name of a theory about the creation of the universe; also used to describe what occurs on the day when a significant financial market removes a swathe of old-fashioned rules and regulations. It has since come to symbolise the effect on a market of abrupt and far-reaching change. The phrase started to be used in the financial world to describe the DEREGULATION of the LONDON STOCK EXCHANGE on October 27th 1986. From that date:

- STOCKBROKERS were obliged to abandon their long-standing fixed scale of COMMISSION;
- for the first time foreigners were allowed to own a majority stake in a UK BROKER; and
- DUAL CAPACITY was introduced, allowing brokers to be MARKET MAKERS and vice versa.

The biggest bang on the day, however, came from the Stock Exchange's newly computerised dealing and quotations system, which collapsed under the strain. The US equivalent of Big Bang was called Mayday and took place on May 1st 1975, the day on which minimum commissions were abolished on the NEW YORK STOCK EXCHANGE.

Bill of exchange

A written instruction to a buyer (an importer) to pay a seller (an exporter) a defined amount of money before a certain date. In the UK, a CHEQUE is a bill of exchange and is still governed in important respects by the Bill of Exchange Act of 1882. In the United States, a bill of exchange usually refers only to a foreign transaction. There, a written order from one party requesting another to pay a certain amount to a third party is a draft.

Bill of lading

The set of documents relating to goods while they are in transit. The documents contain a brief description of the goods and where they are going. The bill of lading is signed by the carrier who, on receipt of the goods, gives the bill to whoever the shipper (the owner of the goods) has instructed. Usually the shipper instructs a forwarding AGENT or BROKER to handle the formalities. Where payment for the goods is by LETTER OF CREDIT, the money will only be made available if the bill of lading conforms to the conditions laid down in the letter of credit.

Black Monday

STOCKMARKET history is riddled with black days. Black Monday was October 19th 1987, when virtually all the world's stockmarkets tumbled by all-time record amounts. Black Tuesday was October 29th 1929, the blackest day of the Great Crash. Others talk of Black Thursday, October 24th 1928, when the markets first began to fall abruptly.

Black-Scholes formula

A model for pricing OPTIONS developed by Fischer Black and Myron Scholes, two Chicago academics. To gauge whether an option is fairly valued, the model considers such things as the VOLATILITY of a SECURITY'S RETURN, the level of INTEREST rates, the relationship of the price of the underlying SHARE to the STRIKE PRICE of the option, and the amount of time before the option expires. Black and Scholes came up with their theory in 1975, the year that formal trading in options began on the

CHICAGO BOARD OF TRADE. Their formula has since gained almost universal acceptance because it is nearly as successful as rival formulae that are infinitely more complicated.

B

Black Wednesday

September 9th 1992, the day when speculators in the FOREIGN-EXCHANGE markets forced the pound to abandon the EXCHANGE RATE MECHANISM.

Blend fund

A UNIT TRUST or MUTUAL FUND that holds a combination of SHARES, BONDS and liquid MONEY MARKET instruments to balance its RISK and RETURNS. It also refers to a fund invested mainly in EQUITIES that favours neither GROWTH STOCKS nor VALUE STOCKS in its PORTFOLIO. As a result, fund managers are free to switch between the two if they see opportunities in any sector of the market. A blend fund is therefore more diversified than a specialised one whose performance may be more volatile.

Block trading

Trading in big blocks of SHARES. On the NEW YORK STOCK EXCHANGE any deal of more than 10,000 shares or any quantity of shares or BONDS worth $200,000 or more is called a block trade. Certain STOCKBROKERS specialise in such trades and, in the United States, are known as BLOCK HOUSES. The number of blocks of shares traded daily is watched closely by ANALYSTS. It shows how active in the market financial institutions are compared with private investors.

Blue chip

A company known nationally, or internationally, for the quality of its products and services and for its ability to generate PROFIT through bad times as well as good. This usually also means that it has rarely, if ever, missed a DIVIDEND payment. Such companies and thus their shares are often therefore also a constituent of a main STOCKMARKET INDEX (such as the FTSE 100, S&P 500 or France's CAC 40) and are seen by investors as a BELLWETHER of sentiment in the stockmarket.

Blue-sky laws

Legislation passed by individual states in the United States regulating the sale of corporate securities. The laws, so called because a judge apparently once compared the value of one SECURITY to a patch of blue sky, are intended to protect investors from FRAUD.

Bond

An INTEREST-bearing instrument issued by governments, corporations and other established organisations. A bond is evidence of a DEBT on which the issuer usually promises to pay INTEREST at regular intervals and to repay the amount of the original LOAN at a specified date in the future. So, unlike an EQUITY holder, who is a part owner of the company, the holder of a corporate bond is a creditor. Bonds are usually sold at a DISCOUNT (or PREMIUM) to their face value. The discount (or premium) reflects the difference between the interest rate on the bond's COUPON and the current market interest rate. Companies or organisations seeking to issue bonds in the international debt markets often get a better reception from investors if they have first sought a CREDIT RATING from an agency specialising in such things. This usually guarantees the issuer a more favourable interest rate. (See also BEARER SECURITY and JUNK BOND.)

Gentlemen prefer bonds.
Andrew Mellon

Bonus issue

See SCRIP ISSUE.

Book

The accounting record of a business or of an ISSUE of SECURITIES. Book-keeping is the maintaining of the ledgers and other books of record of a business. With every issue of securities or syndication to lenders of a LOAN, at least one BANK (or firm of BROKERS) is appointed for a fee to manage, or run, the book. These days, not only is such an exercise carried out with the aid of computers, but, assuming there is sufficient demand, it can also be undertaken 24 hours a day around the world.

Book runner

An INVESTMENT BANK or SECURITIES firm that is responsible for the documentation and general management of an ISSUE of securities to investors or the syndication to lenders of a LOAN.

Book value

The value of a company's ASSETS as expressed in its BALANCE SHEET, which itself is only a snapshot of assets and LIABILITIES at a particular time. This can be less than the assets' market value since accounting conventions may dictate that the assets be included in the accounts at their purchase price. INFLATION alone may have ensured that this is less than the assets' current market value.

Bought ledger

The division of a company's accounts department that deals with its payments to creditors. In order to smooth a company's

CASH FLOW, this division usually attempts to buy time before making payments to suppliers and the like.

B

Brady Bond

Dollar-denominated BONDS issued by the governments of emerging economies, particularly those in Latin America. Named after Nicholas Brady, who was Treasury secretary in the United States during the 1980s, the bonds were developed as a way of bailing out countries that had defaulted on their external DEBT. By issuing new debt supported by Treasury bonds carrying no INTEREST, Brady bonds effectively GUARANTEE the repayment of the PRINCIPAL on the LOAN, if not the interest on them. The idea worked well until, in 1999, Ecuador became the first country to DEFAULT on interest payments due on its Brady bonds. Thereafter, even Brady bonds were regarded as vulnerable to default.

Branch

A retail outlet of a BANK; the places around the country where it collects DEPOSITS, makes LOANS and arranges money transaction services. Electronic banking (via ATMS and the internet) is increasingly making branches (and the people who work in them) redundant. Cutting the number of their branches – or, as some banks have done, starting a business from scratch without any – not only reduces costs but can also lead to greater satisfaction for customers. Many customers find that, when they need one, a friendly voice at the end of the telephone can be just as helpful as a bank teller behind a glass screen. Others complain that they can no longer talk to staff at their local branch because calls are routed to anonymous call centres. Nevertheless, surveys show that customers rate efficiency most highly, however it is delivered.

Bretton Woods Agreement

The pact made in 1994 between 44 countries at Bretton Woods **B**
in New Hampshire in the United States to create a system of
fixed exchange rates. The agreement, which became law the following year, remained in existence until 1971 when the system
was scrapped and currencies were allowed to float. To help the
world economy reconstruct itself after the ravages of the
second world war, the conference also hit upon the idea of establishing the INTERNATIONAL MONETARY FUND and the International Bank for Reconstruction and Development (usually
known as the WORLD BANK), both of which are still doing their
jobs.

Bridging loan

A LOAN that spans the short period from now to the time when
a more long-term credit FACILITY can be arranged. Bridging
loans are commonly used for house purchases before a long
term MORTGAGE has been set up, although the increasing
speed with which banks can offer and approve mortgages has
reduced the need for such loans. Bridging loans are also used to
help developing countries in financial distress (see BANK FOR
INTERNATIONAL SETTLEMENTS).

Broker

An individual or firm that buys and sells FINANCIAL INSTRU-
MENTS on behalf of others. A broker is an AGENT who works
for investors and financial institutions. Brokers earn a COM-
MISSION based on the value of the transactions undertaken.
Commission rates used to be fixed, but in most major markets
they are now deregulated. So, to a large extent, brokers compete
for business on the basis of price as well as the quality of their
service. A broking firm that specialises in SHARES, BONDS,
COMMODITIES or OPTIONS must be recognised by the exchange with which it is dealing. Such recognition helps to

B

ensure best practice and high standards of professionalism. (See DEALER.)

Budget: a method of worrying before you spend instead of afterwards.
Anon

Budget

A plan or estimate of revenue and expenditure for a specific period in the future. In a balanced budget, revenue and expenditure are equal.

In many large companies, budgets are produced annually, with income and expenditure broken down into monthly (or even weekly) estimates that take into account economic and industrial cycles. A budget starts with estimates of sales and income, followed by estimates of the costs of labour, materials, administration, production, research, distribution and so on required to secure that level of sales.

National budgets do the same for countries. In this case, government spending departments usually bid for the money they reckon is needed to deliver the commitments laid down by the government as a whole. A country has a budget deficit when expenditure exceeds revenue and a budget surplus when estimated expenditure is less than estimated revenue.

CAPITAL budgets are compiled for periods of more than a year. They include estimates of the future level of capital expenditure, and of any borrowing required to meet it.

In general the art of government consists of taking as much money as possible from one part of the citizens to give to the other.
Voltaire

Budget account

See ACCOUNT.

Building society

A type of MUTUAL institution that grew up in industrial towns
in the UK in the 19th century (and from which many, such as
Bradford, Burnley, Halifax, Leeds and Leicester, took their
names). Building societies were designed initially to do little
more than take in SHORT-TERM savings and put them out as
long-term LOANS (or MORTGAGES) for house purchase. In
recent years, however, they have been allowed to compete with
BANKS, offering money-transmission services and loans for
things other than house purchase. In return, banks have en-
croached on the building societies' traditional turf, marketing
mortgages to their own customers. Some building societies have
abandoned their mutual status (that is, being owned by their depositors) and have become banks, with their shares listed on the
STOCKMARKET. Traditionalists claim that this undermines their
ability to offer more competitive RATES OF INTEREST on mortgages and savings products because they must now make a
profit for their shareholders. Modernists retort that the dynam-
ics of the market (such as a bank's size, cost of funds and so on)
have a greater influence on their cost structure and therefore on
their ability to offer competitive rates to savers and borrowers
alike.

Bull

A person who expects the price of a SECURITY (or of a securities market as a whole) to rise. The opposite therefore of a BEAR.
Bulls will buy SHARES now expecting to be able to sell them
later at a higher price and at a PROFIT. Bulls who are losing their
nerve are known as stale bulls.

Bulldog bond

A BOND that is denominated in sterling but issued by a non-UK
borrower.

Bullet

B A LOAN on which all the PRINCIPAL is repaid in one go at the end of the period of the loan. During the life of the loan the borrower pays INTEREST only. Although they are not called bullets, some retail mortgages are effectively the same, in that they rely on investment plans, called endowment policies, to pay off the loan in full at the end of its life.

Bundesbank

Germany's CENTRAL BANK. As central banks go, the Bundesbank has a long tradition of being independent of government. Since Germany is a member of the EUROPEAN MONETARY SYSTEM and the European System of Central Banks (ESCB); the president of the Bundesbank also sits on the General Council of the EUROPEAN CENTRAL BANK.

Bunny bond

A BOND where the holder has the option to receive INTEREST in CASH or in the form of more of the same bond.

Bureau de change

A small office trading in FOREIGN EXCHANGE, often found in places where travellers first set foot on foreign soil, such as airports and railway stations, as well as in shopping areas. A bureau de change makes a PROFIT by charging a COMMISSION (usually a percentage of the amount exchanged) or by the TURN it makes on the buying and selling of the currency, that is, the difference between the price it pays for the foreign currency and the price at which it sells it. Evidence that bureaux de change have been used as conduits to launder money made from drug dealing and to transfer CASH used by terrorists has rekindled authorities' efforts to ensure that they are properly regulated. International agencies affiliated to the OECD want national governments to encourage bureaux de change to report any suspicious transactions.

B

Buy-back

An agreement in a sales CONTRACT under which the seller agrees to buy back an ASSET if certain conditions are (or are not) met within a certain period of time: for example, an agreement to buy back a house if the purchaser has to move on within a certain period; or an agreement to buy back a shareholding in a company if it fails to meet a certain level of sales or if the authorities change the regulations under which it operates.

The term is also used to describe the purchase by companies of their own SHARES. They do this to improve their EARNINGS PER SHARE (total PROFITS divided by the total number of shares in the issue). The fewer shares there are in issue, the better the earnings appear.

Buyer credit

A medium- to long-term LOAN granted by a foreign buyer of exported goods. The loan is given by the exporter's BANK and usually carries the GUARANTEE of the exporter's national EXPORT CREDIT agency.

Buyer's market

A market in which there is a plentiful supply of commodities (or securities, or whatever) and in which, as a consequence, prices are weak and can often be negotiated downwards. Contrast with SELLER'S MARKET.

Cable

The name given by traders to the pound/dollar exchange rate. It stems from the days when New York relayed the rate to London via a transatlantic cable.

Call

A demand made by a company that a shareholder must pay the amount due on a certain date for SHARES that have been issued as PARTLY PAID. It can also be the right to redeem BONDS before their scheduled MATURITY date. Such dates are usually specified in the prospectus for a bond ISSUE.

Call option

A CONTRACT to buy a certain number of SHARES at a stated price (the STRIKE PRICE) within a specified period of time. A call option will be exercised when the SPOT PRICE rises above the strike price. If it is not exercised, the option expires at the end of the specified period. Call options are usually taken out by investors who think the price of a SECURITY will rise significantly. By buying call options, investors stand to make a bigger profit for a smaller outlay than if they were to buy the underlying security. By selling call options, the owners of securities can also generate extra income but have to relinquish ownership if the strike price is met. For example, if an investor is optimistic about the prospects for a share, he or she might buy a call option for, say, $15, giving him or her the right to buy the underlying security at $350. Assume too that the market price of the security is $320. The investor would be in profit if the share price rose above $365, covering the $350 exercise price and the $15 cost of the option.

Call premium

The price of acquiring a CALL OPTION. A call option gives the holder the right (but not the obligation) to purchase, say, 100 shares of a SECURITY at a fixed price before a specified date in the future. For this right, the buyer of the call option pays the seller, called the WRITER, a fee, called a PREMIUM, which is forfeited if the buyer fails to exercise the right within the agreed period. (See also OPTION.)

Camel

An acronym for the five things that banking supervisors look for most keenly when examining a BANK:

- CAPITAL adequacy
- ASSET quality
- Management quality
- EARNINGS
- LIQUIDITY

The increasing sophistication of financial markets has encouraged regulators to give banks more flexibility in running their businesses. This helps banks to balance the RISKS they take and to match the MATURITY of their LOANS with the DEPOSITS they take in. As the LENDER OF LAST RESORT if a bank or financial institution fails, a CENTRAL BANK likes to have as much warning as possible of impending danger.

Cap

A ceiling imposed on the amount of INTEREST and/or CAPITAL that is to be repaid on a LOAN. With an adjustable-rate mortgage in the United States, there can be several different caps:

- an annual adjustment cap, which places a restriction on the amount of interest that can be paid in one year;

- a life-of-loan cap, which places a ceiling on the amount of interest that can be paid on the loan throughout its life;
- a payment cap, which limits the amount by which the monthly payments can rise from year to year.

C

Capital

The money used to build a business. Capital is raised by issuing SHARES and/or long-term DEBT instruments. The balance of a company's ORDINARY SHARES, PREFERENCE SHARES and long-term debt constitutes its capital structure. Together with its retained PROFIT, these make up the company's CAPITAL EMPLOYED. The key relationship between debt and EQUITY is known as GEARING or leverage. For financial institutions, capital is a safety net against sudden losses arising from BAD DEBT, bad management or skulduggery and fraud. (See also WORKING CAPITAL.)

Capital adequacy

A measure of a financial institution's ability to withstand CREDIT and market RISKS. The Basel Committee on Banking Supervision (a body composed mainly of the governors of the CENTRAL BANKS of the Group of Ten wealthiest countries) sets down rules with which banks must comply. Banks must set aside in their accounts part of their CAPITAL to cover the risk of DEFAULTS caused by the failure of the companies they are lending to or a collapse in the financial markets as a whole. In the past, these standards have been mechanical rules that have stipulated the size of the financial buffer that banks must maintain. In recent years, however, regulators have realised the need for more sophisticated systems that can monitor the level of risk to which banks may be exposed. For example, since the late 1980s banks have been allowed to use VALUE AT RISK models to determine the amount of capital they must hold to cover the risks they are running. The Basel committee plans new rules (expected to be introduced in 2006) which will distinguish more clearly between different sorts of LOANS. These may reduce but are unlikely to eliminate altogether the danger of banks getting into trouble.

Capital allowance

The part of the amount paid for capital ASSETS that can be set off against INCOME for the purposes of calculating a company's taxable PROFIT. The demand for capital equipment in a company can be controlled to some extent by governments' fine-tuning of these allowances, both by the amount and by the things that they can be set against. For example, allowances might vary as to the period over which the capital expenditure can be set off (say 20% a year for five years) or by the percentage that can be set off (say 60% in year one, but no more). The degree to which capital allowances apply and how they are used varies from country to country.

Capital asset pricing model

A model of the relationship between the expected RISK of a SECURITY or investment PORTFOLIO and the RETURN that investors can expect from it. The model is based on the theory that investors will demand a PREMIUM for taking on increased risk. The expected return from an ASSET or security is therefore equal to the return derived from a risk-free security (such as a government BOND) plus a premium for the extra risk. Although the model has limitations, particularly in assessing the likely VOLATILITY of individual securities, it is still widely used as a tool in managing portfolios of investments.

Capital employed

The CAPITAL in use in a business. There is no universally agreed definition of what this includes, but it is usually taken to mean NET ASSETS (that is, current assets plus fixed assets less

C

current LIABILITIES) plus bank LOANS and OVERDRAFTS. The RETURN on capital employed is a measure of how efficiently a company is employing its capital to generate a return. The ratio is usually calculated as the PROFIT before INTEREST and tax divided by the difference between total assets and current assets.

Capital flight

See FLIGHT CAPITAL.

Capital gain

The PROFIT from the sale of a CAPITAL ASSET (such as a BOND or a SHARE). In most countries, capital gains are subject to special tax rules. Assets sold for a PROFIT and held for more than a year are usually subject to a special rate of tax that is related to the amount of income tax the seller pays. Often there is relief for certain provisions that can be set off against the total. For example, relief is often linked to the rate of INFLA-TION. Lower rates of tax can also apply if assets are held for longer than a year. In some countries, capital gains are treated in the same way as income, so it does not matter as much when investors buy or sell assets.

October: This is one of the particularly dangerous months to invest in stocks. Other dangerous months are July, January, September, April, November, May, March, June, December, August and February.
Mark Twain

Capitalisation

The attribution of a CAPITAL value to a stream of income. This value is the amount that would have to be invested now in order to produce a particular income stream in the future (see also MARKET CAPITALISATION). In accounting, the term means recording costs as ASSETS rather than as expenses. For example, a firm might capitalise research and development costs. In STOCK EXCHANGE parlance, it is the aggregate market price of all of a company's ORDINARY SHARES.

Capital market

Any market in the long-term FINANCIAL INSTRUMENTS (such as SHARES and BONDS) that make up a company's CAPITAL.

Capital ratio

The ratio of a BANK'S CAPITAL and RESERVES to its total ASSETS. In most countries, this figure is not allowed to exceed a ceiling set by the CENTRAL BANK. In the United States, capital ratio requirements apply also to BROKERS and DEALERS operating in the financial markets. This is so as to ensure that their total borrowings do not exceed a certain proportion of their liquid assets, such as CASH, or its equivalent, such as short-term FINANCIAL INSTRUMENTS.

Captive

INSURANCE companies (or FUND MANAGERS) that are set up inside large multinational groups for the purpose of handling all the multinational's own insurance or fund management needs. A captive insurer is expected to handle all the parent group's business (and to be cheaper than buying the services from outside). Although in theory such captives are free to accept business from outside the group, in practice they rarely do. A company will consider setting up a captive when it has sufficient demand, specialised needs, easy access to CAPITAL and a desire to keep the PROFITS from the business within the group. Even so, captive insurers will take only a proportion of the RISKS that they underwrite. Most will be reinsured with outsiders.

Carry back

The capacity to shift tax advantages, or PENSION payment privileges, back into a fiscal year that has ended. For example, in some circumstances, contributions to a pension fund can be carried back to previous years if an allowance has not been met.

Carry forward

The capacity to shift tax advantages, or PENSION payment privileges, forward into a year that has not yet begun. For example, in certain circumstances, companies may carry losses forward to set against tax due on PROFITS earned in subsequent years. This is why some loss-making companies are more valuable than their business models might suggest.

CARs

Short for Certificate for Automobile Receivables (see ASSET-BACKED SECURITIES).

Carve-out

See EQUITY CARVE-OUT.

Cash

Ready money; not just NOTES and coins but also liquid ASSETS that can readily be turned into notes and coins without loss. In a company's financial statement, cash is usually grouped with cash equivalents, which are highly liquid SECURITIES with a known value and MATURITY. The demand for cash varies throughout the year, being strongest, for example, in Christian countries at Christmas time, or at Chinese New Year in China and parts of Asia.

Cash flow

The amount of money flowing through an organisation (or, indeed, an individual) in a given period. For a company, cash flow is the sum of its net borrowings plus money from any SHARE issues, plus its trading PROFIT, plus any DEPRECIATION. A cash flow statement, sometimes also called a funds flow statement, shows how a company balances the flows of CASH in and out of its business. Cash flow and profits are two different things. A company can be recording rising profits year by year while its cash is ebbing away, particularly if it is unable to get in the money owed by its debtors. Alternatively, a company may be cash rich but making little or no profits.

Profit is an illusion, cash flow is fact.
Anon

Cash machine

See AUTOMATIC TELLER MACHINE.

Cash market

See SPOT PRICE.

Cash on delivery

Commonly known as COD, cash on delivery refers to goods and services that must be paid for in full at the time that they are handed over to the buyer. In the United States, the term is "collect on delivery".

Catastrophe bond

A BOND issued in the CAPITAL MARKETS by a REINSURANCE

C

company. Reinsurers, like the INSURANCE companies they insure, need to lay off part of the RISK they take on. One way of doing this is to issue bonds to investors which pay out if (and only if) there is a catastrophe – for example, a hurricane or an earthquake which causes millions of dollars-worth of damage and therefore large claims against the insurance and reinsurance companies. A big advantage of catastrophe bonds is that the money is placed in TRUST and called upon as and when the claims are triggered. Most catastrophe bond issues come in TRANCHES; for example, a total of $200m-worth of COVER divided into two tranches of $100m. Typically, the second tranche can be called upon only when the first tranche is exhausted by claims.

CATS

See CERTIFICATE OF ACCRUAL ON TREASURY SECURITIES. It also stands for Computer Assisted Trading System, a piece of software developed by the Toronto Stock Exchange.

CBOE

See CHICAGO BOARD OPTIONS EXCHANGE.

CBOT

See CHICAGO BOARD OF TRADE.

CD

See CERTIFICATE OF DEPOSIT.

CDO

See COLLATERALISED DEBT OBLIGATION.

C

Central asset account

US terminology for ASSET MANAGEMENT ACCOUNT.

Central bank

The institution at the hub of a country's monetary and financial system. Each major developed country has one (see BANK OF ENGLAND, BUNDESBANK and FEDERAL RESERVE) but they do not all do the same things. Central banks carry out some combination of five different functions:

- they act as banker to a government;
- they act as banker to commercial banks;
- they supervise the banking system;
- they print and issue a country's currency;
- they are the LENDER OF LAST RESORT, a back-stop that can print money in a severe financial crisis.

There have been three great inventions since the beginning of time: fire, the wheel and central banking.
Will Rogers

Certificate of accrual on Treasury securities

A US financial invention. Certificates of accrual on Treasury securities (CATS) are Treasury BONDS that pay no INTEREST during their life. They are therefore sold at a deep DISCOUNT to their face value, and redeemed at their full face value at MATURITY. For example, a parent seeking to provide for a ten-year-old child going to college at age 18 might buy CATS with a face value of, say, $15,000 for a price of $62.222 per

100, or a total of $9,393 including commission. On the child's 18th birthday, the bond matures and pays the face value of $15,000. As with ZERO-COUPON BONDS, CATS are popular with investors who need money after a specific date and not before (for example, people about to retire or students about to go to college).

Certificate of deposit

A certificate issued by a BANK to indicate ownership of a DEPOSIT of as little as $100 or as much as $100,000. A certificate of deposit (CD) is a NEGOTIABLE INSTRUMENT that can be bought and sold on a SECONDARY MARKET between the time it is issued and the time that it is redeemed. CDs pay INTEREST at MATURITY and are bought and sold according to the YIELD offered. In the United States, they are also issued by SAVINGS AND LOAN INSTITUTIONS, and deposits are protected by the FEDERAL DEPOSIT INSURANCE CORPORATION.

CFTC

See COMMODITY FUTURES TRADING COMMISSION.

Charge

There are at least two meanings.

- Property pledged or taken as SECURITY for a LOAN, as in "the BANK that lent them the money to buy a house has a charge on the house".
- The cost of goods or services, particularly of financial services – for example, bank charges, the fees paid to banks by their customers for services. The basis for these charges was often opaque. Although regulators in most developed countries have made strides in recent years (for example, by insisting on clearer labelling on itemised

statements), customers still sometimes find it hard to trace exactly what they are being charged for.

Charge card

A plastic card that allows its owner to buy goods before paying for them. Department stores issue charge cards to customers that apply for them. The customers can then spend as much as they like in the store until the day each month when they have to pay, in full, the outstanding DEBT charged to their card. Some charge cards have a CREDIT facility, which allows the repayment to be spread over time. (See also CREDIT CARD and GOLD CARD.)

Chartism

See TECHNICAL ANALYSIS.

Cheque

A BILL OF EXCHANGE drawn on a BANK and payable on demand, although it usually takes three or four days to clear (see next entry). Despite the increasing use of plastic cards, direct transfers of funds and AUTOMATED TELLER MACHINES, cheques are still widely used, by both companies and individuals.

- A cheque is "stopped" when a bank refuses to clear it, that is, refuses to transfer the funds as requested (often because the funds are not there). The bank then returns the cheque to the BRANCH it came from.
- A post-dated cheque is one with a future date on it, before which it cannot be cleared.
- A crossed cheque can only be paid to a payee's bank ACCOUNT; it cannot be paid in CASH.
- A blank cheque is one where the amount to be paid is left blank, to be filled in by the payee.

C

Cheque clearing

The process by which BANKS (and, increasingly, specialist contractors working for banks) DEBIT and CREDIT the ACCOUNTS of customers on which cheques are drawn. A has an account with bank X; B has one with bank Y. When A writes a cheque to B, the cheque passes between bank X and Y. The banks then clear it by debiting X's account and crediting Y's account. Cheque clearing began in the coffee houses of London's Lombard Street where clerks gathered to exchange pieces of paper. These days, most of the work of transferring funds is done by computers. Even so, most transactions still, mysteriously, take three or more days to clear.

Chicago Board of Trade

The largest FUTURES exchange in the world. The Chicago Board of Trade (CBOT) and the CHICAGO MERCANTILE EXCHANGE (CME) between them handle about half of all the world's trading in futures. The CBOT has had the edge in financial futures and the CME in commodities. The CBOT began life in 1848 as a market for grain and later launched the first CONTRACT on the future price of grain. It subsequently pioneered the trading of financial futures and OPTIONS. Futures on Treasury BONDS and NOTES still make up a large part of its volume. Like the CME, the CBOT has links with markets in Europe and Asia, and trades in many of its contracts 24 hours a day. It also has a market to trade over the internet in paper, plastic, glass and other waste materials.

Chicago Board Options Exchange

The largest OPTIONS exchange in the United States and a subsidiary of the CHICAGO BOARD OF TRADE. The Chicago Board Options Exchange (CBOE) was the first to offer listed options on the S&P 100 INDEX in 1983. The CONTRACT gives the buyer the right to buy or sell the dollar value of the index at MATURITY.

It has since become one of the most popular contracts of its kind and dominates the market for options on indices. As well as options on individual SHARES, the CBOE trades in a range of innovative products such as long-term EQUITY participation securities (or LEAPS, options which last for up to five years) and EXCHANGE TRADED FUNDS (which allow investors to buy or sell shares in an entire PORTFOLIO of SECURITIES).

Chicago Mercantile Exchange

The Chicago Mercantile Exchange (CME) is the world's second largest exchange for the trading of FUTURES and OPTIONS on futures. Established in 1919, the "Merc", as it is known, was the first to trade in livestock futures (pork bellies and the like). Now it is best known as a market in futures, and options on futures, of INTEREST rates, STOCK indices (such as the S&P 500), FOREIGN EXCHANGE and COMMODITIES. The Merc still has trading FLOORS, where the majority of its contracts change hands, but it also has an electronic system, called Globex, which operates more or less 24 hours a day worldwide.

Chinese wall

A notional partition between two parts of a financial institution that are supposed to act independently of each other in order to avoid conflicts of interest between them. For example, it may be a divide between the corporate finance side of an INVESTMENT BANK (involved in new SHARE issues) and its fund management side. Without separation, the FUND MANAGERS might be tempted to buy the corporate financiers' new ISSUES in order to help the bank sell something that was not going well, not because they were a good investment for the fund. Or fund managers within a firm whose investment banking division is advising a client that is pondering a TAKEOVER bid might be tempted to buy the shares of the target company. When the takeover is announced, the target company's shares may jump in value and the fund managers, having inside knowledge not available to other investors, may make a tidy PROFIT.

Since the boom and subsequent bust of the dotcom market, regulators have also been keen to avoid conflicts between the advisory and broking arms of banks. Because their salaries and bonuses were pegged to the overall profitability of the bank, some investment ANALYSTS were found to be publicly touting particular new issues of shares which, privately, they considered rubbish. Other people, such as lawyers, erect Chinese walls to help them act independently on behalf of clients who may be in the same business or industry. As with banks, experience shows that such walls can be paper thin.

Churn

To trade excessively in the SHARES of a client's account, with the result that the BROKER generates a larger amount of COMMISSION income (based on turnover). Investors are most at risk from churning where they give FUND MANAGERS discretion on their behalf to buy and sell shares within certain limits. In the United States, churning is illegal if it can be proved that the purchases and sales in question were largely inappropriate for the client.

Circular transaction

Where two companies carry out reciprocal transactions artificially to inflate each other's accounts. For example, company A sells to B $1m-worth of goods and B reciprocates by immediately selling a similar amount to A. After the transaction nothing has changed except for the stated turnover of each company, which has become $1m higher than it would otherwise have been.

The City

The name traditionally given to the part of the City of London that is roughly bounded by St Paul's Cathedral to the west and the Tower of London to the east. It is also the collective name given to the many financial institutions in the area, as in "the City expects INTEREST rates to fall". The City (also sometimes known as the Square Mile) sprang up where it is because in the past all BANKS had to be based within walking distance of their supervisor, the BANK OF ENGLAND. These days, the throng of banks and SECURITIES houses that make the City of London the world's busiest international FINANCIAL CENTRE are just as likely to be housed in tower blocks further east in Canary Wharf or elsewhere in London.

City banks

The (shrinking) band of large BANKS that dominate Japan's financial system. They not only lend vast amounts to Japanese industry (and not much to Japanese consumers), but they are also intertwined with the big industrial and financial conglomerates (called *zaibatsu*) which contributed so much to Japan's post-war economic success. Yet what was a strength in the past has also become a weakness. The banks' extensive shareholdings in their customers are a boon when share prices are buoyant but a headache for the banks and the government when they are not. The lower the value of the banks' shareholdings, the thinner is the layer of fat protecting them from possible insolvency. The banks' holdings in industrial groups have also made it harder for the banks to write off bad LOANS when the economy falters and for the industrial groups to raise new CAPITAL with which to restructure themselves.

Class action

A lawsuit brought by one party on behalf of a group of individuals sharing the same grievance, for example, a legal action (alleging fraud, say) initiated by one shareholder on behalf of all shareholders. In the United States, where such actions are most common, companies insure themselves against the risks of having to pay compensation to successful claimants.

C

Clean price

A price for a BOND which does not include any INTEREST that may have accrued on it between the date of the most recent interest payment and the date of the price QUOTATION. (See also DIRTY PRICE.)

Clearing bank

A type of commercial BANK in the UK with authority to clear CHEQUES. Into this category fall the country's largest high-street banks as well as a handful of others with specialist pedigrees. (See CHEQUE CLEARING.)

Clearing house

A firm or agency that handles the processes involved in transferring money or SECURITIES from one owner to another. A clearing house enables those institutions that use it to NET off their CREDITS and DEBITS against each other at the end of each working day. So between two parties there needs to be only one consolidated transfer each day. As STOCK EXCHANGES have merged and become bigger, so clearing houses have followed suit. In 2002, EUROCLEAR and CREST joined forces to create Europe's largest clearing house. The combined operation covers about 60% of trades in European EQUITIES and around half of all deals in FIXED-INCOME SECURITIES. (See also AUTOMATED CLEARING HOUSE.)

Clearstream

A company that clears, settles and holds SECURITIES for financial organisations around the world. Clearstream is Europe's biggest clearing and settlement house. Each day it handles hundreds of thousands of transactions involving investors in 80 locations. For a fee, it makes sure that, when an investor buys or sells an EQUITY or a BOND, the correct payment is made and cleared with the buyer's BANK, and any certificate or documentary evidence is transferred. Clearstream will also hold securities for institutions and credit any DIVIDENDS or INTEREST paid on them.

Although considered unglamorous by many DEALERS and investors, clearing and settlement has become an increasingly important link in the smooth running of markets. With more and more deals done electronically, the chances of FRAUD or simple mistakes have become much greater.

Closed-end fund

A fund that has a fixed number of SHARES that can be bought and sold like those of any other company listed on a STOCK EXCHANGE. So investors who want to buy into the fund have to purchase its shares in the SECONDARY MARKET. Like an OPEN-ENDED FUND (such as a UNIT TRUST or MUTUAL FUND), a closed-end fund offers investors a spread of ASSETS managed by a professional team. However, unlike an open-ended fund, which simply issues new units whenever a new investor comes along, a closed-end fund must seek approval from its shareholders to increase the number of shares in issue. As a result, the shares can trade at either a PREMIUM or a DISCOUNT to the value of the underlying assets that the company owns. This is because investors' perceptions of the prospects for a particular fund do not always square with the value placed by the market on the underlying assets. In the UK, a close-end fund is called an INVESTMENT TRUST.

Closing price

The official STOCK EXCHANGE price of a SHARE, BOND or other SECURITY at the close of the exchange's trading day. Such prices can still change in AFTER-HOURS trading, and any changes are treated as though they occurred the following day.

CLS Bank

A BANK based in New York and owned by dozens of other banks worldwide which settles the $2 trillion or so that changes hands each day on the FOREIGN-EXCHANGE markets. Irrespective of time zones, where possible CLS Bank aims to settle the following day deals done in seven main currencies: US dollar, Australian dollar, Canadian dollar, euro, sterling, yen and Swiss franc. Most transactions are cleared during a five-hour window when most of the CENTRAL BANKS of the countries with the participating currencies are open for business. The bulk of CLS's business is accounted for by five main shareholders, which between them account for nearly half the daily turnover in the foreign-exchange markets. Other users, such as BROKERS and FUND MANAGERS, have to deal through one of the five.

CLS is the main champion of CONTINUOUS LINKED SETTLEMENT, a technique that has not only speeded up the settlement of transactions in foreign-exchange markets but also removed much of the counterparty RISK (that is, of one or other side not paying) that traders are exposed to when dealing in it.

CME

See CHICAGO MERCANTILE EXCHANGE.

COB

See COMMISSION DES OPÉRATIONS DE BOURSE.

COD

See CASH ON DELIVERY.

Co-financing

A technique for bringing the international muscle of institutions such as the WORLD BANK or the Asian Development Bank together with the financing clout of commercial BANKS. Projects in developing countries are co-financed jointly by the international institution and a group of commercial banks. It gives banks the comfort of knowing that borrowers rarely DEFAULT on LOANS from the World Bank and other such bodies. The World Bank or other institution benefits from the extra money, albeit on a quasi-commercial basis, that the commercial banks can bring to a project.

Collar

There are several meanings.

- When trading OPTIONS, the simultaneous selling of an OUT-OF-THE MONEY CALL OPTION and the buying of an IN-THE-MONEY PUT OPTION. In so doing, a trader will create a collar by limiting both the upside and the downside on the deal.
- When underwriting a new ISSUE of SECURITIES, a collar sets the minimum INTEREST rate required by a buyer of BONDS and the lowest price that a bond issuer will accept.
- When one company is taking over another, it may insist on a collar which protects the acquirer from having to put up more CASH (or more of its own SHARES if it is paying partly or wholly in EQUITY), should the price of its shares fall in the time between the agreement of the terms of a deal (or its acceptance by shareholders) and its closing.

Collateral

Property or ASSETS which are provided by a third party as

C

SECURITY for a borrower, as in "my parents let me use their house as collateral for a LOAN". The fine distinction between collateral (which is provided by a third party) and security (which is provided by the borrower) still exists in the UK and certain other jurisdictions. But in the United States, the terms are virtually indistinguishable; collateral NOTES or collateral surety are pledges of assets to support a loan.

Collateralised debt obligation

An INVESTMENT-GRADE SECURITY issued to investors in the CAPITAL MARKETS. Collateralised debt obligations (CDOs) are made up of a pool of existing BONDS or LOANS (for example, bonds issued by utilities in various EMERGING MARKETS). These are first transferred to a new company, or SPECIAL-PURPOSE VEHICLE, which then issues CDOS to investors supported by the COLLATERAL of the original bonds or loans. By transferring some of the RISK to EQUITY in the new company, the issuer is able to raise part of the new CDOS to investment grade. Typically, investors are offered various TRANCHES of DEBT and equity, some riskier than others. CDOS are usually divided into two sorts: collateralised bond obligations, which are based on bonds of different types; and collateralised loan obligations, supported by loans. Issuers of CDOS aim to profit either from the difference in YIELD between the underlying securities and the new ones issued to investors, or simply, as with BANKS, by spreading their risk to other investors.

Collect on delivery

US terminology for CASH ON DELIVERY.

COMEX

A US commodities market founded in 1870. Formerly known as the Commodities Exchange, COMEX is now a division of the

New York Mercantile Exchange. It is the leading market in the trading of FUTURES and OPTIONS on metals, specialising in aluminium, copper, gold and silver. Together with the London Metals Exchange, COMEX dominates worldwide trading in metals.

C

Comfort letter

A letter required by US securities legislation. Written by an independent AUDITOR, it guarantees that the information contained in a PROSPECTUS has not altered materially in the period between the preparation of the prospectus and its distribution to the public. Comfort letters can also be written by the parties to legal agreements covering points related to the substance of the agreement.

Commercial paper

SHORT-TERM DEBT instruments issued by top-notch BANKS and corporations. Born in the US financial markets, commercial paper spread rapidly in Europe and East Asia in the 1980s. It has a maturity of 5–365 days (most frequently 30–90), and is issued in dollops as small as $10,000 or as large as $1m. It is usually sold at a DISCOUNT to its face value and rarely bears INTEREST. When issued in the EUROMARKET, such instruments are known as Eurocommercial paper. Lenders like the fact that it is issued only by the soundest banks and companies and is often backed by additional lines of CREDIT.

Don't confuse selling with art.
Jack Taylor

Commission

The reward of an AGENT, usually expressed as a percentage of the sales that the agent generates on behalf of his or her client.

In most industries there are accepted rates for different types of business. Any negotiation of commission is done around these BENCHMARKS.

C

Commission des Opérations de Bourse

The official watchdog of the Paris Bourse (STOCK EXCHANGE). The Commission des Opérations de Bourse (COB) is a government agency that supervises new LISTINGS on the bourse, monitors TAKEOVERS and looks out for INSIDER DEALING and other infringements of the SECURITIES laws. It also takes an interest in accounting standards and efforts to make companies more transparent to investors. The COB's power and influence have grown in line with the rapid growth of the French STOCK-MARKET.

Commitment fee

A payment made to a lender in return for the guarantee of a LOAN (up to a certain size) as and when needed. The fee is usually a fraction of 1% of the amount committed.

Commodity

A raw material that is usually sold in bulk on either the SPOT MARKET (that is, for CASH against immediate delivery) or an EXCHANGE (where a CONTRACT expiring within a month is also reckoned to be on the spot market). Common commodities are grains, metals and certain foodstuffs (such as pork bellies, orange juice, coffee and cocoa). The most valuable commodities of all (by turnover) are oil and GOLD.

Commodity Futures Trading Commission

The US regulator of trading in COMMODITY FUTURES and

OPTIONS. Set up by Congress in 1974, the Commodity Futures Trading Commission (CFTC) ensures the integrity of the market and guards against manipulation, abusive trade practices and FRAUD.

Commodity trading adviser

An intermediary in the United States licensed to advise on the whys and wherefores of trading in COMMODITIES. Commodity trading advisers (CTAS) must be registered with the COMMODITY FUTURES TRADING COMMISSION, the market's main regulator.

Common stock

US terminology for ORDINARY SHARE.

Compensating balance

An amount that a customer is asked to deposit with a BANK when the bank makes a LOAN to the customer. On the surface this sounds rather odd. Why borrow money from a bank simply in order to put it back into the bank? The rationale for compensating balances lies in a time when there were strict limits on the RATE OF INTEREST that could be charged to lenders. Banks that wanted to charge more would insist that, in addition to paying the top rate, borrowers must deposit a certain amount (interest free) with the bank. This free balance would compensate for the interest payments that the bank was unable to collect on the loan.

Compliance officer

An employee of a SECURITIES firm who is appointed to make sure that the firm follows the (increasingly complex) rules laid down by the regulators of financial markets. Failure to comply with such rules can lead to the guilty division, or sometimes the whole firm, being banned from carrying on its business. So even during tough times, the compliance departments of INVEST-MENT BANKS and securities firms invariably escape cost cutting, especially since tightened rules following excesses during the dotcom bubble of the late 1990s forced banks and their corporate customers to be more aware of CONFLICTS OF INTEREST.

Composite insurer

An INSURANCE company which sells both casualty insurance (against damage to household contents, automobiles, travel plans and so on) and life insurance. In theory, this gives such companies a good spread of business and makes them less liable to the effects of calamities such as floods and hurricanes. In practice, the PREMIUMS they charge for cover, especially on bigger RISKS, and the cost to them of reinsurance, are highly cyclical, so their PROFITS still go up and down.

Concert party

A group of investors who act together to try to gain control of a company. Each buys a small stake which, when combined with the others, gives them control. In most jurisdictions with developed financial markets, parties of investors seeking to change a company's management or force it somehow to alter course must make their intentions clear. It is illegal for those acting in concert (and in secret) to manipulate a company's SHARE PRICE for their own gain.

Conflict of interest

An occasion where the interests of a person or firm in one guise are in conflict with the interests of a person or firm in another guise. For example, a BANK advising a company in its battle against a TAKEOVER will have a conflict if it is also a shareholder in the bidding company. Similarly, an ANALYST who is likely to be rewarded for helping a company with its FLOTATION may have a conflict if he or she is also expected to make an independent recommendation of the company's merits to would-be investors. CHINESE WALLS between different parts of the same INVESTMENT BANK or SECURITIES firm are designed to reduce such conflicts of interest. But they can never be high enough to stop conflicts altogether. The excesses of the dotcom boom (and subsequent bust) forced regulators on both sides of the Atlantic to re-examine the nature of possible conflicts and to tighten up the rules where they could.

Consensus

The common name for the International Agreement for Guidelines on Officially Supported Export Credit. The consensus is an agreement between member countries of the OECD on how far they will go in subsidising the RATE OF INTEREST on loans to buyers of their country's exports. The maximum interest rates that they agree to permit vary according to whether the importing country is rich, intermediate or poor.

Consortium bank

A BANK owned by a group of other banks from a number of different countries. Consortium banks were popular in the 1970s when they were seen as a way to gain a foothold in the markets represented by all the banks in the consortium. Many of these consortia have since been disbanded because banks either become confident enough to go into new markets on their own or decided that the markets were not sufficiently interesting.

Consumer credit

A LOAN granted to enable somebody to buy consumer goods such as cars, washing machines and such like. Many countries have consumer-credit laws designed to prevent consumers from being exploited. In the United States, at least 12 different government agencies are concerned in some way with ensuring that consumer credit is granted fairly. In most developed markets, governments insist that lenders quote the RATE OF IN-TEREST charged to consumers in a standardised form; in the UK it is called the annualised preference rate (APR).Yet, as many consumers find to their cost, such quotes can still be misleading.

Contango

When the prices for future delivery of COMMODITIES are higher than the prices for present delivery. This is the opposite of BACKWARDATION and may be known as forwardation.

Contested bid

See HOSTILE BID.

Continuous linked settlement

A method of settling deals done in the world's FOREIGN-EXCHANGE markets which has speeded up the time taken to clear transactions. Before continuous linked settlement, each party to a transaction to buy, say, dollars and sell Swiss francs was credited or debited separately and through a different route. Continuous linked settlement, pioneered by CLS BANK, has helped to remove much of the risk of one or other side defaulting on its payment and of muddles delaying the settlement of trans-actions. With $2 trillion or so traded each day on the foreign-exchange markets (much of it among fewer than a dozen big banks), delays can become expensive. Under continuous linked settlement, CLS Bank aims to clear the bulk of bargains struck in seven main currencies the following day. With ever closer links between currency and DERIVATIVES markets (for example, when trading in currency OPTIONS), speed is of the essence.

C

Contract

In general, a legally binding agreement between two parties that one will supply goods or services to the other for a specified price. A contract is also the unit in which OPTIONS are traded, usually with an option representing 1,000 shares of the underlying SECURITY. In FUTURES, a contract is an agreement to buy or sell specific amounts of a COMMODITY in the future.

Contract for difference

The generic name given to SWAPS that are traded to exploit the difference between the fixed price of a FINANCIAL INSTRUMENT agreed between two parties and the floating average of that price over the same period. As with most forms of swap, the contract is based on an exchange of income payments, or the right to such payments, which can benefit both parties. Some contracts for difference (CFDS) have specific uses. For example, a Brent CFD is a SHORT-TERM swap that enables investors to HEDGE their exposure to the difference in price between a CONTRACT to deliver crude oil at a certain date in the future and the price in the CASH MARKET on the same date.

Convertible

The capacity of one FINANCIAL INSTRUMENT to be converted into another. The expression usually applies to PREFERENCE SHARES or BONDS that can be exchanged for a set number of ORDINARY SHARES at a preordained price. Convertibles are attractive to investors who want more income than they can easily find from EQUITY, together with the potential for a greater uplift in value than bonds will normally allow. The advantage for the issuer is that, to the right audience, such instruments can be easier to sell.

C

Corporate bond

A BOND issued by a corporation. Unlike bonds issued by governments or government agencies, corporate bonds are taxable for most investors. They generally also have a term MATURITY, that is, all bonds issued together become due at the same time. Like government bonds, corporate bonds are traded on STOCK EXCHANGES, their prices are quoted in the news media and the companies that issue them can be rated by agencies for their CREDIT standing. Most corporate bonds are regarded as riskier than those of governments or supranational agencies, so they usually offer a higher YIELD.

Correspondent bank

Before BANKS opened their own BRANCHES around the world, they managed their international business by setting up a network of loose relationships with other banks in different countries. The correspondent banks provided services in their home market for the others in the network, and vice versa.

Cost of capital

The RATE OF RETURN that a company could earn if it chose another business with an equivalent RISK – in other words, the OPPORTUNITY COST of employing the CAPITAL where it is. Measures of this kind are used to decide whether investments are worth making or businesses are worth starting up. The cost of capital is also the weighted or average cost of a company's DEBT and various types of EQUITY: ORDINARY SHARES, PREFERENCE SHARES, DEBENTURES, BONDS, LOANS and so on.

C

Countertrade

See BARTER.

Coupon

A piece of paper attached to a BEARER SECURITY giving the bearer the right to the income (INTEREST or DIVIDEND) that comes with the security. To collect the income due, the bearer must detach the coupon and present it to the paying AGENT of the issuer of the security.

The word "coupon" is also used to refer to the interest rate itself. So a bond with a 10% coupon will pay $10 for every $100 of face value per year, usually in two six-monthly instalments. Registered bonds, many of which pay interest through electronic transfers, are gradually replacing coupon bonds, particularly in the United States, although the term lives on. (See REGISTERED SECURITY.)

Covenant

A promise contained in a TRUST deed or other agreement involving the ISSUE of SECURITIES that a certain thing will or will not be done. Designed to protect the lender's interest, covenants cover, for example, the split between DEBT and EQUITY for a CAPITAL raising, and the frequency with which DIVIDENDS or INTEREST are to be paid.

Cover

Funds to provide protection against loss (as in INSURANCE cover), or to guarantee payment of a LIABILITY (as in DIVIDEND COVER). Dividend cover refers to the number of times that a company's EARNINGS PER SHARE covers its dividend per share.

Covered warrant

A FINANCIAL INSTRUMENT that bestows on the holder the right, but not the obligation, to buy or sell an underlying ASSET such as an ORDINARY SHARE in a company. If the warrant is European-style, it can be exercised only on the date it expires; if it is American-style, it can be exercised at any time up to and including the date of expiry. (See AMERICAN-STYLE OPTION and EUROPEAN-STYLE OPTION.) As with an OPTION or a FUTURE, a warrant gives the holder GEARING, that is, exposure to the underlying asset for less than the cost of buying it outright. So the price (or PREMIUM) paid for a warrant is usually less than the cost of the underlying asset; and the holder can lose only the amount paid. Unlike warrants issued by a company, covered warrants do not create extra shares.

When will the market bottom?
Frankly, when investors stop asking the question.
Richard Bernstein

Crash

What happens when a STOCKMARKET falls precipitously, as in the United States in 1929 and on BLACK MONDAY in many markets in 1987. J.K. Galbraith, in his classic book, *The Great Crash 1929*, gave five main reasons for the 1929 fall.

1 The poor distribution of money in American society. The top 5% of the population was reckoned to be receiving 33% of all personal income.
2 Bad corporate structure. The 1920s was a decade of stockmarket fraud; crooks bled companies of huge amounts of money.
3 Bad banking structure. There were too many independent units; the failure of one led others to collapse in a domino effect.
4 The United States' foreign balance. There was a declining trade surplus for the first time in modern history.
5 The poor state of economic intelligence at the time. The government made decisions that were contrary to the best interests

of the economy, and too little was known about the true state of the economy.

Putting these and other failings right has done much to prevent similar falls occurring. But, as Black Monday in 1987 shows, anything can happen if investors lose confidence in the markets. The decline in share prices from 2001 onwards was painful – share prices on most major STOCK EXCHANGES halved in value – but it was not a crash.

In '29 when the banks went bust
Our coins still read "In God We Trust".
E.Y. Harburg

Credit

A LOAN or the ability to raise a loan, as in "he bought the washing machine on credit" and "her credit at the bank is good". The term covers all forms of loans, BONDS, obligations on CHARGE CARDS and CREDIT CARDS, as well as LETTERS OF CREDIT and other forms of standby commitment from banks.

Credit card

A rectangular piece of plastic that empowers its owner to buy goods and services, and to buy them on CREDIT. The use of credit cards, which should not be confused with CHARGE CARDS, has grown rapidly in recent years. Most credit cards are issued by BANKS and retailers. The business is dominated by two powerful brand names, Visa and Mastercard. These are marketing organisations to which the banks that issue cards are affiliated. Most credit cards offer a grace period (usually 25 days) during which INTEREST charges do not accrue. Thereafter, a holder pays interest on the remaining balance until it is paid off. Most credit cards also allow their holders to obtain a CASH advance; some charge a fee for this service, and interest is generally payable from the date of the advance until it is repaid in full. Despite attempts by regulators to standardise the basis on which interest rates are quoted, it can still be hard to compare one card with another.

C

Credit default swap

A bespoke DERIVATIVE that allows the buyer to purchase a form of INSURANCE from the seller against the risk that a third party will DEFAULT on its payment. Suppose there are two counterparties to a deal: a MARKET MAKER and an investor. They first decide on the ASSET that is to be the third party; for example, a BOND issued by a company or perhaps a sovereign borrower. The market maker agrees to make regular payments to the investor for two years (the life of the bond), each one co-inciding with the INTEREST payments received on the bond. If the third party defaults at any time during the two years, then the market maker would make the regular fixed payment to the investor and hand over the bond in exchange for the equivalent of the bond's PAR value plus any remaining interest. Credit default swaps are somewhere between a CASH instrument and a derivative and, believe it or not, are reckoned to be among the most straightforward types of credit derivative.

Credit duration

A measure (expressed as a figure) of how long it takes to repay a BOND's purchase price in present-day values. This depends on a combination of the present value of its CASH FLOWS (both INTEREST and repayments of PRINCIPAL over the bond's life), the proportion of the bond's current price that these cash flows form and the period left to run before the bond matures. Bonds with a low COUPON (interest rate) generally have a longer duration and are therefore more sensitive to changes in the RATE OF INTEREST. So when rates are volatile it may pay an investor to choose a bond with a lower duration.

Credit enhancement

A technique used by issuers of BONDS to make it easier and cheaper to raise DEBT. Companies issuing bonds in the debt markets can ask banks to provide LETTERS OF CREDIT to support an ISSUE, so raising their CREDIT RATING by a notch or two. Municipal authorities can do the same by insuring an issue of new bonds with a specialist agency such as America's Municipal Bond Investors' Assurance. These agencies or banks charge a fee in return for assuming part of the RISK associated with the issue. The effect is to reduce the RATE OF INTEREST or COUPON paid to the holder of the bond. This is because a buyer will generally think a higher credit rating reduces the risk of a DEFAULT (that is, of the issuer being unable to pay interest or to repay the bond in full when it becomes due).

Credit insurance

Protection against the chance of abnormal losses from unpaid accounts receivable (that is, amounts owed to a person or company by creditors). Banks lending to a company against the security of its accounts receivable will often insist on INSURANCE of this kind. Individuals with MORTGAGES or large amounts of CONSUMER CREDIT may also be asked to take out similar COVER to protect them against death or disability.

Credit line

A credit limit agreed between a customer and a BANK which the customer can draw upon as and when required.

Credit note

A written message informing a customer that his or her account with a supplier has been credited (and by how much). Credit notes are frequently used when a customer returns goods as being below standard, or when there has been a short shipment.

Credit rating

A formal assessment of a company's creditworthiness, and of its ability to meet payments on time. A credit rating is often obtained by a trader dealing with a new customer for the first time. It may come from a client's bankers or from existing suppliers, or from one of the specialist agencies (such as Dun & Bradstreet) that provide such ratings for a fee. Agencies (such as Moody's or Standard & Poor's) also assign formal credit ratings to the issuers of BONDS, be they governments, national or supranational agencies, or companies. The higher the rating, the lower is the risk of default. The highest (and therefore safest) rating is usually AAA (triple A) and the lowest is D. Issuers that are downgraded to junk are called FALLEN ANGELS; those that make the opposite journey are known as RISING STARS.

Credit risk

The risk that a BOND, LOAN or some other form of CREDIT will not be repaid when it becomes due.

Credit union

An organisation in which a group of people with a common bond (such as employees of the same company or members of a trade union) get together to pool their savings. Since credit unions do not try to make a PROFIT, most can offer higher deposit rates and lower borrowing rates to their members than commercial BANKS. Surprisingly, credit unions are popular in the United States, where they are regulated by the National Credit Union Administration. They are also a popular way of redistributing money in developing countries where borrowers have little SECURITY and banks are reluctant to lend.

CREST

The LONDON STOCK EXCHANGE'S SHARE settlement system, now owned by EUROCLEAR, a former rival based in Brussels.

CRM

Short for customer relationship management: the management of an institution's relationship with its customers. CRM involves measuring the profitability of different customer segments and offering appropriate services to each one. Typically, customers go through a cycle of borrowing (when they are young), saving (when at the peak of their earning power) and dissaving (when they are in old age). The trick for a financial institution, as with any business offering a service, is to maximise the value of the relationship at each stage.

Cross default

A condition that may be attached to a DEBT or a SECURITY. If the borrower or issuer DEFAULTS on any of its other debts or securities, this automatically counts as a default in respect of the debt or security that contains the cross-default clause. The lender then has the right to pursue repayments as if the borrower or issuer were in default on its debt or security.

CTA

See COMMODITY TRADING ADVISER.

Cum div

A SHARE being sold together with the right to a DIVIDEND that has been declared but not yet paid. In most cases, shares are deemed to be cum div up to a few days before the register of eligible shareholders is closed. Then the share goes ex-dividend, or EX-DIV. Similarly, CUM RIGHTS is a share that is being sold together with the right to take up a new offer of shares; and ex-rights refers to one that does not.

C

Current account

See ACCOUNT.

Current ratio

The ratio of a company's current LIABILITIES to its current ASSETS.

- ▪ Current assets = CASH, bank deposits and other items that can quickly be turned into cash
- ▪ Current liabilities = SHORT-TERM LOANS and trade CREDIT
- ▪ Current assets − current liabilities = working capital (see also CAPITAL EMPLOYED)

The current ratio is used as a guide to a company's SOLVENCY. It has only limited use in comparing companies across industries, however. The appropriate current ratio for a company depends on the sector to which it belongs and on the normal terms of trade in that industry. These terms can vary greatly.

Cushion bond

A BOND that can be retired early – that is, it can be called in before it reaches MATURITY. There is a stated price (the CALL price) at which such bonds can be called. This inevitably holds down the price of the bond in the SECONDARY MARKET. As a result, cushion bonds are less volatile than other bonds of a similar maturity, making them suitable for investors wanting to reduce their RISK.

Custodian

Somebody (usually a BANK but sometimes a lawyer) who holds an investor's SECURITIES on that investor's behalf. A custodian handles everything that arises from the ownership of the securities, such as the collection of income, voting at meetings, exercising rights and so on. Some institutions, such as the Bank of New York, have built sizeable businesses around such services. They often cater for INSTITUTIONAL INVESTORS who have little experience of investing in foreign markets and who may invest outside the United States primarily through AMERICAN DEPOSITARY RECEIPTS.

Cyclical stock

A STOCK that rises quickly when investors expect the economy to turn up and falls again when it shows signs of turning down. Cyclical stocks include engineering, cars, and paper and packaging. In contrast, non-cyclical stocks, such as food and pharmaceuticals, vary less with movements in the economy. Canny investors try to anticipate an upturn in the economy by switching out of defensive, non-cyclical stocks into cyclical ones. Movements of this kind can occur surprisingly quickly when the telltale signs emerge.

Daily trading limit

A limit imposed by many COMMODITIES and OPTIONS
markets on the extent to which individual CONTRACTS may
rise or fall in value during a single day. Each STOCK EX-
CHANGE sets limits according to the sensitivity of the instrument and the volumes traded. For example, the CHICAGO
BOARD OF TRADE limits daily movements up or down in its
Treasury bond FUTURES contract to two points ($200). The idea
is that this helps to maintain an orderly market.

Day trader

A retail investor who deals on the STOCKMARKET via online
brokers. Day traders came to epitomise the boom (and subsequent
bust) of the dotcom era. Most make a living from trading in and
out of STOCKS on a daily basis, something that in the past only
professional investors with expensive equipment could do. Although day traders can make money by selling the market SHORT
(selling borrowed stock and then buying it at a lower price), it is
generally easier to prosper when stockmarkets are rising.

Dealer

An individual or firm acting as PRINCIPAL when buying or
selling SECURITIES. Unlike a BROKER, who acts on somebody
else's behalf, a dealer trades on his or her own account and
bears the RISK involved in a transaction. By law in the United
States customers must be told when they buy securities from a
broker who is acting as a dealer, because most financial-services
firms operate both as brokers and principals. (See also DUAL
CAPACITY.)

Debenture

A long-term DEBT instrument which is often secured on the

general creditworthiness of the issuer rather than on any specific ASSET. When a company goes bust and is liquidated, debenture holders (like most other BOND holders) take precedence over ordinary shareholders in claiming a right to any of the company's remaining assets.

D

Debit card

A piece of plastic much like a CREDIT CARD, except that it gives the holder no CREDIT. A debit card is passed through an electronic reading device at a point of sale and in this way debits the holder's bank ACCOUNT automatically (and immediately) with the value of the sale. As with credit cards, banks usually charge a fee to withdraw CASH via a debit card from another bank's ATM machine. Some banks also levy a surcharge for withdrawing money from an ATM abroad. Even so, it is still usually cheaper to withdraw money via a debit card from a local ATM machine than to change one hard currency into another.

A borrower is servant to the lender.
Proverbs 22:7

Debt

An obligation of one person to pay something (usually money) to another.

There are but two ways of paying debt: increase of industry in raising income; increase of thrift in laying out.
Thomas Carlyle

Debt service ratio

The ratio of a country's annual repayments on its foreign DEBT to the value of its annual HARD-CURRENCY EARNINGS from exports. The ratio is used as a guide to a country's creditworthiness, or lack of it. For many Latin American countries in the 1980s the ratio was well over 100%. All their hard-currency export earnings (and more) went to service the debt to foreign banks and governments. Even in 2001, Latin America's ratio of debt service to exports as a whole was over 50%, twice as high as that of other regions. It is perhaps not surprising, therefore, that Argentina chose at the end of that year to DEFAULT on its debt to foreign banks and institutions.

Blessed are the young, for they shall inherit the national debt.
Herbert Hoover

Default

Failure to repay a LOAN or a BOND according to the terms of a CONTRACT. The first step in default is usually to cease payments of INTEREST on the loan, let alone repayments of any PRINCIPAL owed. Once a borrower is in default there are various legal moves that a lender can make to try to recover the money, or to get hold of any underlying SECURITY backing the loan. In most cases, it is in the creditors' interests to club together to find a way of rolling over or working off the amount owed.

Sovereign debt – the obligation of nations – was widely thought to have the least chance of default. In fact, it was more volatile and carried a greater risk than the debt of companies or even individuals.
Michael Milken

Defeasance

The placing of ASSETS, like CASH or TREASURY BILLS, in TRUST by the issuer of a BOND. All the INTEREST and PRINCIPAL due on the bond are subsequently repaid out of these assets by the TRUSTEE.

Defined benefit pension

A PENSION that promises to pay a specified amount to each beneficiary after a set number of years of service. Also known as a final-salary scheme because the benefit in retirement is a proportion of the employee's final salary when he or she retires. Either the employer or the employee can contribute to such pensions (usually it is both) but, importantly, the investment RISK lies with the employer. So, whatever happens, the retiree when eligible is guaranteed a minimum pension. This is fine while STOCKMARKETS are rising and surpluses are accumulating to the pension scheme; it is not so fine for the company when markets are falling and deficits are piling up. Regulations forcing companies to reflect in their accounts any shortfall in the funding level of their pension scheme, and to make it up if necessary, have put extra pressure on such schemes, particularly in the UK. The result is that many are being closed to new entrants who instead are being offered DEFINED CONTRIBUTION PENSIONS.

Defined contribution pension

A PENSION in which an employee elects to contribute a proportion of his or her salary until retirement. In most cases an employer will make contributions too, but, unlike a defined benefit pension, the investment RISK lies entirely with the employee. So the employer bears no responsibility for making up any shortfall. Called 401(k) plans in the United States, where they were started, defined contribution pensions are designed to shift to the employee not just the investment risk (that is, whether the scheme makes or loses money) but also responsibility for managing it. The cost of administering pensions and the unpredictability of the STOCKMARKET have persuaded an increasing number of countries and companies to opt for defined contribution pensions. Japan, with one of the world's fastest-ageing populations, and countries in continental Europe are embracing the idea.

Delivery

The transfer of title of a FINANCIAL INSTRUMENT from one owner to another. Hence the delivery date, delivery month and so on – the time when delivery is to be made. In COMMODITY markets, there are three main classes of delivery:

- **current delivery** – delivery in the current calendar month;
- **nearby delivery** – delivery in the next calendar month;
- **distant delivery** – delivery in a month that is further away.

Dematerialise

In finance, the word is used to describe the process of transferring into electronic form something that was previously recorded on paper. Thus it can be said that SHARES and BONDS are gradually being "dematerialised", as increasingly the certificates that investors used to hold are stored in electronic form (see EUROCLEAR). It can also be said that banks themselves are dematerialising as their branches become fewer and fewer, and their dealings with customers increasingly take place through ATMS or online.

Deposit

There are several meanings.

1 Money left as SECURITY before receipt of a service, such as a tenant might give a landlord before moving into a furnished property, or a telephone company might demand before connecting a line for a new customer.
2 Natural resources found underground, as in South Africa's rich mineral deposits.
3 Money left with a BANK for safekeeping. Such deposits come in many different forms.

- **Demand deposit.** Money that can be withdrawn on demand or without notice.
- **Savings deposit.** A sort of piggy bank account, designed for regular savings that are rarely withdrawn. It pays INTEREST but at below market rates.
- **Time deposit.** A deposit that can be withdrawn only after a specified period of time; for example, a three-month deposit or a six-month deposit. These deposits pay interest at close-to-market rates and are also known as fixed deposits.

Deposit insurance

A safety net for those depositing their savings with banks. One of the first deposit insurance schemes was set up by New York State in 1829. Since then most developed countries have established schemes that protect depositors from the possibility that their BANK will collapse. The RISKS can be real. During the Great Depression in the 1930s, more than 10,000 (admittedly small) banks in the United States went bust or closed their doors. To protect savers from losing their money, the FEDERAL DEPOSIT INSURANCE CORPORATION guarantees deposits up to $100,000 should the bank fail. Savers' deposits and those of their families are aggregated so that the rules are applied fairly between depositors. In the UK, depositors get back only a proportion of their total savings.

Does deposit insurance encourage banks to be reckless with their deposits? Yes and no. Evidence suggests that banks generally collapse in countries which have unstable economies (or governments) and whose financial markets lack transparency. Some countries, such as Germany, encourage banks to snoop on each other to keep them on their best behaviour.

Deposit protection

An INSURANCE scheme into which BANKS pay a PREMIUM to protect depositors against loss should the bank go bust. Such schemes usually give limited protection, covering small DEPOSITS up to a certain fixed amount and insuring larger deposits only up to that amount. This tempts big depositors to spread their money around several institutions to get the maximum insurance COVER. The main argument against deposit protection schemes is that they give badly run institutions a competitive advantage. (See FEDERAL DEPOSIT INSURANCE CORPORATION.)

Depreciation

The effect of the passage of time (wear and tear or technical obsolescence, for example) on the value of tangible ASSETS such as machinery; recognition that the value of an asset at one end of an accounting year is different from its value at the other end. Accountants deduct an amount from a company's annual PROFIT to take account of depreciation.

There are three ways of calculating depreciation for the purposes of a company's books.

- **The straight-line method.** An estimated scrap value of an asset at the end of its life is subtracted from the original cost. This is then divided by the number of years of useful life that the asset is supposed to have. For example, a computer bought for $1,000 with a five-year life would be depreciated at the rate of 20% a year:

Year	Annual depreciation ($)	Year-end value ($)
1	900 × 20% = 180	1,000 − 180 = 820
2	900 × 20% = 180	820 − 180 = 640
3	900 × 20% = 180	640 − 180 = 460
4	900 × 20% = 180	460 − 180 = 280
5	900 × 20% = 180	280 − 180 = 100

- **The reducing balance method.** A fixed percentage of the value of an asset last year is set aside out of profit each year.
- **The inflation-adjusted method.** This tries to take

account of the fact (ignored by other methods) that the cost of replacing the asset will usually be greater (if only because of inflation) than its original cost. An amount adjusted for the rate of inflation during the year is set aside out of profit each year.

D

All these methods ignore the fact that in a fast-changing technological world most assets are unlikely to be replaced with anything like themselves. In some cases (with computers or telecommunications, for instance) the cost of replacement may be considerably less than the original cost, inflation notwithstanding.

Deregulation

The process of removing legal or quasi-legal restrictions on the types of business done, or on the price charged, within a particular industry. The aim of most deregulation is to boost competition by increasing the freedom of players within the industry. In recent years, industries such as airlines, banking, stockbroking and telecommunications have been deregulated around the world. In the United States, the removal of INTEREST-rate ceilings (called Regulation Q) was one example of price deregulation. In the UK, the introduction of DUAL CAPACITY in the STOCKMARKET was an example of non-price deregulation.

Governments aim to strike the right balance. Regulation, after all, is often there to protect consumers. For example, if airlines are allowed to compete too fiercely, safety standards may fall with fatal consequences. Likewise, if BANKS compete too fiercely, their DEPOSITS may be put at risk. Sometimes (as many believe happened in the US energy market) the pendulum swings too far towards deregulation. The abuse of free markets by Enron, an energy trader that went spectacularly bust in 2001, caused regulators to reconsider tightening the rules.

Derivatives

A general term for financial ASSETS that are "derived" from

other financial assets. For example, an OPTION to buy a Treasury BOND: the option (one financial asset) is derived from the bond (another financial asset). The value of the option depends on the performance of the bond. This can be taken a stage further. For example, the value of an option on a FUTURES CONTRACT depends on the performance of the futures contract, which, in turn, will vary with the value of the underlying contract or SECURITY. Derivatives exist for assets (like EQUITIES or bonds) as well as for INTEREST rates, currency exchange rates and STOCKMARKET indices. The main advantage of derivatives is that they give investors leverage in the market in which they are trading. This can either enhance their RETURNS or help to HEDGE risks.

Regulators worry that the market for derivatives undermines the market for the original underlying asset. This happened in late 1987, when so-called PROGRAM TRADERS (those using computers to determine when and how to profit from ARBITRAGE) were widely believed to have contributed to the VOLATILITY of the market and the steep fall in SHARE prices on BLACK MONDAY. Regulators can reduce the risk of this happening by encouraging markets to become as liquid as possible. Unlike the futures contracts for agricultural products on which they are based, the supply of financial derivatives is virtually unlimited. So it would be difficult, if not impossible, to corner the market in, say, options on dollar/yen interest-rate contracts.

> *Financial weapons of mass destruction.*
> Warren Buffett on derivatives

Devaluation

A sudden, downward jerk in the value of a currency vis-a-vis other currencies; the opposite of revaluation. Governments devalue a country's currency when its costs have risen faster than those of its competitors, or when its exports are no longer competitive in price. Devaluations are often exacerbated by the activity of speculators in the FOREIGN-EXCHANGE markets. They buy and sell currencies in anticipation of, and to profit from, a devaluation. Governments are often forced to devalue their currencies when the system of fixed exchange rates under which they are operating becomes untenable. To sustain a fixed exchange rate, a country must have enough RESERVES, often in dollars, to purchase all offers of its currency at the established exchange rate. When a government is unable or unwilling to do so, as happened in Argentina in 2001, it must devalue its currency to a point which it can support. This caused problems for many Argentinians who had taken out dollar-denominated loans, notably MORTGAGES, in the belief that the value of the peso would remain tied to the dollar. Devaluations also hit exporters selling goods at prices set in the devalued currency.

It does not mean, of course, that the pound here in Britain, in your pocket or purse or in your bank, has been devalued.

Harold Wilson, British prime minister, after the pound was devalued

Dilution

When a company ISSUES more SHARES, and sells them for less than their market price, the value of each existing share is diluted. The total value of the company is being divided into a larger number of little pieces (that is, shares). Hence the value that attaches to each piece gets smaller. Companies talk about their fully-diluted EARNINGS PER SHARE. This refers to the earnings per share when all shares are included: ORDINARY SHARES plus any CONVERTIBLE securities (that is, convertible into shares), as well as all WARRANTS and stock OPTIONS.

Direct

A general word for the way in which financial services are sold by telephone or over the internet rather than face-to-face by an AGENT (in INSURANCE) or OVER THE COUNTER (in banking), as in "direct insurance" or "direct banking". There has been rapid growth in the direct selling of financial services in recent years. This has enabled many firms to cut out middlemen, with the result that agents' COMMISSIONS have been greatly reduced. Hopes that intermediaries of any sort could be cut out by using the internet led to the launch of numerous such services during the dotcom boom. Many have since closed or merged with others, but the idea lives on and is increasingly popular with many consumers.

Direct debit

An instruction from a BANK's customer asking the bank regularly to debit his or her ACCOUNT with the amount demanded by a named creditor. Direct debits are designed to make it easy to pay regular but varying bills (like those of utilities).

Dirty price

A price for a BOND which includes the amount of INTEREST that has accrued on the bond since the date of the last interest payment. (See also CLEAN PRICE.)

Discount

As a verb it means to sell at a reduced price; as a noun it refers to the reduction in price itself. A CASH discount is a reduction in price given to someone who pays immediately for goods in cash or a cash equivalent. A trade discount is a reduction in price given to someone who is in the same trade as the vendor – for example, by a wholesaler of garments to a fashion boutique. When a bill is sold for a discount to its face value, the discount represents the interest forgone between the time of the sale and the date that the bill matures. A BOND trading at less than 80% of its PAR value is said to be trading at a deep discount. This usually means that the COUPON (that is, RATE OF INTEREST) is far below the market rate or the quality of the bond's CREDIT is in question.

Discount rate

The rate at which a CENTRAL BANK discounts government BONDS and other first-class DEBT instruments to commercial banks; or the rate at which central banks lend to commercial banks, using government bills as COLLATERAL. In SECURITIES markets, it is also the RATE OF INTEREST used to determine the present value of a stream of future income. In theory, the rate should rise the riskier the source of the stream of income becomes. Assume the rate is 10%; then ask what value today will produce $1,000 in a year's time at that rate. The answer is $909 ($1,000 divided by 1.1, which is the figure you get if you compound 1 at the rate of 10% for a year). The method is used by ANALYSTS to compare one income stream with another, or to weigh up the attractions of different types of investment.

Discount window

A FACILITY provided by CENTRAL BANKS whereby commercial banks can lodge their surplus RESERVES or top up their reserves against the SECURITY of their top-quality ASSETS.

Discretionary account

An account that an investor has with a BROKER which gives the broker discretion to buy or sell SECURITIES on behalf of the investor without consultation. This discretion usually applies within certain pre-agreed limits and is reviewed regularly.

Disintermediation

The exclusion of financial intermediaries from the process of allocating savings. For example, a company may choose to raise EQUITY, or issue BONDS, directly in the financial markets, rather than borrow from a BANK. A government may choose to raise revenue by issuing attractive savings bonds that are sold directly to the public, rather than by the traditional method of selling Treasury bonds to banks.

To some extent disintermediation is a function of the economic cycle. Market rates generally move ahead of banks' IN-TEREST rates. So when rates are rising, investors prefer to put their money directly into the markets, and borrowers are happy to pay marginally more for easy access to this money. When rates are falling, bank rates lag behind market rates. Investors then switch their money out of the markets and into financial institutions. The opportunities for disintermediation can be expected to increase the wider the variety of sophisticated instruments is made available in the markets.

Distribution channel

The route by which a company sells its products or services. A BANK may have a variety of distribution channels, starting with its BRANCHES, followed by its direct-mail operations, its telephone selling and its electronic dealings via the internet. The relative importance of these channels changes over time. Banks are faced with a difficult decision about what to do with all their expensive branches (and the expensive employees in them). Customers want the convenience of being able to make transactions by telephone or via the internet, only occasionally needing to use a branch.

Dividend

The part of the EARNINGS of a company that is distributed to its shareholders. Payment of a dividend is not automatic. It is decided on by the company and declared by the board of directors. Companies listed on STOCK EXCHANGES in the United States usually report their earnings, and therefore declare dividends, every three months; in Europe, it is generally every six months. Dividends on PREFERENCE SHARES are paid at a fixed rate; all others may vary with the performance of the company. Some companies, usually described by ANA-

LYSTS as growth companies, plough most of their earnings back into the business because they are growing fast and so pay few, if any, dividends. Others, known as value companies, usually have more mature businesses and therefore generate more CASH which can be distributed as dividends to shareholders. Each type of SHARE appeals to different types of investor. Most companies find that cutting their dividend from one year to the next carries considerable risk. Their share price may fall and consequently the cost of raising new CAPITAL in the markets may rise. As a result, those that do pay regular dividends go to great lengths to maintain the payout from year to year. This can have the effect of squeezing CASH FLOW that might better be used for other purposes.

Dividend cover

The number of times that a company's annual DIVIDENDS can be divided into its annual EARNINGS. So if a company's after-tax earnings in a year are $20m, and it pays out $2.5m in dividends, that year its dividend cover is eight.

This is similar to the dividend payout ratio, a concept popular in the United States. The dividend payout ratio is the percentage of the company's earnings paid to shareholders in CASH. With companies in old, mature industries (called VALUE STOCKS), it is generally high (and the dividend cover is therefore low). But for young growing businesses (or GROWTH STOCKS) that need CAPITAL for reinvestment, it is usually low (and the dividend cover is high).

Documentary credit

A method of financing trade. BANKS provide the buyer of goods with CREDIT to pay the exporter on the strength of documents which prove that the buyer has proper title to the goods. This is useful when documents reach the buyer more quickly than the goods themselves.

Dotcom stocks

During the internet boom, which ended with a bump at the beginning of 2000, part of the strategy of dotcom companies (those with the suffix .com in their registered name) was to aim for an INITIAL PUBLIC OFFERING of their shares as soon as possible. Once public, such companies became known as dotcom stocks. Although many of them made no PROFITS, until the technology boom turned to bust their shares rose ever higher.

Double-taxation agreement

It is a fundamental principle of tax law in most countries that the same income should not be taxed twice. Consequently, there is a network of agreements between pairs of countries that seek to avoid taxing income in one country when it has already been taxed in another. This applies in particular to income that arises in one country but is then remitted to a resident in another. Double taxation can also occur when income passes from one taxable entity (such as a corporation) to another (such as a shareholder). Attempts to reduce the double taxation of DIVIDENDS (paid out of a company's taxed income to taxable individuals) have been less popular with governments than attempts to eliminate the taxation of the same income in two fiscal jurisdictions.

Dow Jones Indexes

Dow Jones, the company which publishes the *Wall Street Journal*, also gives its name to the most famous STOCKMARKET INDEX in the world. The Dow Jones Industrial Average (introduced in October 1896) is a closely watched index based on the average prices of a selection of about 30 companies quoted on the NEW YORK STOCK EXCHANGE. It gives an indication of the rate and direction in which the market as a whole is moving. Other less widely reported indexes include the so-called Global Titans, companies big enough to stand out internationally, a Composite Average and indexes covering sectors such as transport and utilities. This is just the tip of the iceberg. In all, Dow Jones licenses around 3,000 indexes used by investors for different products and in different markets around the world. In a joint venture with the Deutsche BÖRSE, EURONEXT Paris and the Swiss Exchange, the company also calculates the STOXX series of indexes of European companies in dollars and EUROS. These are calculated on the same basis as the Dow Jones Global Indexes, so that investors can compare one with another.

Downgrade

A reduction in the RATING of a company or of its DEBT securities. Companies whose ratings are reduced to the point where they are no longer INVESTMENT GRADE, and whose bonds therefore become JUNK BONDS, are known as FALLEN ANGELS.

Drawdown

Making use of funds that have been made available under a bank FACILITY.

Dual capacity

The ability of the same financial institution to be both STOCK-BROKER (that is AGENT) and stock JOBBER or MARKET MAKER (that is PRINCIPAL). (See also BIG BANG.) In any business, being both agent and principal inevitably leads to potential CONFLICTS OF INTEREST. In stockbroking, for example, it presents opportunities to put good deals (retrospectively) on a company's own books and bad deals on the books of clients.

Dual-capital trust

See SPLIT-CAPITAL INVESTMENT TRUST.

D Due date

The date on which a payment of INTEREST or PRINCIPAL becomes due.

Due diligence

The thorough search of a business done either by a potential manager of a new ISSUE of the company's SECURITIES, or by a company intending to take over the business through a merger or a sale. The purpose of due diligence (normally carried out by accountants, lawyers or financial experts) is to check that the company's sales figures and general performance are as it claims they are. In the case of a possible TAKEOVER this is a deliberate exercise. The company carrying out the due diligence has made no binding commitment to buy the business that it is examining. Should it back out of the negotiations, it may have obtained commercially-sensitive information for nothing. Nevertheless, only rarely can a vendor hope to sell a business without giving the purchaser some chance to look at the books in advance of a sale.

Dutch auction

An auction in which the auctioneer's prices fall rather than rise. In such an auction, the first person to bid wins whatever it is that the auctioneer is selling. The name comes from the system used in the Dutch flower markets, and it is also, occasionally, used as a method of selling SECURITIES.

Earnings

The PROFIT of a company after deducting for tax, profits belonging to outside shareholders (minorities), extraordinary items and DIVIDENDS to preferred or preference shareholders. Earnings are normally expressed per share, that is, the amount divided by the total number of ORDINARY SHARES in issue. This figure can be refined still further: from basic EARNINGS PER SHARE before share OPTIONS, WARRANTS and CONVERTIBLE SECURITIES are taken into account, to fully diluted earnings per share, the resulting figure after all these have been deducted.

Earnings before interest, taxes, depreciation and amortisation

A measure of a company's financial performance (arrived at by taking income minus expenses, excluding tax, INTEREST, DEPRECIATION and amortisation). EBITDA, as it is usually known, came into favour during the 1980s when bankers supporting LEVERAGED BUY-OUTS needed a measure that showed a company's ability to service its DEBT. Because it eliminates the effects of financing and depreciation, EBITDA can be a useful way of comparing companies in different industries. Hence EBITDA's popularity during the internet boom, when investors used it to compare the performance of technology companies in different industries or sectors. Because it is relatively easy to calculate, EBITDA is too often used instead of measures relying on operating CASH FLOW. It can be dangerous to rely too heavily on EBITDA and ignore changes in a company's working capital.

Earnings per share

A measure of the TOTAL RETURN earned by a company on its ORDINARY SHARE capital: the NET PROFIT of the company divided by the number of ordinary shares in issue. Net profit is the gross profit (receipts minus costs) less INTEREST charges, DEPRECIATION, payments to holders of PREFERENCE SHARES and tax. A company that makes a net profit of $10m and has

2m shares outstanding has earnings per share (EPS) of $5. EPS is a helpful guide to a company's past, present and future performance.

EASDAQ

See NASDAQ EUROPE.

EBITDA

See EARNINGS BEFORE INTEREST, TAXES, DEPRECIATION AND AMORTISATION.

E-commerce

Commerce that is carried out electronically, particularly via the internet. Although consumers and businesses liked the idea of e-commerce, its development was restrained by the difficulty of finding secure methods of payment on the internet. It took time to convince consumers that their CREDIT-CARD details would not become accessible to any casual hacker after they had keyed them into an order form on a website. The hype that accompanied the internet boom, when companies offering virtually anything online were feted by investors, has given way to more sober times. Companies with marginal businesses have collapsed and many of the survivors have merged. Many of the companies that have benefited most from e-commerce are small firms with a niche idea that have suddenly found an international market for their product or service. Some of the most successful ways of using the internet are hidden from public view. For example, suppliers of spare parts for airlines or car companies now find they can move millions of products at the touch of a button; these exchanges connect business to business.

Econometrics

The use of computer analysis to describe the relationship between the main economic forces such as CAPITAL, RATES OF INTEREST and labour. Economists can test the relationship between these influences and determine what is likely to happen to the economy if one or more elements change.

E

Economic and Monetary Union

The process, known as EMU, of bringing together the currencies and monetary policies of the member states of the European Union so that the whole block lives and works with a single currency (the EURO) and is governed by a single central bank (the EUROPEAN CENTRAL BANK). The timetable for EMU, laid down in the Maastricht treaty, began in earnest in 1999. The treaty established certain criteria (on budgetary deficits and the like) which member states must meet if they are to participate fully in EMU. The 11 members of the euro zone – Austria, Belgium, Finland, France, Germany, Ireland, Italy, Luxembourg, the Netherlands, Portugal and Spain – which came into being on January 1st 2000, were joined by a 12th, Greece, on January 1st 2001. The process, mapped out ten years earlier, reached its conclusion on January 1st 2002, when all 12 states dropped their individual currencies and adopted the euro. On that date the euro became not just scriptural – that is, something in which companies could deal and which institutions could borrow – but also a currency with NOTES and coins that people could touch.

Efficient market theory

The theory that excess RETURNS from the STOCKMARKET for a given level of RISK are always arbitraged away (that is, equalised), so investors can only make what the market allows. If this is so, why is there a whole industry – investment management – dedicated to the idea that such returns are possible? Good question. At its crudest, the efficient market theory says that the prices of SECURITIES quickly reflect all the available information about them and that prices will automatically adjust to this information. This is true to a point when markets are big enough and liquid enough for no single investor (or group of investors) to have an effect on prices. Some markets – such as New York and London – are efficient most of the time but not always. Canny investors may profit when they are not.

E

EFTPOS

See ELECTRONIC FUNDS TRANSFER AT THE POINT OF SALE.

Egibi

Probably the first recorded BANK in history. Mr Egibi, the bank's founder, lived in Damascus in the latter part of the reign of the Babylonian king Sennacherib (705–681BC). A stone tablet recording the bank's first loan is in the British Museum.

Electronic funds transfer at the point of sale

A way of paying for shopping electronically, commonly abbreviated to EFTPOS. A plastic DEBIT CARD gives the retailer access to a customer's bank ACCOUNT. The account is debited immediately with the cost of the goods or services purchased. Customers still receive a receipt with the amount of the transaction and, if necessary, can verify the payment seconds later by checking the balance on their account at a nearby ATM or CASH MACHINE.

Electronic purse

Any method of storing money electronically and of carrying it around like a purse. Hence a plastic DEBIT CARD, with an embedded microchip in which is stored value that can be spent on goods or services, is an electronic purse. (See also SMART CARD.)

Embedded value

The CAPITAL value of an INSURANCE contract to an insurance company, as measured by the annual PREMIUM income minus the annual cost of managing the policy multiplied by the number of years that the policy has to run. Thus a policy with seven years to run that brings in a premium income of $35 a year for an institution whose average cost of running a policy is $20 a year has an embedded value of $105 [($35 − $20) × 7].

Emerging market

A STOCKMARKET in a fast-developing country (such as Taiwan, India or even China) that has little history of domestic CAPITAL MARKETS. In the late 1980s and early 1990s, some of the emerging markets grew rapidly. Their growth was fuelled by an increasing supply of new SHARES – from local PRIVATISATIONS and from the FLOTATION of old-established family firms – and by the increasing demand from western investors for STOCKS whose prices would increase in value more quickly than many of those in their domestic markets.

As western markets rebounded in the mid-1990s, the growth of emerging markets slowed down. They were dealt a further blow by Asia's economic crisis, which began with the devaluation of the Thai baht in July 1997. This caused stockmarkets in the region to tumble, many to the point where their WEIGHT-INGS in world indices compiled by Morgan Stanley Capital International and others were so small that international investors began to lose interest in them. Since then many Asian markets have rebounded, and new markets in eastern Europe have also attracted investors' attention.

Employee Retirement Income Security Act

Introduced in the United States in 1974 to govern the operation of most private PENSION and benefit plans. Among other things, the Employee Retirement Income Security Act (ERISA) established a Pension Benefits Guarantee Corporation and set up guidelines for managing pension plans. Those flouting the rules may be subjected to strict audits by the Department of Labour. Since most qualifying plans pay no tax and over the years have grown to dominate investment markets, ERISA funds are courted for their business and treated with a respect that matches their influence.

Employee stock ownership plan

A US scheme designed to encourage employees to buy STOCK in the companies that they work for. There are tax advantages to employee stock ownership plans (ESOPs); companies can deduct for tax purposes any DIVIDENDS paid to employees under them. Most developed countries have similar schemes.

EMS

See EUROPEAN MONETARY SYSTEM.

EMU

See ECONOMIC AND MONETARY UNION.

Endorsement

The signature on the back of a CHEQUE (or similar FINANCIAL INSTRUMENT) which transfers ownership of the instrument from the signatory to the bearer. A bearer instrument, such as an open cheque, does not need endorsement.

Endowment mortgage

A MORTGAGE linked to an ENDOWMENT policy. During the life of the mortgage, the mortgagee pays only INTEREST on it. However, he or she also pays PREMIUMS on a policy which matures at the same time as the end of the LOAN. The CAPITAL sum assured by the policy should cover the PRINCIPAL that has to be repaid on the mortgage. This is fine in theory, but it does not always work in practice if the RETURN on the premiums invested fails to match the value of the principal outstanding. During the gung-ho days of the 1980s and 1990s, when STOCK-MARKETS were on average rising strongly, some home buyers were tempted into taking out endowment mortgages which assumed investment returns of 8–10% a year. When markets fell in 2000 and subsequent years, some homeowners were left with a shortfall.

Enterprise value

The value of a company's EQUITY plus the DEBT that it employs (that is, the total amount of CAPITAL at its disposal). The measure is usually used in conjunction with a company's EARNINGS BEFORE INTEREST, TAX AND DEPRECIATION AND AMORTISATION (EBITDA) compared with the amount of free CASH that it is generating. The ratio of enterprise value to EBITDA is often used instead of the PRICE/EARNINGS RATIO for companies whose accounts have large amounts of DEPRECIATION or amortisation.

Eonia

See EURO OVERNIGHT INDEX AVERAGE.

EPS

See EARNINGS PER SHARE.

E

Equity

The ownership interest of shareholders in a company, as in "he launched a new company last year and has 20% of the equity". On the company's balance sheet, equity is what is left over when all the company's external LIABILITIES have been deducted from the ASSETS. Hence the use of the term equity to refer to an ORDINARY SHARE in a company, private or public.

Equity has also come to mean the excess of surplus value of a capital asset over and above the DEBT still owed on the asset. For example, the amount by which the market value of the SECURITIES in a customer's MARGIN ACCOUNT with a BROKER exceeds the debt still owed on the account; or the amount by which the market value of a house exceeds the MORTGAGE on the house. (See also NEGATIVE EQUITY.)

Equity carve-out

The sale by a parent company of a minority stake in one of its subsidiaries by means of an INITIAL PUBLIC OFFERING. The usual purpose of an EQUITY carve-out is to give the STOCK-MARKET a chance to value separately a particular part of the company which is growing faster than the rest. (See also TRACKING STOCK.)

ERM

See EXCHANGE RATE MECHANISM.

Escrow account

A bank ACCOUNT kept by a third party on behalf of two others who are (usually) in dispute about its rightful ownership. The disputing parties try to set out conditions under which they will agree to let the money be released. When the conditions have been met, the third party releases the funds.

ESOP

See EMPLOYEE STOCK OWNERSHIP PLAN.

ETF

See EXCHANGE TRADED FUND.

Ethical investing

The practice of investing only in the SHARES of companies that meet certain ethical and environmental criteria. There is no firm definition of what these criteria are, but most ethical funds exclude, among others, the shares of manufacturers of tobacco and munitions. Ethical funds measure their performance against specific indices, such as the FTSE4Good Index. Also called socially responsible investing (SRI), ethical investing has its supporters but is no guarantee of profitability. Detractors argue that by excluding the shares of some companies, such funds are riskier and more prone to VOLATILITY.

Eurex

An electronic platform that has become one of the world's largest markets for the trading of DERIVATIVES. Eurex was formed in 1996 from a merger of the DTB German FUTURES exchange and SOFFEX, the Swiss OPTIONS and financial futures exchange. Since then it has grown on both sides of the Atlantic to dominate trading in long-term INTEREST-rate futures. Its biggest selling point is that traders can deal more or less when they like and wherever they are.

Euribor

See EUROPEAN INTERBANK OFFERED RATE.

Euro

The name of the single European currency. Under the terms of the Maastricht treaty, it was introduced in 11 EU member states – Austria, Belgium, Finland, France, Germany, Ireland, Italy, Luxembourg, the Netherlands, Portugal and Spain – in stages from January 1999, when the exchange rates between the euro and the currencies of the countries that joined it were first fixed.

For the first couple of years the euro was used mainly by BANKS, companies and other commercial organisations in dealings among themselves. Greece joined the group on January 1st 2001, a year before the launch on January 1st 2002 of euro NOTES and coins in the participating countries. By pre-stocking with euros more than 170,000 ATMS, vending machines and other outlets throughout the euro zone, the authorities were able to withdraw most national currencies within a couple of months of the start of the year. Indeed, the changeover went remarkably smoothly. What lingered were gripes about the inflationary effect of the euro's introduction. Before the changeover, the governments involved had insisted that when the new notes and coins were introduced, some prices would be rounded up and some would be rounded down. Consumers were sceptical, and rightly so. In the event, nearly all prices were rounded up and stayed up, thus to the cost of living.

Euro conversion rates

Currency	€1 =
Austrian schilling	13.7603
Belgian franc	40.3399
Finnish markka	5.94573
French franc	6.55957
D-mark	1.95583
Greek drachma	340.750
Irish punt	0.787564
Italian lira	1936.27
Luxembourg franc	40.3399
Netherlands guilder	2.20371
Portuguese escudo	200.482
Spanish peseta	166.386

Eurobond

A BOND issued by a company, government or supranational organisation with two peculiar characteristics:

- it is issued in a market other than that of its currency of denomination;
- the banks or investment houses that issue it sell it internationally, not just in the domestic market.

Thus if Germany's Deutsche Bank were to issue a dollar-denominated bond for France's Alcatel and sell it around the world, it would be a Eurobond. If it were to sell the bond only in Germany, it would be a foreign bond. Eurobonds are peculiar in having no home base whose government could support them should the market collapse.

Euroclear

Europe's largest clearing and settlement system for SHARES and BONDS. In 2002 Euroclear merged with CREST, the LONDON STOCK EXCHANGE's former settlement system, to form a pan-European service for institutional and retail investors alike.

Eurocommercial paper

COMMERCIAL PAPER which is issued by a company in a EUROCURRENCY, that is, in a currency other than the one where the company is domiciled or has its principal base. (See COMMERCIAL PAPER.)

Eurocredit

A LOAN denominated in the currency of one country but made to a company or other borrower in another country. This would include a loan in yen to a US company or one in EUROS to a Japanese borrower.

Eurocurrency

Currency deposited by companies, BANKS or federal governments outside their own country. Usually, this means the currency of a non-European country (that is, dollars) deposited in Europe.

Euromarket

A market for Eurocredits, EUROCURRENCIES and EUROBONDS, that is, SECURITIES in the currency of one country but held in another – for example, the market for dollar deposits (or Eurodollars) in Europe; or the market for sterling (or Eurosterling) in the United States. There were two coincidental and complementary influences on the development of the Euromarket: fear of the consequences of a cold war between Russia and the United States which encouraged investors to switch deposits to western Europe; and restrictions on US banks which encouraged them to conduct part of their business in London.

Euronext

A company that owns the Paris, Amsterdam, Brussels and Lisbon stock exchanges as well as the London International Financial Futures Exchange (LIFFE), which is part of its DERIVATIVES division, Euronext.LIFFE. Since 2002, Euronext has also had links with the TOKYO STOCK EXCHANGE. The aim is to build a common platform so that the various exchanges share the same technology and trading and clearance systems. As NASDAQ found to its cost, international tie-ups of this kind are more easily described than made. In 2002, NASDAQ had to retreat from an expensive attempt to establish an offshoot in Japan.

Euro.NM

An association of European STOCKMARKETS that are designed for smaller companies. The members are the second-tier markets in Amsterdam, Brussels, Frankfurt and Paris. The exchanges banded together in 1996, partly to defend themselves from competition from London's AIM, which had ambitions to be the CAPITAL MARKET of choice for growing companies in Europe, and from EASDAQ, which was subsequently taken over and renamed NASDAQ Europe. The association aims to offer common rules and regulations so that companies and those who invest in them have to contend with as little bureaucracy as possible. The formula worked well until the dotcom boom turned to bust in 2000. Since then, fewer companies have sought LISTINGS and business has been leaner. So much so that, in 2002, the Deutsche BÖRSE closed down its Neuer Markt, originally set up to attract young technology companies.

Euro Overnight Index Average

A weighted average of the rate at which all unsecured lending takes place in the EURO zone. The rate is calculated by the EUROPEAN CENTRAL BANK at the end of each trading day from data supplied to it by a panel of reporting banks, which is why it is called an overnight average. Eonia, as it is known, is used as a BENCHMARK for pricing transactions in the CAPITAL MARKETS throughout the euro zone and anywhere that DERIVATIVES denominated in euros are bought and sold. It was introduced at the same time as EURIBOR, the benchmark used by the money markets, following the euro's introduction in January 1999 as a notional currency that could be exchanged between banks and financial institutions.

European Bank for Reconstruction and Development

An institution owned by governments and international organisations which was set up to channel aid to eastern Europe.

Created largely on the initiative of the European Union, the European Bank for Reconstruction and Development (EBRD) has 40 member countries. It opened its doors for business (in London) in 1991 with plans to grant 40% of its LOANS to eastern Europe's public sectors and 60% to the growing private sectors. In all, EBRD lends money to around 27 countries from central Europe to central Asia and is the region's largest single investor. Large capital projects are usually the beneficiaries of its cheap loans, for example, the restructuring of the Slovak railway, an oilfield in the Arctic Circle jointly developed by the Russians and Finns, and a dam in Kazakhstan.

European Central Bank

The European Union's central bank and guardian of the EURO. The European Central Bank (ECB) is the successor to the EUROPEAN MONETARY INSTITUTE and operates as a sort of Euro-Fed, a European version of the FEDERAL RESERVE System. Like the Fed, the ECB is made up of representatives from EU member countries' central banks, which form the European System of Central Banks (ESCD). The ECB's main duty is to maintain price stability, a job that many think it often takes too literally, especially when the largest economies within the EU need stimulating.

European currency unit

An artificial creation based on a basket of European currencies. The European Currency Unit (or ecu) was invented by the European Community in the 1970s and came into force with the signing of the Maastricht treaty in 1992. Its original purpose was to act as a reserve ASSET and as a means of settlement in the EUROPEAN MONETARY SYSTEM. The ecu ceased to exist on January 1st 1999 when the EURO was created; any ecus then in use became euros at the rate of one to one.

European Interbank Offered Rate

The rate at which prime banks in the EURO zone lend to each other. Euribor, as it is known, is the BENCHMARK used by money markets throughout the euro zone and anywhere that euros are bought and sold. It is calculated each day from data supplied by a panel of big banks. Euribor was first quoted on January 4th 1999, the first day that the euro was traded after its introduction as a notional currency at the beginning of 1999. (See also EURO OVERNIGHT INDEX AVERAGE.)

European Investment Bank

A BANK created in 1957 by the Treaty of Rome (the treaty which first established the existence of what has become the European Union). The European Investment Bank (EIB) acts as a development bank for Europe, using its good name to borrow cheaply in the international CAPITAL MARKETS and then lending these (cheap) funds to borrowers in the EU and associate member states. Most EIB loans are for 7–10 years. The bank has certain priorities. It favours lending to:

- depressed areas where the infrastructure and industry need upgrading;
- projects that will help to develop European technology;
- infrastructure projects that involve more than one EU member country, such as a bridge or the Channel Tunnel;
- projects that further a particular interest of the EIB.

The result is a diverse range of borrowers, such as projects to build roads in Sweden and Greece or to develop renewable energy in Scotland, and start-up companies involved in biotechnology in Germany.

European Monetary Institute

The forerunner of the EUROPEAN CENTRAL BANK (ECB) made

necessary by ECONOMIC AND MONETARY UNION and the single European currency. The European Monetary Institute (EMI) was established in 1994 and based in Frankfurt. Its aim was to strengthen the co-ordination of monetary affairs between European Union member states and to set up the infrastructure necessary for the proper functioning of European monetary policy and a single European currency. The EMI was superseded by the ECB in June 1998.

E

European Monetary System

A scheme to manage the way in which European currencies' exchange rates move against each other. The European Monetary System (EMS) started on March 13th 1979 as the successor to the snake, the first concerted attempt to dampen fluctuations in exchange rates since the dollar had been allowed to float freely in 1971. The Maastricht treaty (signed in 1992) laid out plans to take the EMS several giant steps further. It provided a schedule to implement ECONOMIC AND MONETARY UNION through a system of permanently interlocked exchange rates and a single monetary policy. It led ultimately to the adoption of the European currency, the EURO.

European-style option

An OPTION that can only be exercised on the date that it expires; the opposite of an AMERICAN-STYLE OPTION, which can be exercised at any time between the date it is purchased and its expiry. Most options in the United States are American-style, but Europe deals in both. For obvious reasons, American-style options are more flexible.

Exchange control

The method by which governments attempt to control the flow of currency in and out of their country, both foreign currencies and their own currency. Many countries maintained strict exchange controls after the second world war. The UK abolished them in 1979, and France even later.

Exchange Rate Mechanism

A central part of the EUROPEAN MONETARY SYSTEM. The Exchange Rate Mechanism (ERM) was an agreement to maintain within limits the exchange rates of member states of the European Community. This guaranteed a degree of monetary stability within the boundaries of what later became the European Union. However, it also created strains, as the UK found to its cost when the pound was forced out of the ERM by speculators in 1992.

Exchange traded fund

A MUTUAL FUND (UNIT TRUST) which tracks a particular STOCKMARKET INDEX and can be bought and sold like a SHARE. One of the most widely held exchange traded funds (ETFS) is Standard & Poor's Depositary Receipt (SPDR, or spider) which tracks the shares of companies that make up the S&P 500 index. One SPDR is worth a fraction of the value of the S&P 500. Investors receive DIVIDENDS quarterly, based on the accumulated amounts held in TRUST, less any expenses charged by the fund.

Ex-div

An indication given next to a quoted share price showing that the price excludes payment of a DIVIDEND that has been declared by the company but not yet paid. Ex-div means that the dividend is to be paid to the previous owner of the share. (See also CUM DIV.)

E

Exercise

Making use of a right that is available under the terms of a CON-TRACT; for example, exercising an OPTION to purchase a SHARE at a certain price within a certain time. The right in question may also be the conversion of a CONVERTIBLE SECURITY into a share.

Exercise price

See STRIKE PRICE.

Expiry date

The last day on which a particular right (to buy shares at an advantageous price, for example) can be exercised.

Export credit

A LOAN to an exporter to tide it over the period between the time when its goods are sent abroad and the time when it receives payment for them. With exports of large CAPITAL goods, that time may be anything up to several years. Most western governments have agencies which provide loans, often at subsidised rates, to exporters. The UK's Export Credit Guarantee Department (ECGD) was originally set up in 1919 to help companies rebuild trade after the disruption of the first world war. In the early 1990s, the arm of the ECGD dealing with SHORT-TERM CREDIT (up to two years) was sold off, and it now competes with other insurers in the private sector. In recent years the ECGD has helped exporters manufacturing things as diverse as double-decker buses for Hong Kong, low-cost housing for Romania, road improvements in Vanuatu and a pharmaceuticals plant in Croatia. In underwriting such risks, the ECGD aims to break even.

External funds

SOURCES OF FUNDS that are available to a company from outside the company itself. Thus the proceeds of a BOND issue or a bank LOAN are external funds; retained PROFIT is an internal source of funds. (See INTERNAL FUNDS.)

E

Extrinsic value

When pricing OPTIONS, the amount by which the PREMIUM (the price the buyer has to pay) exceeds the INTRINSIC VALUE of the option. For example, if the premium is $20 and the EXERCISE PRICE of the option is $410, then the extrinsic value (sometimes called time value) will be $10. This is also known as the amount by which the option is IN THE MONEY. In this case, the option would not be worth exercising at $410, but it would be if the price rose to, say, $425.

Facility

A banking service (such as an OVERDRAFT facility) that is made available to customers for their use as and when they please. A facility letter is a letter from a BANK confirming in writing the details of a specific LOAN that has been made available.

Factoring

The business of collecting someone else's DEBTS on their behalf. A company sells its receivables (that is, its unpaid invoices) to a factor (often the subsidiary of a BANK) at a DISCOUNT. The factor then sets out to collect the money owed. Its PROFIT comes when it has collected more than the discounted price that it pays for the debts. A company that sells its debts to a factor gets a helpful boost to its CASH FLOW, does not have to worry about BAD DEBTS and should be able to spend less on its in-house accounts function. Factoring may also include any or all of the following:

- maintaining the company's sales ledger;
- managing the company's CREDIT control, that is, making sure that it does not give customers excessively long periods to repay;
- the actual collection of unpaid debt;
- INSURANCE cover against bad debt.

Factoring is divided into disclosed and undisclosed. Disclosed factoring, in which the factor lets the debtors know that that it is collecting payments on behalf of the client, is increasingly common. Undisclosed factoring (also known as confidential invoice discounting) allows the client to conceal the fact that it has employed a factor.

Fallen angel

A company with BONDS outstanding in the market that is

downgraded from INVESTMENT GRADE to speculative grade. This usually happens because a RATING agency decides that the quality of the company's CREDIT (that is, its ability to repay its DEBTS) has deteriorated. Being reduced from investment grade to junk status increases a company's cost of borrowing and therefore the effective RATE OF INTEREST paid on any bonds held by investors. The prospects of fallen angels are harder to assess than those of companies judged from the outset to be speculative. This is because ANALYSTS do not know whether to believe the forecasts of sales and PROFITS produced by companies whose CREDIT RATING has been downgraded. (See also JUNK BOND.)

F

Fannie Mae

The name used by the Federal National Mortgage Association, a company created in 1938 by Congress to support the SECONDARY MARKET in MORTGAGES. Like FREDDIE MAC (the Federal Home Loan Mortgage Corporation), it buys mortgages from BANKS and other providers, repackages them as SECURITIES and sells them in the market. Fannie Mae's aim is to maintain the pool of money available to mortgage providers, thus ensuring that those who want them can find competitively priced home loans. As a result, it has sometimes owned as much as 10% of all US mortgages. Although Fannie Mae started life as a government agency, it was split in two during the 1960s. One half became GINNIE MAE (the Government National Mortgage Association), a federal agency; the other was acquired by its own shareholders and became what is now known as Fannie Mae. Fannie Mae is still the largest buyer of US mortgages and one of its most active borrowers in the DEBT market.

FCM

See FUTURES COMMISSION MERCHANT.

FDI

See FOREIGN DIRECT INVESTMENT.

FDIC

See FEDERAL DEPOSIT INSURANCE CORPORATION.

Fed funds rate

The rate at which US BANKS lend their surplus RESERVES to each other overnight. The reserves are generally non-INTEREST-bearing DEPOSITS held with the FEDERAL RESERVE. Banks lend them in order to meet their required CAPITAL RATIO, or the level of their CAPITAL and reserves compared with their ASSETS (LOANS). A target for the Fed funds rate is set by the Federal Open Market Committee, the body that sets the Fed's monetary policy. As the main BENCHMARK for SHORT-TERM interest rates in the United States, the Fed funds rate is taken as a sensitive indicator of the way in which US interest rates in general are moving.

Federal Deposit Insurance Corporation

A deposit protection fund, established in the United States in 1933 in the depths of the Great Depression. The Federal Deposit Insurance Corporation (FDIC) insures DEPOSITS up to a limit of $10,000 per deposit at banks that take out INSURANCE with it. The FDIC believes in identifying new RISKS to the financial system as well as dealing with existing ones. A similar body does a similar job for the country's savings and loans associations. It used to be called the Federal Savings and Loan Insurance Corporation, then the Resolution Trust Corporation and now goes by the name of the Savings Association Insurance Fund.

Federal Reserve

Commonly known as the Fed, the CENTRAL BANK of the United States and thus the guardian of the value of the dollar. The Fed is both the regulator of banks in the United States and the controller of the money supply. The Federal Reserve System works through 12 regional federal reserve banks spread across the country. Each is owned by banks in its area, and each has nine directors serving a three-year term of office. At the pinnacle of the system is the Federal Reserve Board, consisting of seven governors based in Washington, DC. The US president appoints each governor for a 14-year term, a long time for people who are rarely young when they start the job. The Fed has the usual central-bank responsibilities for MONETARY POLICY and FOREIGN EXCHANGE. It is also the supervisor of bank holding companies in the United States. In practice, the Fed keeps an eye on all US banks, for which it is LENDER OF LAST RESORT. Since the dollar holds sway in many countries and territories outside the United States, the Fed is also the de facto custodian of the value of the currencies of many other countries and territories.

Fiduciary deposit

A Swiss speciality in which a BANK takes a DEPOSIT for the purpose of lending it to someone else, entirely at the depositor's own risk. One of the big benefits for the bank is that the deposit remains off its balance sheet (so it does not have to set aside expensive RESERVES in order to meet CAPITAL RATIO requirements). Yet the bank still makes a TURN on the transaction. The advantage for the depositor is a higher RATE OF INTEREST and the veil of Swiss SECRECY. Most fiduciary deposits are simply passed on to other banks and become straightforward EURO-CURRENCY deposits.

Financial centre

Any place, for historical or fiscal or political reasons, in which a large amount of financial business is transacted. Well-established financial centres include London, New York, Tokyo, Frankfurt and Paris. They have been joined by others in East Asia such as Hong Kong and Singapore. Then there are "special-purpose" centres, such as the Cayman Islands, where the attractions are low or no tax and greater opaqueness. Two things that most financial centres have in common are light regulation and a willingness on the part of the authorities to see international business grow. It also helps – as with Hong Kong – to be near a much bigger place such as Mainland China, which, by and large, has yet to realise the benefits of such an approach.

Financial instrument

Documentary evidence of the ownership of a financial ASSET; for example, a BILL OF EXCHANGE, CERTIFICATE OF DEPOSIT, government BOND, STOCK and so on.

Financial intermediary

An individual or institution that mediates between savers (that is, SOURCES OF FUNDS) and borrowers (that is, users of funds). The chain from original source to ultimate use can be a long one, with many intermediaries along the way.

Financial Services Authority

The UK's omnipotent regulator of financial services. The Financial Services Authority (FSA) was set up under the Financial Services and Markets Act 2000. Unlike most regulators, the FSA covers both retail and wholesale business; that is, services for professionals as well as consumers. So it is just as likely to pronounce on the regulation of, say, securities DERIVATIVES as

CREDIT UNIONS run for and by individuals. A company limited by GUARANTEE with a board of directors appointed by the government, the FSA pays for itself through a levy on the industry that it regulates. Because of its size and scope, it is rarely out of the limelight.

Financial services institution

Any firm in the financial services industry, such as a commercial BANK, INVESTMENT BANK, an investment company, or a FUND MANAGER. Often abbreviated to FSI.

Financial Times

A daily newspaper printed on pink paper. It is the bible of the European financial community in much the same way that the WALL STREET JOURNAL is for the United States. The Financial Times is printed in 18 cities around the world and has several different editions, for example, in the UK, the United States and Europe.

Financial year

The 12-month period covered by a company's accounts. On occasions, a financial year can be a period of more or less than 12 months. For example, when a company wants to change the ending of its financial year from (say) inconvenient May to more convenient December, it will have to have a financial year of either seven months or 19 months (7 + 12).

Fixed-income security

A SECURITY that pays a FIXED RATE of INTEREST. This includes government, municipal and CORPORATE BONDS which pay a fixed rate of interest until they mature. It may also refer to preferred or PREFERENCE SHARES which pay a fixed DIVI-

DEND. Such instruments protect the holder during periods of low INFLATION but do nothing to guard against the erosion of buying power during times of rising inflation. The prices of fixed-income securities rise and fall according to demand, like any other, as well as being determined by the value of the remaining interest payable until maturity.

F   Fixed rate

A rate of INTEREST that remains the same all the way through to the MATURITY of the FINANCIAL INSTRUMENT to which it attaches. (See also VARIABLE RATE.)

Fixing

The setting of the GOLD price in London twice a day – at 10.30am and 3pm – by several big gold DEALERS which are all market-making members of the London Bullion Market Association. Although fixed for transactions that take place at the time, the price is not set in stone and can fluctuate between fixings. The gold price is fixed in sterling, although it is most often expressed as the dollar equivalent. A smaller number of traders gather once a day by telephone to fix the silver price.

Flight capital

Money that rushes out of a country when political or economic uncertainty undermines people's faith in a currency's ability to maintain its value. Such money generally heads for stable places such as Geneva or Miami, and for stable currencies such as the Swiss franc or the dollar. The expression is also sometimes used to cover untaxed and illegal money that stems from sources such as fraud or drug dealing.

Flip-flop bond

A BOND that can be turned into another type of DEBT instrument at the investor's discretion, and can then equally easily be flipped back into the original form of investment.

Float

There are three meanings.

1 The number of SECURITIES issued by a company or its BANK that are free to be traded; that is, securities that are not held by investors who are unlikely or unable to sell them. The fewer the number of SHARES available to be traded, the lower the level of LIQUIDITY in a particular security.
2 Money that appears in the accounts of banks from CHEQUES in the process of being cleared. Money being shunted from one account to another will disappear from the account from which it is debited sometimes days before it reappears in the account being credited. Customers transferring money from one account to another may understandably be annoyed if they lose INTEREST as a result.
3 CASH held in the till by a retailer or other such business using NOTES and coins.

Floating charge

SECURITY given by a borrower to a lender that floats over all the borrower's ASSETS. So if the borrower fails to repay the LOAN, the lender can claim any of the borrower's assets, up to the value of the loan.

Floating rate

A RATE OF INTEREST that changes with the cost of funds. Since BANKS and other financial institutions must charge their customers a margin over their own cost of funds, interest rates throughout the banking chain – from CENTRAL BANK to retail customer – move up and down depending on the demand for funds. The starting point is usually the base or prime rate at which banks lend to their best customers.

Floating-rate note

A BOND with a COUPON whose RATE OF INTEREST varies in line with a market rate of interest such as the LONDON INTER-BANK OFFERED RATE (or LIBOR). A floating-rate note (FRN) often has a long or sometimes even infinite MATURITY. Also called adjustable-rate notes, FRNs appeal to borrowers who expect interest rates to fall. At such times borrowers do not want to be locked into paying the FIXED RATES of interest that apply to traditional bonds. FRNs were invented by lenders in the EUROMARKETS and have since become popular among banks dealing in international markets.

Floor

There are two meanings.

1 A minimum RATE OF INTEREST on a FLOATING-RATE NOTE.
2 The place in a STOCK EXCHANGE where trading actually takes place, or where it used to. Thus the tag given to a floor trader: somebody who trades (or who used to trade) on the floor of a stock exchange.

Flotation

The launch of a new BOND or EQUITY issue on a CAPITAL MARKET. All markets have rules governing the way flotations must take place, most of which are designed to protect investors from FRAUD. It is the job of a regulator, such as the SEC in the United States or the FSA in the UK, to make sure the rules are observed. This adds to the cost of a flotation, which usually requires the services of an INVESTMENT BANK or sponsoring STOCKBROKER to underwrite (or assume the RISK for selling) new SHARES in the company that is being floated. To qualify for a flotation, companies usually have to satisfy the authorities, or STOCK EXCHANGE on which their shares are to be listed, that they have audited accounts and articles of association drawn up by lawyers. (See also INITIAL PUBLIC OFFERING.)

F

Footsie

See FTSE 100.

Forced savings

Savings which accrue without the consumer making a conscious decision to save. This can happen in all sorts of ways. For example, governments levy taxes which go towards paying PENSIONS, or certain expenditure is prohibited, as when restrictions are imposed on foreign travel.

Forecasting

The instinct to try to predict the future is found everywhere, particularly in things financial. Any certainty about the future which is not widely known promises huge gains to those who do know. For this reason, ANALYSTS spend their waking hours trying to discern what is happening to the economy and therefore how particular industries and companies are likely to fare. Companies' PROFITS may lead or lag behind changes in the business cycle, but over time they generally track the rate of growth in a country's gross domestic product (GDP). Using various models, analysts try to forecast a company's EARNINGS and how this might affect their valuation. At a certain SHARE price, they can then determine whether a company is undervalued or overvalued compared with its peers and the average for the market. The answer will suggest whether investors should buy or sell its shares.

Foreign bond

A BOND denominated in a currency foreign to the issuer, and sold in the domestic market of the currency of issue – for example, a Swiss franc bond issued by a Japanese company and sold in Switzerland. (See also EUROBOND.)

Foreign direct investment

The purchase by a commercial organisation of ASSETS overseas for the purpose of investment. Such assets might include greenfield sites, where a factory or office is to be built from scratch, or a sizeable stake (usually over 50% if regulations allow) of an existing company that is already operating in the foreign market. Flows of foreign direct investment (FDI) can have a profound effect on a developing economy. Maintaining the economy's equilibrium in the face of a flood of investment can be as difficult as coping with the consequences when, for whatever reason, the flow is suddenly turned off.

Foreign exchange

The means through which payments are made between one country and another. BANKS and their customers are the mainstay of the foreign-exchange (forex) markets. The markets started out as the servants of trade but, during the past 20 years or so, they have undoubtedly become one of its masters. Every day in the forex markets traders place buy-and-sell orders worth more than $2 trillion, most of them in pursuit of SHORT-TERM (that is, overnight) gain. This is more than the value of all the cars, wheat, oil and other products bought and sold in the real economy every day.

As well as dealing in physical currency (for example, from

dollars to yen or vice versa), traders routinely use DERIVATIVES (FUTURES, OPTIONS and the like) to give them extra leverage or to HEDGE against the RISK of possible losses. This gives the markets power not just to influence events but sometimes also to profit from them. In 1992, George Soros made $1 billion from betting correctly that the UK would be forced out of Europe's EXCHANGE RATE MECHANISM.

Forfaiting

Also known as *à forfait*, the business of discounting a FINAN-CIAL INSTRUMENT that is being used to finance the export of capital goods. BANKS buy the instruments at a DISCOUNT and then trade them. The forfait market grew up in Switzerland, where it concentrated on buying east–west trade DEBT, but its name became increasingly anglicised (from *à forfait* to forfaiting) as the market shifted to London in the 1980s.

Forgery

A counterfeit coin, NOTE or document that tries to pass as something that it is not. Forgeries often involve the copying of other people's signatures. To make forgery as difficult as possible, the printing of notes has become a highly specialised task that involves sophisticated technical processes.

Forward contract

An agreement to buy a specified quantity of a COMMODITY or currency at some specified future time and place. A forward contract in the FOREIGN-EXCHANGE market might involve an agreement to buy £100,000-worth of sterling in dollars; that is, to pay now (in dollars) for the delivery of £100,000 in three months' time. The exchange rate to be paid for this sterling will reflect market expectations about the appreciation or DEPRECI-ATION of sterling against the dollar over the next three months.

A PREMIUM over the spot rate will indicate that sterling is expected to appreciate and a DISCOUNT will indicate an expected depreciation.

Forward cover

The process of covering future payments or receipts, either by buying now (in the FUTURES markets) the currency that is required for the payment, or by selling now a receipt that is due in the future. This is particularly valuable in volatile FOREIGN-EXCHANGE markets where fluctuations in rates can wipe out an ordinary business's profit.

Forward rate agreement

An agreement between two parties to protect themselves against movements in INTEREST rates in a particular currency. The CONTRACT ties in both parties for a particular period of time and covers a specified rate. Should interest rates move away from the agreed rate, then one party pays the other the difference between the two rates.

Franked income

Income paid from a company's PROFITS on which tax has already been paid. This matters to investment companies in countries such as the UK, where DIVIDENDS are paid NET of the basic rate of tax. If they can show that income is franked, INVESTMENT TRUSTS escape having to pay tax twice.

Fraud

An act of deception aimed at gaining financial benefit illegally, at the expense of others. Fraud can be the result of many different kinds of deception, from lying in documents to support a

TAKEOVER or new ISSUE of SECURITIES, to false accounting in a company's accounts, to pretending to be a registered BROKER, to simply forging CHEQUES.

As the corporate scandals that erupted in the United States at the beginning of the 21st century show, shareholders and employees alike rely to a large extent on the integrity of people who run big international companies. If such people choose to bend or break the law, the consequences can be far-reaching. People's jobs and PENSIONS can be wiped out, and regulators are forced to introduce complicated new rules to prevent abuses from happening again.

> *A clean glove often hides a dirty hand.*
> English proverb

Freddie Mac

The name used by the Federal Home Loan Mortgage Corporation, an unusual body that is owned by its stockholders but operates under a charter from Congress. Freddie Mac was set up in 1970 to boost home ownership in the United States. Like FANNIE MAE (the Federal National Mortgage Association), Freddie Mac does this by buying MORTGAGES from BANKS and other providers, repackaging them as SECURITIES and then selling them to investors in the market. Securitising mortgages in this way replenishes the money available to banks to lend to home buyers in the retail market and thus helps to encourage home ownership. Freddie Mac also buys mortgages for investment on its own account. To raise the money to do this, it is an active issuer of its own BONDS and securities in the DEBT market.

FRN

See FLOATING-RATE NOTE.

Front running

An illegal practice where a BROKER buys a SECURITY after gaining inside or privileged information. When the information becomes public and the price of the security goes up, the broker sells at a PROFIT. For example, a banker may buy shares in XYZ company in advance of a general offer for all the SHARES by another company which he or she happens to be advising. Such practices are not only illegal but can often be detected by studying dealing records.

Fruits and suits

A popular combination for the successful launch of an internet-based INITIAL PUBLIC OFFERING during the boom years of the technology bubble. Fruits are net-wise individuals who wear casual clothing and are not particularly savvy about finance. Suits are numeric individuals who wear ties and convince their investors that the combination of high-tech fruits and high-finance suits will earn them a fortune. Such winning combinations proved less appealing after the high-tech bubble burst at the beginning of 2000, since when fruits are just as likely again to wear suits and vice versa.

FSA

See FINANCIAL SERVICES AUTHORITY.

FSI

See FINANCIAL SERVICES INSTITUTION.

FTSE 100

A STOCK INDEX introduced by the FINANCIAL TIMES and the

LONDON STOCK EXCHANGE, known affectionately as the Footsie, on January 1st 1984. It is a computerised index of 100 big UK companies. The Footsie was designed to fill a gap between the FT ORDINARY SHARE index (started in 1935), which contained a mere 30 companies, and the FT all-share index, which contains hundreds and was then calculated only infrequently.

The Footsie has become by far the most widely followed index on the London market. Companies are periodically included or excluded depending on their STOCKMARKET CAPITALISATION as their fortunes wax and wane. Being included in the index can have a big impact on a company's SHARE price because, once it is included, TRACKER FUNDS (which track the market) are effectively obliged to buy the company's shares in proportion to its weight in the index. Conversely, if a company is ejected from the index, trackers will invariably dispose of their shares.

The first stock-index FUTURES and OPTIONS to be traded in London were based on the Footsie. The index started life at a level of 1,000.

Fund manager

A firm or individual that manages other people's money with the aim of gaining a certain (and often minimum) RETURN on it. The industry is broadly divided into two: those who specialise in managing institutional money – that is, funds placed with them by financial institutions of one sort or another, often firms' own PENSION FUNDS; and those who specialise in managing retail money – that is, the savings and investments of individual investors. Fees on the latter are generally higher and therefore more attractive, mainly because the money comes from lots of smaller savers and is therefore more costly to administer.

There are also active and passive fund managers. Active managers attempt to beat various BENCHMARKS by managing their PORTFOLIOS of investments (which can be made up of FIXED-INCOME SECURITIES as well as EQUITIES). Passive managers aim only to track the same indices and so perform in line with the market. Active managers rely on well-tried but still fallible methods to assess the RISK of investing in certain markets and types of SHARES. One of the best ways of spreading RISK is to diversify your investment.

Fungible

The quality of things like NOTES and coins where any one specimen is indistinguishable from any other. A person owed $1 does not bother which particular dollar note he or she receives, even if it is crumpled or frayed at the edges. Anything to be used as money (be it cowrie shells, beads or GOLD pieces) has to be fungible.

Futures

Contracts to buy something in the future at a price agreed in the present. First developed in agricultural COMMODITY markets, such as those for wheat or pork bellies, futures then spread into financial markets. There are now futures in such things as government BONDS, STOCKMARKET indices and even BANK DEPOSITS. Futures (and OPTIONS) markets have added greatly to the LIQUIDITY of financial markets. By selling futures banks can spread the RISK they take on from lending; and investors can assume the same RISK by buying CONTRACTS in the futures markets. Futures (and options) have also found it easier to cross borders than the physical SECURITY or commodity that underlies them. So, for example, futures contracts on European indices are routinely traded in the United States whereas the underlying securities are not.

There has been fierce competition among FINANCIAL CENTRES to become the world's leading futures markets. Traditional centres have not had it all their own way. Chicago has given New York a run for its money; Frankfurt has challenged London; and in East Asia Singapore has sometimes beaten Hong Kong. Increasingly, specialist companies such as Euronext.LIFFE, part of EURONEXT (which owns several exchanges), are likely to dominate the DERIVATIVES business internationally, partly by establishing electronic platforms which form the basis of a market.

Futures commission merchant

A person or company authorised to buy and sell FUTURES or OPTIONS in the United States. Those filling this role must be licensed by the COMMODITY FUTURES TRADING COMMISSION. The job of a futures commission merchant (FCM) is similar to that of a BROKER in the SECURITIES markets. As well as accepting orders to buy and sell futures, an FCM can hold a client's money or securities in a MARGIN ACCOUNT. Some firms may be authorised to deal on a client's behalf in both the CASH and futures markets.

Gearing

The indebtedness of a company expressed as a percentage of its EQUITY capital, referred to in the United States as leverage. A highly leveraged company is one with a lot of borrowings compared with its equity. The more long-term DEBT that a company has, the greater is the financial gearing. Shareholders benefit to the extent that the RETURN on the borrowed money exceeds the INTEREST cost. In theory, the SHARES should rise correspondingly in value. (See also LEVERAGED BUY-OUT.)

General policy

An INSURANCE policy that gets around a trader's need to insure each shipment separately. The trader and the insurer agree in advance on cover up to a certain ceiling. The trader then merely advises the insurer of the nature and value of shipments as and when they are made and until (in total) they reach the ceiling.

Gilts

Short for gilt-edged SECURITY, so called because the original certificates for UK government BONDS had gilded edges and were literally as good as GOLD. Like Treasury securities in the United States, gilts are regarded as having no RISK of DEFAULT. They are therefore used as a BENCHMARK against which the YIELDS, or INTEREST rates, of other, riskier bonds are set. Gilts, like Treasuries, have a variety of maturities depending on the borrowing needs of the government of the day. Gilt FUTURES (that is, futures contracts based on UK government bonds) are traded on EURONEXT.LIFFE. CORPORATE BONDS with a high CREDIT RATING (that is, with little likelihood of default) are sometimes described as gilt-edged securities; STOCKS of a similar or better standing are usually referred to as BLUE CHIPS.

Ginnie Mae

The name used by the Government National Mortgage Association, a US government institution designed to support to the housing market. Ginnie Mae was formed in 1968 when its parent organisation, FANNIE MAE (the Federal National Mortgage Association) was split into two. Ginnie Mae remained within the government, while Fannie Mae was hived off to investors. The job of both is to encourage home ownership. Ginnie Mae does so by buying MORTGAGES, bundling them up and reissuing them as SECURITIES for investors to buy. This ensures both that there is always a ready buyer in the market for mortgages and that Ginnie Mae has the money to buy them. Ginnie Mae also raises money in the financial markets.

Giro

A payment system organised by a group of BANKS, or by postal authorities. It enables institutions to make payments among themselves without perpetually shuffling CASH from one to another. A giro system transfers funds among ACCOUNTS which the participating institutions hold at the giro's central CLEARING HOUSE.

Glass-Steagall Act

A law put forward by Senator Carter Glass and Representative Henry Steagall in 1933, a milestone in US banking legislation. The law prevented any commercial BANK in the United States from underwriting and dealing in SECURITIES. Securities business was left as the exclusive preserve of INVESTMENT BANKS. The strict divide was created in the wake of financial scandals in the late 1920s and early 1930s. Some banks had used depositors' money to support the price of securities that they were underwriting, sometimes with disastrous consequences for depositors. Many investors who bought the shares of dud dotcom companies during the technology boom of the late 1990s felt similarly short-changed. They discovered that some ANALYSTS employed by investment banks had worried more about the fees the bank would receive from a successful INITIAL PUBLIC OFFERING of the shares than about delivering an objective recommendation of the company's worth. Changes in the way financial markets operate and pressure from the new breed of financial-services conglomerates finally caused the Glass-Steagall Act to fray at the edges, and it was repealed in 1999.

G

Global custody

A service for the worldwide settlement and safekeeping of SECURITIES. The industry sprang up in 1974 when the EMPLOYEE RETIREMENT INCOME SECURITY ACT became law in the United States, forcing US pension funds to separate the management from the custody of the underlying investments. The term "global custody" was coined by Chase Manhattan Bank, which first designed services to satisfy the new law. In those days custodians helped investors to buy, sell and hold securities from a handful of foreign markets; these days it could be as many as 100 markets. With more and more countries encouraging employees to build up their own PENSIONS through diversified holdings of BONDS and EQUITIES held in UNIT TRUSTS (MUTUAL FUNDS) and other forms of collective investment, the business of global custody is likely to grow bigger still.

Global market

A market for goods or services that attracts buyers from all over the world. The idea that there might be a global market for everything from Mars bars to MORTGAGES was first popularised during the 1980s. However, many financial markets were global long before that.

▰ Customers of BANKS in London and New York come from all over the world in search of CAPITAL, advice and trade finance.

- ◪ LLOYD's of London has long insured RISKS (especially those at sea and in the air) throughout the world.
- ◪ Hard commodities (metals of one sort or another) and soft commodities (tea, coffee, wheat and the like) from all over the world have long been bought and sold in London and other international FINANCIAL CENTRES.

Gold

The precious metal that individuals most like to hoard when they feel uncertain about the value of money or other forms of investment. CENTRAL BANKS still hold some of their country's RESERVES in the yellow metal. The biggest store of gold is believed to be 80ft below the streets of Manhattan.

For much of the 19th century the UK had a monetary system that was based on gold (the so-called Gold Standard). NOTES and coins were freely CONVERTIBLE into their worth in gold by the central bank; gold was also exported and imported freely to settle accounts between the central banks of different countries. The Gold Standard was finally abandoned in 1914 at the outbreak of the first world war. One of the problems of using gold in this way was its inflexibility: the growth in world trade was restricted by the world's ability to produce more gold.

Accursed greed for gold,
To what dost thou not drive the heart of man.
Virgil, *Aeneid*

Gold card

A plastic card, such as a CREDIT CARD or DEBIT CARD, which offers additional services to those available from the basic version of the card. Gold cards are aimed at high earners who are also high spenders. Most require applicants to have a minimum income, as do platinum cards, which are touted as being better still.

Golden handcuffs

A generous employment contract that persuades managers to stay with a company for a period of time when they might otherwise have thought of leaving; for example, when a company is bought by another or otherwise comes under new ownership.

Golden handshake

G

A generous payment to employees to persuade them to leave a company without making a fuss, even if they have not completed their contract. The term can also apply to senior managers who are leaving a company after a successful tenure. Such managers in the past have been known virtually to write the terms of their own handshake, which can include perks such as the use of offices, clubs and other benefits as well as money or a generous PENSION.

Golden share

A SHARE with special voting rights that give it peculiar power vis-a-vis other shares. The term applies particularly to shares retained by a government after a company has been privatised. If a government wishes to sell off a company in a sensitive industry, such as defence, and yet retain control, it can hold on to a golden share. This might give it the right, for example, to block the sale of certain ASSETS or the sale of the company to a foreign bidder. The beauty of such a share is that, some years down the road, a government can choose not to exercise it if circumstances or priorities change.

Golden week

An unusually short working week on the TOKYO STOCK EXCHANGE which straddles two long holiday weekends.

Goodwill

The value of a business to another over and above the value of its ASSETS – that is, the amount that a purchaser is prepared to pay for the business's good name, customer base and other benefits as a going concern. Goodwill is generally regarded as an INTANGIBLE ASSET and therefore has to be written off over a period (25 years in the United States or 20 years in the UK, or less if you choose).

G

Governance

The government of an organisation, the way in which it is run and controlled. Financial regulators place great emphasis on establishing that there is good governance at institutions under their charge. Such efforts usually centre on ensuring that a company appoints outside, independent directors, who oversee its audit committee, preside over the remuneration of the other directors and see that the board discloses to its shareholders everything it should. This is often more easily said than done, as the spate of corporate scandals in the United States in recent years has shown.

Governments

In the United States, a distinction is sometimes made between governments and government SECURITIES. Governments are securities (such as TREASURY BILLS, BONDS and NOTES) issued by the central government. They are backed by "the full faith and credit" of the US government, which means that all its powers to tax or to borrow can be called upon to repay INTEREST and PRINCIPAL on the LOAN. Government securities are also sometimes issued by government agencies such as the Federal Land Bank. Although these securities are usually highly rated, they do not have the full faith and credit of the US government behind them.

Grace period

The time between the granting of a LOAN and the first repayment of the PRINCIPAL. It is also a period in many LOAN or INSURANCE contracts during which cancellation of the CONTRACT will not occur automatically, even if a repayment is overdue.

G Greenback

Slang for the world's favourite currency: the dollar. The expression arose because the back of US NOTES is green.

Greenmail

The payment of a sum to a corporate raider as part of an agreement to leave the prey alone. Such agreements, which became popular in the merger-mad 1980s, are frowned on by most jurisdictions where TAKEOVERS are possible because they interfere with the smooth working of the CAPITAL MARKETS and of shareholders' rights. Where such tactics are allowed, they are usually accompanied by undertakings by the raider not to buy any more SHARES in the target company and not to pursue the takeover attempt for a period of time.

Gresham's Law

One of the oldest laws in economics, named after Sir Thomas Gresham, financial adviser to Queen Elizabeth I of England in the 16th century. Sir Thomas noted that when a currency has been debased (if, for instance, the metal becomes mutilated) and a new one is introduced to replace it, the new one will be hoarded (and thus taken out of circulation) and the old one will be used for transactions (to use it up). Hence Gresham's Law: that bad money drives out good money.

Grey market

Trading in SHARES in advance of the official start of dealings. Shares are traded in the grey market before they have been allocated to investors. They are traded on the basis of "when issued", denoted by the letters WI.

Group accounts

G

The combination in one BALANCE SHEET, and one PROFIT-AND-LOSS ACCOUNT, of the reports of a number of interrelated companies (a group). A group usually consists of a parent or HOLDING COMPANY and several subsidiaries. The consolidated accounts of a group eliminate intra-group transactions. Anybody looking at the accounts of just one subsidiary would be misled if, say, most of the company's sales were with other companies in the group. This subsidiary may be providing a service or supplying a product only to others within the group.

Group insurance

INSURANCE obtained by an individual as a member of a group rather than as a single individual. An insurance company might, for instance, offer cheaper car insurance to the over-50s (a group) on the grounds that they drive more carefully and are therefore less of a liability than the under-30s (another group).

Growth stock

A SHARE in a company whose EARNINGS are growing at a faster rate than the average for the STOCKMARKET as a whole and, often, for its industry. Such companies rarely pay DIVIDENDS, preferring to reinvest the income in order to feed the machine. So investors must look to CAPITAL GAIN, not income, for their PROFIT. A growth fund, therefore, is a UNIT TRUST

(MUTUAL FUND) which seeks above-average growth by holding the shares of growth stocks. (See also VALUE STOCK.)

Growth investing

A type of investing that relies on CAPITAL GAIN from holding (and then selling) GROWTH STOCKS (that is, those whose EARNINGS grow more rapidly than the average for the market as a whole). The opposite of growth investing is VALUE INVESTING, in which investors seek to profit from stocks that are undervalued compared with the average for the market as a whole and which generally offer a bigger income in the form of DIVIDENDS.

Guarantee

An undertaking by a third party to be responsible for a LIABILITY (a LOAN from a BANK, for instance) should the party to the liability be unable or unwilling to meet the liability on time. To be legally binding, a guarantee must be in writing.

A guarantee differs from an indemnity in the nature of the undertaking. With an indemnity a guarantor takes on collateral responsibility; that is, the same degree of responsibility as the person he or she is guaranteeing. Should the person die, then so does the guarantor's responsibility.

Hammering

An old expression for the failure of a member firm of the
LONDON STOCK EXCHANGE. An employee of the exchange
would hammer for silence on the FLOOR before making an an-
nouncement of a member firm's troubles. In the United States,
hammering has come to refer to intense selling pressure on a
market, when investors believe prices are too high.

Hang Seng Index

The main index of the Hong Kong STOCK EXCHANGE and
therefore of the local market.

Hard currency

A currency that people want to possess because they believe it
will hold its value. Hard currencies (like the dollar, the hardest
of all) are those in which people are happy to denominate international transactions. Hard currencies are more in demand
than soft currencies, and so they often appreciate in value
against other currencies.

Head and shoulders

A recurring pattern on charts that plot the movement of SHARE
prices over time. A head and shoulders occurs when prices
climb to a temporary peak (the left shoulder) before falling
back; prices then rally again (to form the head) before the
market loses momentum. The last part of the pattern involves
another brief rise (the right hand shoulder) before the market
subsides again. The line denoting the overall trend is drawn
across the neck (from left to right). Chartists like to match the
trend in prices against the volume of shares traded at each stage
of the head and shoulders. Volume generally follows prices up
on the left shoulder before tailing off on the head as buyers lose

confidence. At this point it is usually time to sell. (See also TECH-NICAL ANALYSIS.)

Hedge

Something that reduces the RISK of loss from future price movements. During times of high INFLATION, property is the traditional hedge. GOLD too is a popular hedge, but it has not been a reliable store of value in recent years. DERIVATIVES (FUTURES, OPTIONS and the like) provide opportunities for investors and financial institutions to hedge their risks. For example, banks can lay off part of the risk of their loans becoming duff by selling interest contracts in the futures market. A perfect hedge is one which completely eliminates the risk of future losses but at the expense of any possible gain.

Hedge fund

An investment fund that takes a contrarian approach to most investors, often by ARBITRAGING between markets to make a PROFIT. The term "hedge fund" covers a multitude of strategies, some of which are more exotic than others. Many hedge funds have high borrowings to give them LEVERAGE in specialised markets where they hope to exploit inconsistencies in pricing between various FINANCIAL INSTRUMENTS; others focus exclusively on opportunities in the DERIVATIVES markets. Since the late 1990s, hedge funds have tried hard to broaden their appeal by offering alternative strategies to individual investors as well as institutions. This has not stopped many of them losing money when markets have gone against them.

High-yield bond

A BOND that is independently rated below INVESTMENT GRADE and that pays a higher YIELD, or RATE OF INTEREST, to compensate for its greater RISK. Bonds that start off as investment grade but subsequently have their CREDIT RATING down-graded are known as FALLEN ANGELS; those that are upgraded are called RISING STARS. (See also JUNK BOND.)

Hire purchase

A means of paying for high-value consumer goods such as cars or televisions. At the point-of-sale the goods that the consumer wants to buy are first sold to a financial institution, which then rents them to the consumer. After the consumer has made a pre-arranged number of payments (usually monthly) and paid a small service fee, the goods become his or her property. The RATE OF INTEREST charged by the institution is usually higher than the cost of a bank LOAN.

Low interest rates and the increasing use of interest-free CREDIT has undermined the market for traditional hire purchase. During periods of low interest rates, manufacturers of cars and other big-ticket items believe they can make more money by subsidising the cost of credit in order to increase their sales.

Historic cost

The cost of something on the day that it was purchased; its original cost, as opposed to the cost of replacing it or its INFLATION-adjusted cost. Accountants like historic cost because it gives them a real figure to play with. It is not particularly helpful, however, to say in a company's accounts that the value of its premises is the historic cost that was originally paid for them (perhaps 100 years ago). Nor is it useful to know the historic cost of wasting ASSETS like computers or cars. More useful for investors when valuing a company is to know today's value of a company's assets and what it will cost to replace those close to the end of their useful life. (See also DEPRECIATION.)

Holding company

A company set up to hold the SHARES of other companies. These would become subsidiaries if the holding company owned 51% or more of them. Holding companies are often set up in jurisdictions where taxes are lower or regulations are more lax (for instance, an OFFSHORE haven like the Cayman Islands). Such tactics are frowned upon in the United States, even though corporations there often establish holding companies in states that are friendly to business (for example, Delaware).

H

Home banking

Banking done at home by individuals via the telephone or the internet. ACCOUNT holders can thus move money between accounts, pay bills or simply check their balance more or less when they want to and without having to queue up for the privilege. The only time people really need to go to a BANK'S BRANCH is when they have to deposit large amounts of CASH; otherwise everything can be done from afar. This has given financial organisations without branch networks a big cost advantage. And as banks cut back their branch networks, so more people are likely to switch to home banking.

Hostile bid

A TAKEOVER bid by one company for another in which the second company resists the takeover attempt. There are various weapons at its disposal. The most orthodox is to persuade the shareholders that they will be better off in future without being taken over. This usually involves showing how the company will grow and thus increase the value of its business for shareholders. A target company can also appeal to a WHITE KNIGHT, another company often in the same industry with which it could do a deal that would maintain some or all of its independence. Until their use became frowned upon, companies in the

United States could also resort to a POISON PILL, a measure such as a prior agreement with a third company that would make it indigestible to a possible predator. The City of London prides itself on its voluntary takeover code, a rule book presided over by the PANEL ON TAKEOVERS AND MERGERS. The European Commission has tried to come up with its own code so that companies operating across Europe can abide by similar rules. Its efforts have met with varying degrees of success. A hostile bid is also known as a CONTESTED BID.

Hot money

Highly mobile money that flies to wherever it can get the best RATE OF RETURN for a given level of RISK. Hot money has no long-term allegiance to any particular investment, so it flows back and forth across exchanges and can cause wild fluctuations in exchange rates. Such fluctuations have become more and more exaggerated as exchange controls have been removed, and as DEREGULATION has freed money to go where it wants.

Hot money may also refer to the fickle capital that stems from illegal sources such as drugs and which sloshes around OFFSHORE FINANCIAL CENTRES where there are few rules to curb or control it.

Hurdle rate

The RATE OF RETURN which a business or investment opportunity needs to satisfy in order to justify its existence. Such returns are measured in a variety of ways – for example, on the basis of DISCOUNTED CASH FLOW or the cost of the CAPITAL involved compared with the expected return adjusted for the level of RISK involved. The hurdle may be the RATE OF INTEREST on government BONDS, on the grounds that it is the least that investors would expect to get from an alternative investment with a minimum amount of risk. Or it may be a comparable rate of return adopted by firms in the same industry.

IBF

See INTERNATIONAL BANKING FACILITY.

IFA

Short for independent financial adviser; someone in the UK who is recognised by the FINANCIAL SERVICES AUTHORITY (FSA) as fit to give investors financial advice. IFAS provide supposedly independent advice but are paid via COMMISSION from the institution whose product they recommend. The FSA recognised the conflict inherent in this relationship but realised that a complete separation from the product provider was uneconomic: few customers would be prepared to pay the true cost of advice. So the FSA retained a system based on commission but made it as transparent as possible by requiring IFAS quoting for financial products to declare the commission that would be paid to them.

IMF

See INTERNATIONAL MONETARY FUND.

Impact day

The day when details of a new ISSUE, or INITIAL PUBLIC OFFERING, of SECURITIES are announced. This is when the price and number of the SHARES or BONDS on offer to investors is confirmed. At this point there is no going back if the market moves against the offer.

Impaired loan

A LOAN that may not be repaid in part or in full as scheduled; one on which INTEREST payments are in doubt. BANKS with loans they believe to be impaired must examine the borrower's business and financial strength, and assess the chances of the loan being repaid. A borrower which subsequently fails to repay the loan according to the terms of its contract is said to be in DEFAULT.

Income statement

US terminology for PROFIT-AND-LOSS ACCOUNT.

Indemnity

See GUARANTEE.

I

Index

A statistical average of the prices of a number of things. The things may be consumer goods (as in the consumer price index), or they may be STOCKS and SHARES, as in STOCKMARKET indices such as the DOW JONES. Some stockmarket indices reflect a narrow part of the market (averaging the share prices of a handful of the largest, BLUE-CHIP companies, for example); others try to reflect the whole market by averaging most of the shares quoted on it. Yet others include stocks from only one industry or sector (an average of utility or of mining stocks, for example). An index is a useful way of showing by how much, and in which direction, prices are moving. In recent years, investors have moved away from narrow indices (such as the FT ORDINARY SHARE index, which covers the share prices of only 30 companies). Instead, they follow a combination of wider indices (such as the FTSE 100 and FTSE 250) and those devoted to specific sectors or parts of the market (such as the FTSE Smaller Companies Index). One of the most widely used family of indices is compiled by Morgan Stanley Capital International. Fund managers use them as BENCHMARKS against which to measure their performance, for BONDS as well as EQUITIES in different markets and in different sectors of those markets throughout the world.

Index fund

A MUTUAL FUND or UNIT TRUST which invests in a PORTFOLIO of SHARES that matches identically the constituents of a well-known STOCKMARKET INDEX. Hence changes in the value of the fund mirror changes in the index itself. So when companies drop in or out of an index, as they do periodically because of changes in their stockmarket CAPITALISATION, managers of index funds must adjust their portfolios accordingly. For a company that falls out of an index because the combined value of its shares (that is, its capitalisation) has shrunk, the results can be drastic: index funds are forced to sell the company's shares, the effect of which can be to depress their value even more.

Index-linked

Describes the linking of the redemption value (and sometimes even the INTEREST) of a SECURITY or LOAN to a general price INDEX (such as the index of retail prices). This is done to protect the value of the security or loan from the ravages of INFLATION. Whatever interest is paid after the indexing is the "real" RATE OF INTEREST on the loan or security.

Employers may also seek to link their employees' pay to indices such as the consumer price index in the hope that this will act as a restraint. During periods of low inflation, or even deflation, this can still lead to arguments over the level of pay. Not surprisingly, governments then cast about for other indices that prove their point.

Index option

An OPTION whose underlying ASSET is a STOCKMARKET

INDEX, such as the S&P 500 or the FTSE 100. By purchasing the right, but not the obligation, to buy the underlying SHARES, an investor is therefore betting on the overall direction of the market. Buying an index option is an easier and cheaper way of getting exposure to the stockmarket as a whole than buying all the individual shares that make up a particular index. Financial institutions may also use index options to HEDGE their RISK in the EQUITY market; in other words, to lay off to other investors part of the risk that they may already have through the shares that they own.

Index tracking

The process of comparing the performance of an investment PORTFOLIO with the performance of a relevant STOCKMARKET INDEX. If an actively managed investment fund outperforms the index, it can be said to have earned its fee. Otherwise its investors would have been better off investing passively in the constituent parts of the index. This can be done by investing in a TRACKER FUND, which tracks the index. These funds are cheaper because there is no need for a manger to make investment decisions and they are simpler to administer. The index being tracked is said to be a BENCHMARK.

Individual retirement account

A special fund, set up under US tax law, into which an individual can put a certain amount of money each year towards his or her PENSION. Since 2001, there have been two types of individual retirement account (IRA). The first, called a traditional IRA, allows payments (lump-sum or regular) to be paid in free of tax. When a pension is paid out of a traditional IRA, the beneficiary pays tax on it like any other income. The second, called a Roth IRA, offers no relief from tax on contributions but shelters all EARNINGS within it (provided the IRA has been set up for at least five tax years and the holder is at least 59.5 years old before he or she begins to make withdrawals). Contributions to both types of IRA are restricted according to a holder's earnings and other circumstances.

Inflation

A systemic rise in the price of goods and services over time. Economists still differ in their views of what causes inflation. There are two main theories.

- **Cost push**, which asserts that increases in the cost of the factors of production are the main cause. This includes the prices of raw materials and any rise in property rents. More importantly, it includes rises in wage costs. As a result, employers argue that any rise above the rate of inflation is itself inflationary.
- **Demand pull**, which asserts that consumers are demanding more of a product or service than is being produced and are thus pushing up prices. They can only do this if the amount of money in the economy exceeds the growth in production plus the rate of inflation.

Inflation redistributes wealth and income. It hits hardest those on fixed incomes (because the purchasing power of their income is eroded) and benefits most those heavily in DEBT (because the value of their borrowings diminishes the higher the rate of inflation, even though the cost of servicing the debt may rise because of higher INTEREST rates). It also undermines the basis for calculating value. It is not in itself, however, a deterrent to economic growth. Many developing countries have successfully combined high growth with high inflation. Indeed, many economists regard deflation as a bigger threat.

Inflation is the one form of taxation that can be imposed without legislation.
Milton Friedman

Initial public offering

A company's first offering of SHARES to the general public. An initial public offering (IPO), or new ISSUE, of shares is often a difficult time for a company and its founders. Not only do they have to contend with the demands of the INVESTMENT BANKS, BROKERS and other professional advisers acting on their behalf, but they also have to adjust their horizons to the medium and short term, because from the word go, the market will look for evidence of growth in EARNINGS, which in turn is used to justify an increase in the share price. It is not just the company's founders who will seek to cash in some of the rewards of their creation. Venture capitalists and specialists in PRIVATE EQUITY frequently take advantage of an IPO to realise some or all of their PROFITS (if there are any) from backing the company while it was privately owned.

Insider dealing

Dealing in SHARES with the benefit of inside information; that is, information not yet known to the general public. In some circumstances, insider dealing is a crime, but it is a difficult one to prove. In cases where there is a conviction, the courts rely on somebody else – a confidant or fellow director, perhaps – to confirm that the accused did indeed act on knowledge that had yet to reach the public domain. Insider DEALERS can be prosecuted not just for buying shares on good news (and therefore profiting from a rise in their value), but also for selling part, or all, of their holding on bad news (and so successfully reducing their losses).

Stealing too fast.
Calvin Trillin's definition of insider trading

Instalment credit

A LOAN that is repaid over a period in regular, equal instalments. Such loans are most often used to finance consumer purchases, but they are also sometimes used in trade finance. Instalment credit differs from HIRE PURCHASE. In hire purchase, consumers hire the goods until they have paid off the loan; with instalment credit they own the goods throughout the time that they are paying off the loan.

Institutional investor

An institution (such as an INSURANCE company, PENSION FUND or INVESTMENT TRUST) that makes substantial investments by gathering together the small savings of others and acting collectively on their behalf. In recent years, individuals' savings have increasingly been channelled through these institutions and they have come to have great influence in most financial markets. In the UK, for example, they hold more than 70% of all quoted SECURITIES. Institutional investors are stronger in Anglo-Saxon countries where PENSIONS are more frequently funded by accumulated savings from the private sector. However, the increasing cost of paying for people's pensions on a pay-as-you-go basis (particularly with the rising proportion of old and retired people compared with the number of younger ones in work) has forced other countries to follow suit.

Institutional investors are usually divided into those that specialise in retail money, running MUTUAL FUNDS and other investment vehicles aimed at individual investors, and those that specialise in institutional money, such as large companies' pension funds. The fees for managing the former are, by and large, higher partly because it costs more to look after lots of individual savers.

Insurance

A CONTRACT between two parties (the insurer and the insured) in which the insurer (usually an insurance company) agrees to reimburse the insured for clearly defined losses. It does so in return for payments of a PREMIUM. In essence, this is a process for transferring RISK from an individual to a larger group (all those who are paying premiums to the insurer). There are two main types of insurance.

- **Casualty**, where there is no certainty that that the thing insured will occur. Common forms of casualty insurance are against accidents (in cars or boats or planes), against damage to buildings and against sickness.
- **Life**, where the thing insured against is certain to occur: the death of the insured. The only uncertainty is when. This sort of insurance is usually referred to as life ASSURANCE because the event is assured of happening.

Life assurance was traditionally sold directly by sales people to customers in their homes, Casualty was normally sold by agents, who matched a customer's needs with insurance policies available on the market. Both are now increasingly sold DIRECT (by telephone) or via the internet.

When the praying does no good, insurance does help.
Bertolt Brecht

Intangible assets

The ASSETS of a company (such as a brand, franchise, trademark or other form of intellectual property) that cannot be touched, yet have value. In most jurisdictions, attributing a value to such assets increases a company's net worth (by adding to the plus side of the BALANCE SHEET) but does not always add to its EARNINGS. This is because, once valued, intangible assets usually have to be depreciated each year; this is a cost. For this reason, companies that have built up brands from scratch often decide not to value them, particularly if they are increasing in value. However, companies that acquire brands or other forms of intellectual property separately, or when they acquire another company, invariably have to depreciate them over time. (See also DEPRECIATION and GOODWILL.)

Interbank market

A financial market in which BANKS deal with each other; a central part of any efficient financial system. Interbank markets work at two main levels: at the top are CENTRAL BANKS, which use the interbank market to influence INTEREST rates and thus determine the direction of MONETARY POLICY; below that are banks and financial institutions, which exchange funds between themselves and enable the financial system to work efficiently. Banks that get more deposits from their customers than requests for LOANS need a market in which to sell their surplus DEPOSITS to those in the opposite position.

The interbank markets are most tested during times of financial crisis when interest rates rise, pushing up the cost of money for those who need it most. One of the biggest tests in recent years was during 1998 when Russia reneged on its sovereign DEBTS and Long Term Capital Management, a HEDGE FUND, came close to collapse and had to be rescued by a group of banks at the behest of the US FEDERAL RESERVE. Both incidents involved LIABILITIES running into billions of dollars. A subsequent study by the BANK FOR INTERNATIONAL SETTLEMENTS found that, despite the strain placed on the interbank market, interest rates fluctuated only marginally from the base line set by central banks. This suggests that money was able to reach the parts of the market where it was needed.

Interdealer broker

A BROKER that acts as an intermediary between DEALERS in the EQUITY, BOND or DERIVATIVES markets. By broking large blocks of SECURITIES, interdealer brokers help dealers to balance their books and provide LIQUIDITY to a market when and where it is needed. Interdealer brokers do not trade on their own account but are often involved in big transactions, particularly in the bond markets.

Interest

There are two meanings.

1 The price of money over time (see RATE OF INTEREST, AN-NUALISED PERCENTAGE RATE, COUPON, DISCOUNT RATE, INTERNAL RATE OF RETURN, NEGATIVE INTEREST, VARIABLE RATE and YIELD). If the rate of interest is 8% a year, then for someone to borrow $100 for a whole year will cost them $8, when calculated as simple interest. Compound interest involves paying interest on the PRINCIPAL and on accrued interest as well. Hence if interest is due every six months, but is paid only annually, the interest due would be 8% on $100 for six months (which is $4) plus 8% on $104 for the next six months (which is $4.16).

2 Somebody's share in property, as in "she had a 50% interest in the house".

It is not my interest to pay the principal,
nor my principle to pay the interest.
Richard Brinsley Sheridan

Interest coverage ratio

The number of times a company's annual INTEREST payments can be divided into the net operating income. An indication of how sure the company's creditors can be of repayment.

Interest-only loan

A LOAN on which only the INTEREST is paid at regular intervals until the loan matures, at which time the full amount of the PRINCIPAL is repaid. This differs from the case where interest and principal are repaid throughout the life of the loan in a series of regular payments. Interest-only loans are most popular during times of high INFLATION. This erodes the value of the loan so that there is relatively less to pay off when it matures.

Another reason for taking out an interest-only loan is when a borrower cannot afford to repay both interest and principal but anticipates having enough money when the loan matures to pay it off in full.

Interim dividend

Part of a company's DIVIDEND paid at intervals during the year. Interim dividends are usually paid six months into the financial year. Some US companies pay quarterly but rarely more frequently unless, for some reason, a special dividend is declared and approved by the board of directors.

Internal funds

Companies have two sources that they can turn to when they need money:

- external funds from banks, CAPITAL MARKETS and shareholders;
- internal funds from their own CASH FLOW – cash retained within the business and not distributed to shareholders.

Businesses that generate large amounts of cash (as distinct from PROFIT) are able to rely more on internal funds than those, such as PRIVATE EQUITY companies, that have lumpy cash flows. Companies in Anglo-Saxon countries have traditionally raised more money from their shareholders and the capital markets. Companies in continental Europe and Japan have closer links with their BANKS, which often have shareholdings in them. As a result, such companies have relied more on borrowings from banks for a large proportion of their external funds.

Internal rate of return

The RATE OF INTEREST which would discount the flow of revenue generated by an investment, so that the NET PRESENT VALUE of the flow is equal to the CAPITAL sum invested. At its simplest, the internal rate of return (IRR) of a BANK ACCOUNT is the rate of interest received on it.

The IRR is much used in appraising whether investment proposals are viable. In this case, ANALYSTS examine a venture's income stream to arrive at the IRR. This does not always give the same result as using net present value as a yardstick. One project can have a higher net present value than another, yet have a lower IRR.

International Bank for Reconstruction and Development

See WORLD BANK.

International Banking Facility

A type of offshore organisation that has been permitted in the United States since the early 1980s. International Banking Facilities (IBFS) can only carry out large financial transactions and only with non-residents. But these transactions are free from the RESERVES requirements imposed on domestic financial institutions, and in many cases they are also free from state and local taxes.

International Monetary Fund

An institution established as part of the landmark BRETTON WOODS AGREEMENT of 1944. The role of the International Monetary Fund (IMF) was to oversee the system of fixed exchange rates which prevailed at the time. As fixed exchange rates gave way (in most cases) to floating ones, the IMF found a new role for itself. It was deeply involved in sorting out the

DEBT crisis that gripped the developing world during the 1980s, imposing economic conditions on countries before agreeing to new LOANS and the RESCHEDULING of old ones.

It is this "conditionality" that has repeatedly drawn most criticism: in Asia and Russia during the late 1990s and in Latin America during the early 2000s. Some felt the IMF acted too brusquely with former communist states in eastern Europe and later when confronted with the problems of Brazil and Argentina. As soon as the IMF draws up new rules to deal more flexibly and efficiently with the next crisis, it seems to be wrong-footed by the latest set of problems.

With headquarters in Washington, DC, the IMF has over 140 member countries. Originally confined to the capitalist west, they now include many of the former communist states of eastern Europe. Each country pays a membership fee (its quota), which is related to the size of its economy. Members can then borrow up to 25% of their quotas at will; if they want any more they have to accept certain conditions from the IMF on how they run their economy. The managing director of the IMF is traditionally a European and the deputy managing director an American.

International Securities Market Association

Founded in 1969 in Zurich, the International Securities Market Association (ISMA) was originally called the Association of International Bond Dealers (AIDB) but changed its name in 1991. It is a loosely knit club that presides over a market in SECURITIES worth more than $3 trillion. It has more than 800 member firms from over 40 countries that deal in and underwrite international BONDS. The ISMA draws up its own rules and regulations and supervises the activities of its members.

Internet banking

The practice of banking over the internet. During the dotcom boom of the late 1990s, it was confidently predicted that, within a few years, most people would be doing all their banking trans-actions over the internet. It has not turned out quite like that, but an increasing number of customers do favour the speed and efficiency of doing business via the internet or the telephone. Many BANKS set up to cater for such customers also offer MUTUAL FUNDS and other investment products, which can just as easily be researched, bought and sold over the internet. (See also HOME BANKING.)

In the money

A CALL OPTION is said to be in the money when it has a STRIKE PRICE below the current price of the underlying COMMODITY or SECURITY on which the option has been written. Likewise when a PUT OPTION has a strike price above the current price it is said to be in the money. Contrast with OUT OF THE MONEY.

Intrinsic value

The difference between the exercise or STRIKE PRICE of an option and the market value of the underlying SECURITY. For example, if the strike price on a CALL OPTION is $43 to purchase a STOCK with a market price of $45, then the intrinsic value is $2. In the case of a PUT OPTION, if the strike price is $45 and the market value of the underlying stock is $43, then the intrinsic value would also be $2. (See also IN THE MONEY; contrast with EXTRINSIC VALUE.)

Introduction

A way of introducing a company to a STOCKMARKET. No new SHARES are issued, but existing shares (which may have been in the hands of a small number of founders or their families) are distributed and sold more widely. Most such offerings are for small companies LISTING on junior STOCK EXCHANGES.

Inventory

A company's merchandise; finished and unfinished products which have yet to be sold. Such goods are ASSETS so they can be used as COLLATERAL or SECURITY for bank LOANS, which is also called inventory financing.

Inverse yield curve

In the normal structure of INTEREST rates, the rate for long-term FINANCIAL INSTRUMENTS is higher than that for SHORT-TERM ones. Plot this as a graph (rates on the vertical axis, maturity on the horizontal axis) and the curve slopes upwards from the bottom left hand corner to the top right. When there are strong expectations that a currently high INFLATION rate will soon fall rapidly, this curve can slope the other way; the longer the MATURITY, the lower are the rates. Plotting this on the graph is said to produce an inverse yield curve.

Investment bank

A BANK whose main business is acting as an UNDERWRITER or AGENT for companies and other institutions (for example, municipalities or even countries) issuing DEBT or EQUITY SECURITIES in order to raise money. Such banks rarely accept DEPOSITS or make LOANS. Instead they charge fees for advising their clients. They usually also make markets in the securities that they have underwritten and helped to ISSUE as well as act as BROKERS or DEALERS in the securities markets.

Controversially, investment banks' ANALYSTS have provided investors with research and made recommendations about the companies whose securities they have brought to the market. This has led to CONFLICTS OF INTEREST. In order to win lucrative mandates from investment-banking clients, analysts were tempted, particularly during the boom years of the late 1990s, to write favourable recommendations about the companies they follow. The biggest investment banks (the so-called "bulge bracket" banks) are American, with offices in most of the world's FINANCIAL CENTRES.

Investment club

A group of private investors who agree to pool their funds and manage their investments themselves. The advantage of investment clubs is that investors feel that they have more control over their investments, and they save the management fees of a professional FUND MANAGER. Members need the time to analyse the SECURITIES they are investing in, which is probably why such clubs are popular among retired people.

I

Investment grade

The definition given to SECURITIES (usually BONDS) issued by companies or institutions with a certain financial standing. In the United States, certain institutions are not allowed to invest in securities below a certain grade because they are deemed too risky. Bonds that are eligible for investment by such institutions are called investment grade; those that are not are referred to as junk. Because of the higher risk that their issuers will default on repayments to holders, JUNK BONDS carry a significantly higher RATE OF INTEREST than safer, investment-grade securities. The arbiters of whether an issue is investment grade or not are the nationally recognised (and therefore biggest) CREDIT-RATING agencies. (See also FALLEN ANGEL and RISING STAR.)

Investment style

The bias that a manager adopts in running his or her investment fund. Growth funds favour SHARES in companies whose sales or EARNINGS are expected to grow rapidly and therefore have a high RETURN on CAPITAL. Value funds, by contrast, prefer the shares of companies that are cheap compared with their earnings and with the average for the market as a whole.

VALUE STOCKS usually pay high dividends; GROWTH STOCKS pay hardly any at all. A fund that combines both styles and therefore has more freedom to switch between the two is called a BLEND FUND. Investment style was born in the United States but has since taken off in the UK, elsewhere in Europe and in other markets.

> *Sometimes your best investments are the ones you don't make.*
> Donald Trump

Investment trust

I

A company that, like any other, issues SHARES to investors but whose business is also investment. Called a CLOSED-END FUND in the United States, an investment trust (unlike a UNIT TRUST or MUTUAL FUND) has a specified number of shares that make up its CAPITAL. The main advantage of an investment trust (like a unit trust or mutual fund) is that it allows investors to spread their RISK. Another is that (unlike a unit trust or mutual fund) it can also borrow money to give it GEARING or leverage. This can work in shareholders' favour provided the trust's return on its investments is greater than the cost of its capital; if not, it ends up destroying the value of its shareholders' investments.

Most investment trusts offer different types of shares, from ORDINARY SHARES (the riskiest) up to preferred or PREFERENCE SHARES and even LOAN STOCK. They are thus able to offer different things to different investors: income shares for those who want interest on their investment; and capital shares for those who are most interested in CAPITAL GAIN.

Investor relations

The job of keeping investors in a company informed about its activities and performance with the aim of maximising the value of its SHARES. Investor relations consultants start by examining the register of shareholders to find out which institutions are holders of the shares as well as those which are not, but should or could be. Most publicly quoted companies prefer to have a stable and diversified base of investors who, with luck, will hold their shares as they grow in value. To this end consultants channel information to ANALYSTS and the media as well as investors to ensure that a company's business is well understood.

Investor relations was originally just a part of public relations. But as external shareholders have grown in importance for most listed companies, so has the role of keeping them happy, during tough times as well as good.

Invisibles

Traded items that never see the inside of a container for shipping, but which earn foreign currency for their sponsor. Services such as banking, INSURANCE and tourism make up the bulk of a country's invisible trade. Some countries have a big surplus in invisibles because they are especially attractive to tourists or bankers, and sometimes to both. Increasingly, the distinction between visible and invisible trade is becoming blurred. When Sony sells a (visible) mini-disc outside Japan, the price paid for it includes a lot of (invisible) services such as patented know-how, copyright and the like; and when tourists or bankers leave the Bahamas, they will often take (visible) items home with them.

IPO

See INITIAL PUBLIC OFFERING.

IRA

See INDIVIDUAL RETIREMENT ACCOUNT.

ISA

Short for individual savings account, a type of savings and investment account introduced by the UK government in 1999. There are three main types of ISAs, holding a combination of CASH, EQUITIES and INSURANCE. Gains made while investments remain within an ISA are tax free. The government's aim was to build up individuals' savings as part of its plan to free more people from their dependence on state PENSIONS. The money flowed in during the boom years of the late 1990s, but tailed off when EQUITY markets faltered.

ISIN

Short for International Securities Identification Number, a 12-digit alphanumeric code that uniquely identifies each issue of SECURITIES. ISIN codes appear on every security and COUPON. Drawn up under the auspices of the International Organisation for Standardisation (ISO), all such codes are published under ISO 6166.

Islamic banking

Banking run according to Islamic law. This forbids what is known as *riba*, a term that encompasses not just the notion of USURY but also INTEREST. As a result, Islamic banks do not accept DEPOSITS on which they pay interest; instead they have partners (rather like a mutually owned institution), who receive a share of the PROFITS from the businesses into which their money is channelled. Likewise, businesses that receive money from Islamic banks pay no interest; instead the bank shares in the company's profit as if they were partners. Banking according to Islamic principles has become more widespread over the past few decades, particularly since oil wealth has spread through the Arab world, but it dates back to the early part of the seventh century. (See ZAKAT.)

ISMA

See INTERNATIONAL SECURITIES MARKET ASSOCIATION.

Issue

The sale of a new SECURITY. An issue can be made in several ways:

- through an OFFER FOR SALE in which the issuing house (usually an INVESTMENT BANK or BROKER) buys the securities from the company, takes the RISK on to its own and others' books, and sells the securities to the public;
- through a DIRECT sale by the company itself;
- through a PRIVATE PLACEMENT of only part of the EQUITY to a restricted number of investors.

A company's issued SHARE capital is the face value of the shares that it has issued. Issued capital should be distinguished from MARKET CAPITALISATION, which is the value put upon all those issued shares by a STOCKMARKET (that is, the share price multiplied by the number of shares in issue). For example, a company which has issued 10m 10-cent shares has an issued share capital of $1m. If the stockmarket price of its shares is $2, its market capitalisation is $20m.

Jobber

The old name for a MARKET MAKER on the LONDON STOCK EXCHANGE. The long-standing existence of DUAL CAPACITY meant that, before BIG BANG in 1996, a jobber could not be a BROKER, and vice versa. Jobbers could deal directly only with brokers or with other jobbers, not with the general investing public, private or institutional. With Big Bang the distinction between jobber and broker was removed and with it outdated practices that had featherbedded the financial community at the expense of investors. The end of dual capacity brought London's EQUITY markets into line with their (more competitive) counterparts in the United States. Much of the rest of Europe soon followed.

Junk bond

A BOND issued by a US company or institution whose CREDIT RATING is below INVESTMENT GRADE, a ranking provided by the two largest rating agencies: Moody's Investors Service and Standard & Poor's. Because their issuer is rated below investment grade, junk (or HIGH YIELD) bonds offer a higher RATE OF INTEREST to compensate the holder for the extra risk of a DEFAULT.

Junk bonds were the idea of Michael Milken of Drexel Burnham Lambert and came into fashion in the 1980s. He helped financiers such as Ivan Boesky to raise the money needed for a spate of ambitious TAKEOVERS. Milken was eventually indicted for wrongdoing and Drexel collapsed, but not before the two of them had helped to transform the CAPITAL MARKETS in the United States. Bonds that lose their status as investment grade are called FALLEN ANGELS; those that travel in the opposite direction are RISING STARS.

Kaffir

A term for the SHARES of South African gold-mining companies.

Kerb trading

Trading in SECURITIES outside the official opening hours of a market. In the United States, the term refers mainly to the trading of shares not listed on the main board of the STOCK EXCHANGE. As a result, the AMERICAN STOCK EXCHANGE was known for years as the Kerb Market. In Australia, the kerb market was reserved for junior shares in which there was little turnover. The term is also used on the London Metal Exchange to describe trading in FUTURES contracts that takes place at the same time as trading in a COMMODITY for current delivery.

Krugerrand

A GOLD coin created and marketed by South Africa to persuade investors to buy more gold. The first Krugerrand (named after the country's president, Paul Kruger, and its currency, the rand) was minted in 1967. It weighed 1 troy ounce of fine gold. In 1980, a family of coins was created, weighing one-half, one-quarter and one-tenth of an ounce. To maintain tradition, Krugerrands are still minted in 22-carat gold.

KYC rules

Know Your Customer (KYC) rules were laid down by regulators in the United States during the late 1990s to ensure that BANKS obtain basic details about their customers so that they know who is the true beneficiary of any ACCOUNT opened at the bank. The rules were part of a raft of measures aimed at fighting MONEY LAUNDERING, drug trafficking and drug-related crime. The information gleaned from KYC rules is also an important tool in the US government's fight against terrorism.

Laddering

The practice of falsely driving up the price of ORDINARY
SHARES (common stock in the United States) when they are
issued to investors as part of a new ISSUE (or INITIAL PUBLIC
OFFERING). The issuing BANK agrees with certain investors
that, in return for being allocated shares at the issue price, they
will buy additional shares at progressively higher prices. The
demand for the shares created in this way has the effect of
driving up the price artificially high. When the price has reached
a predetermined level, the original investors sell out at a huge
PROFIT, leaving everybody else in the lurch. Although the practice is notoriously difficult to prove in a court of law, it was
used during the boom in technology shares during the late
1990s.

Landesbank

A German financial institution that serves as a mini-CENTRAL
BANK for a region (or *land*). Many *landesbanken* have branched
out from their original role and have since become virtually indistinguishable from mainstream commercial banks based in
Germany. Like others in the United States or elsewhere in
Europe, some *landesbanken* have diversified into investment
banking, SECURITIES trading and even INSURANCE.

Laundering

See MONEY LAUNDERING.

LBO

See LEVERAGED BUY-OUT.

LENDER OF LAST RESORT   189

Lead manager

A BANK which leads the organisation of a SYNDICATED LOAN or of a new ISSUE and the underwriting of SECURITIES. The lead manager does most of the hard work in the negotiations with the borrower and guarantees to take up the largest part of any issue that is left unsold. In return, it gets the biggest fee and top billing on the TOMBSTONE. The lead manager also ranks at the top of the league tables of issues underwritten by such banks. Although it is rarely given as a reason for winning a particular mandate, INVESTMENT BANKS like to be seen to be at or near the top, especially for lucrative international deals in the DEBT or EQUITY markets.

Leasing

The hiring of CAPITAL goods or equipment by manufacturing companies in order to avoid the all-at-once cost of purchasing them. A financial institution buys the capital goods, sets the capital cost off against its taxable income and leases the goods to the manufacturer. Much of the tax benefit to the leasing institution is passed on to the lessee in the form of lower charges. Leasing is particularly attractive when:

- the lessee has used up all its available capital allowances (because of its own heavy expenditure on capital risks);
- the lessee does not have the CASH to make a capital purchase;
- the lessee does not want to be burdened with the responsibilities of ownership.

Lender of last resort

The ultimate responsibility of a CENTRAL BANK is to act as a lender of last resort to a country's financial system, typically to provide BANKS under its charge with enough money to stop a run on any particular one of them. All banks are illiquid, that is, the average MATURITY of their LOANS exceeds the average maturity of their DEPOSITS. Should all depositors demand their money back immediately and simultaneously, there is no bank that could meet their demands. They could not call in their loans fast enough. In such a situation the lender of last resort pumps limitless amounts of money into the system until depositors are reassured that they will be repaid as and when they wish.

A single central bank may be able to stem a run on a local bank in a small state such as Hong Kong; indeed, it has happened more than once there over the years. But in today's global market, many doubt whether any single authority in a large western country would have sufficient resources to act in this way if called upon to do so. Closing the banks, as happened in Argentina in 2002 after the country defaulted on its debt to international lenders, may solve the problem for a while but sooner or later the central bank has to find a solution.

L

Letter of credit

An arrangement with a BANK to make money available to a customer abroad. The customer's ACCOUNT is debited with the required amount, and the bank then instructs its relevant CORRESPONDENT BANK to make the money available whenever the customer wants it. As a security check, the bank will send its correspondent a copy of the customer's signature.

Leverage

See GEARING.

Leveraged buy-out

The TAKEOVER of a company in which most of the cost is paid for with borrowed money. Usually the ASSETS of the company being taken over are used as SECURITY for the loan (which may be for up to 70% of the purchase price). The acquiring company pays the INTEREST out of the CASH FLOW of the company being bought. That is mainly why many successful buy-outs are of companies with a healthy cash flow.

Liability

A claim on the ASSETS of an individual or company. A liability (such as a DEBT) shows up once it has been incurred. In a company's BALANCE SHEET, assets are always equal to liabilities, plus a balancing amount of shareholders' funds.

Liability management

The business of managing a BANK'S LIABILITIES (particularly its DEPOSITS). The trick is to structure them so that the RISK, MATURITY and LIQUIDITY are related as closely as possible to the (changing) demand for LOANS (that is, ASSETS). At the same time, of course, the bank must aim to make money on each and every one. For companies, liability management usually applies to their exposure to foreign currencies. The risk that a company's EARNINGS may suffer because of a fall in the value of foreign currencies can be hedged in a variety of ways. One way is to take out currency or INTEREST-rate swaps in the FUTURES and OPTIONS markets.

Libor

See LONDON INTERBANK OFFERED RATE.

Lien

Obtaining certain rights to property until the time that the DEBT owed by the owner of the property has been repaid. For as long as a lien exists on a property, the owner loses the right to sell it, even though he or she may retain legal ownership of it.

Life assurance

See ASSURANCE and INSURANCE.

Life company

Short for life ASSURANCE company (see also INSURANCE).

LIFFE

Short for London International Financial Futures Exchange (see EURONEXT).

Limit order

An order from a client to a BROKER to buy or sell a specific number of SHARES at a specified price or better. Usually there will be a time limit on a limit order. (See also STOP ORDER.)

> *I made my money by selling too soon.*
> Bernard Baruch

Line of credit

A LOAN facility made available to a debtor by a creditor on condition that the debtor uses it to buy goods or services from the creditor. BANKS also provide customers with lines of credit to enable them to make a series of purchases which have been agreed with the bank in advance.

Liquidation

The winding up of a company's affairs and the distribution of its remaining ASSETS after it has ceased trading. After deducting the costs of the liquidation, the assets are divided among the company's creditors. Preferential creditors (such as the tax man and employees) get first call. What is left is divided among the remaining creditors, each according to the amount they are owed. The liquidation process can be lengthy, particularly if there are contested claims to the company's assets.

Liquidity

The degree to which an ASSET or SECURITY can be bought or sold without affecting its price. A highly liquid SHARE is one in which there is a lot of trading (both buying and selling). An illiquid share is one in which a large order to buy or sell will quickly affect the price. As a result, investors trading in illiquid securities must do so with caution, otherwise the price will move up or down against them. The RISK of illiquid stocks is that the price will tumble before investors can sell them.

L

Listing

The addition of a company's CAPITAL to the list of SHARES and other SECURITIES such as DEBT instruments that are traded on a particular STOCK EXCHANGE. A company's securities are usually listed after it has been floated as part of an INITIAL PUBLIC OFFERING of its shares. Listed companies must abide by strict rules governing the amount and frequency of information that they must make available to shareholders. In the United States, listed companies must report to their shareholders every three months; in Europe, most exchanges insist that a company reports its results every six months.

Lloyd's

An INSURANCE market based in London which began in the 18th-century coffee house of a man called Lloyd. The market, which started as an association of UNDERWRITERS, has since grown many times over. Until the late 1990s, the market was supported by thousands of so-called NAMES, wealthy individuals who pledged their ASSETS in support of SYNDICATES that underwrote insurance RISKS. Many were attracted by the tax benefits that accompanied membership but found to their cost that they could also lose large amounts of money. Names still exist but are now in a minority to corporate members of Lloyd's who operate in a similar way. Uniquely, Lloyd's has reported its results three years in arrears, mainly to enable its underwriters to take into account claims against it before closing off its accounts.

In its early days, Lloyd's specialised in marine risks, but it now covers most areas of the insurance market, particularly REINSURANCE. Its strength, though, is in specialised risks such as aviation, employers' liabilities and the like. The fact that the market is made up of dozens of syndicates makes it agile and fast-moving. Yet this does not make it immune to the cycles of boom and bust that seem to characterise the international insurance market.

Loan

A transaction in which the owner of property (usually money) allows somebody else (the borrower) to have use of it. As part of the transaction, the borrower usually agrees to return the property after a certain period and to pay a price for having the use of it. When the property lent is money, that price is called INTEREST.

Loan stock

Part of a company's CAPITAL issued in the form of INTEREST-bearing long-term LOANS or BONDS. Loan stock can be granted to an individual or institution that lends money to a company. It is usually unsecured (that is, it is not held against a particular ASSET or assets as SECURITY) and carries a fixed RATE OF INTEREST.

London Bullion Market Association

A body that represents the group of GOLD DEALERS who meet twice a day in London to fix the gold price. (See also FIXING.)

London Interbank Offered Rate

The rate of INTEREST, commonly known as LIBOR, which prime banks in the EUROMARKETS pay each other for DEPOSITS. LIBOR is usually quoted for deposits of one, three, six and 12 months and as such is used as a BENCHMARK for the pricing of BONDS issued in the DEBT markets.

London International Financial Futures Exchange

See EURONEXT.

L

London Stock Exchange

For years, the London Stock Exchange (LSE) was second only in size worldwide to the NEW YORK STOCK EXCHANGE. Overtaken by Tokyo in the 1990s, it remains the largest exchange in Europe and trades in the SECURITIES of an increasing number of non-UK companies.

Since it became a formal exchange in 1773, the LSE has become increasingly international and at one stage even called itself by that name. But it has found it difficult to change. Twice in recent years it has pulled out of merger deals with the Deutsche Börse; in 2000, the LSE became the potential TAKEOVER target of the Swedish stock exchange, which is somewhat smaller; and in 2001, it failed to acquire London's futures exchange, LIFFE. Like other exchanges the world over, the LSE is now owned by a company whose SHARES can be bought and sold by investors. These days, the FLOOR is no longer the centre of trading, which takes places on screens and via the telephone.

Long

Investors are said to be long in a SECURITY when their supply of the STOCK plus their commitment to buy it is greater than their commitment to sell it. A term usually applied to speculators who therefore believe the market may rise; the opposite of SHORT.

Longs

UK government SECURITIES with a MATURITY of more than 15 years, also called long-term STOCK. Such GILT-EDGED SECURITIES (GILTS) may be purchased by individuals or institutions (such as PENSION FUNDS) seeking to balance their LIABILITIES over a similar period. In the United States, long bonds are those with maturities of more than ten years. But "the long bond" is the 30-year Treasury bond.

LSE

See LONDON STOCK EXCHANGE.

Lutine bell

A bell salvaged in 1859 from a frigate called *Lutine* that had been lost at sea 60 years earlier. The bell hangs in the main hall of the LLOYD'S INSURANCE market. Its tolling foretold gloom when news arrived of a ship formerly reported as "missing, fate unknown". Traditionally, one ring of the bell was for bad news, two for good. These days the bell is rung before important announcements to the market.

M&A

See MERGERS AND ACQUISITIONS.

Management buy-out

A TAKEOVER of a company by a group of its own managers or, in rare cases, by a team of managers from outside. The managers set up a new company, which buys the old one with money borrowed from a mixture of BANKS and PRIVATE EQUITY firms. The banks use the ASSETS of the company as COLLATERAL for their LOAN.

A management buy-out (MBO) invariably raises a company's DEBT and reduces its EQUITY. As a result, it is often called a LEVERAGED BUY-OUT. This makes it doubly vulnerable to any rise in the RATE OF INTEREST: first, because such a rise is likely to damage its business; and second, because it adds to the cost of servicing the debt.

During the 1980s, MBOs frequently balanced a pile of debt on an equity base that made up as little as 10% of the total. Even with MBOs of established businesses generating a lot of CASH, this often led to problems, particularly when interest rates went up. These days, MBOs are more often constructed on a broader equity base making up, say, 35–40% of the total CAPITAL. In such cases, the managers and private equity firms who put up the equity have more at risk but also more control of the company's destiny.

Marché à terme des instruments financiers

France's successful financial futures exchange, commonly known as the MATIF, established in 1996. As well as FUTURES in traditional agricultural products such as wheat, the MATIF enables buyers and sellers to trade in a range of financial futures and OPTIONS on INTEREST-rate CONTRACTS in EUROS. The MATIF is owned by EURONEXT, a pan-European company that owns several stock and futures exchanges.

Margin account

An account which an investor holds with a BROKER, allow-ing it to buy SECURITIES on CREDIT. An investor with such an account pays only a certain percentage of the market price of the securities; the balance is borrowed from the broker whose COLLATERAL is the value of the securities held in the account. The minimum amount that must be held in such an account is called the margin requirement. Such arrangements are fine while the prices of the securities in the account are stable or, better still, rising. The opposite is true when they fall in value. To cover the cost of borrowings from the broker, an investor has to sell part or all of the securities in the account. In falling markets this can be tricky, because the more an investor sells, the more likely it is that the price of the security will continue to drop in value. (See MARGIN CALL.)

Marginal cost

The cost incurred by adding one more unit of a product or service. A firm that is selling many financial services (LOANS, INSURANCE contracts, UNIT TRUSTS or SECURITIES, for example) may well be able to sell one more unit at virtually no extra cost beyond that of the few pieces of paper needed to record the transaction. Marginal cost is quite different from AVERAGE COST, which is the total cost involved in providing the product or service divided by the number of units sold.

Margin call

A demand for extra money from a BROKER to an investor who has not paid the full amount owed for investments held in a MARGIN ACCOUNT. The demand may arise because the market price of the investment has fallen, triggering a need to reduce the amount of the LOAN extended to the investor. Most such loans are extended when the account is opened to enable investors to buy more SECURITIES than they are able to (or want to) pay for in full at the time.

Mark down

There are three main meanings.

1 To adjust downwards the value of SECURITIES in which IN-VESTMENT BANKS are making markets because of a general selling pressure.
2 To reduce the price at which UNDERWRITERS offer BONDS after the market has shown a distinct lack of interest at the original price.
3 To reduce the price of a product or service.

Market capitalisation

The market value of a company's issued SHARE capital; that is, the quoted price of its shares multiplied by the number of shares in issue. The shares of quoted companies are divided into three main types:

- large caps – companies with large market CAPITALISATIONS;
- mid caps – companies with medium-sized capitalisations;
- small caps – companies with small capitalisations.

Since the STOCKMARKET'S capitalisation moves up and down with the value of the STOCKS that are traded on it, there is no hard and fast rule. But in London the 100 largest stocks are regarded as the large caps, the next 250 as mid caps and the remainder as small fry. Investment funds generally specialise in one or the other and measure their performance against the relevant market INDEX. A TRACKER FUND, which tracks a particular index, by definition must hold the shares of all companies that make up the index.

Market maker

A DEALER in SECURITIES who is prepared to buy and sell (that is, make a market in) the securities of a particular company. Market makers frequently stand ready to deal in the shares of several companies, particularly those traded on OVER-THE-COUNTER markets such as NASDAQ. Being a market maker obliges a BROKER to buy or sell at least 100 SHARES of a company in whose shares it trades. As a result, big orders for certain stocks placed by institutions often have to be filled by more than one market maker. (See also JOBBER.)

Mark to market

The recording of the value of a SECURITY or investment PORT-FOLIO according to its market worth. Most US institutions mark to market each quarter; UNIT TRUSTS and MUTUAL FUNDS do so every day in order to arrive at a NET ASSET VALUE per unit.

M

Matching

The process by which a BANK aligns its ASSETS (that is, its LOANS) with its LIABILITIES (its DEPOSITS). The alignment involves matching three main things: currency, MATURITY and geography. Banks with perfectly aligned assets and liabilities do not make much PROFIT. A banker's skill lies in judging the right degree of mismatch to maximise profit for an acceptable level of RISK.

MATIF

See MARCHÉ À TERME DES INSTRUMENTS FINANCIERS.

Maturity

The date on which the PRINCIPAL of a redeemable loan becomes repayable.

- ◪ **Original maturity.** The length of time from the issuing of a SECURITY or LOAN to the date of the last repayment.
- ◪ **Residual maturity.** The time left from today to the final repayment.

So a BOND due to mature on January 1st 2010 will return the principal and final INTEREST payment on that date. Some loans do not have a REDEMPTION DATE. They continue for as long as the interest owed on them is paid.

Mayday

The day of New York's BIG BANG, May 1st 1975.

M

MBO

See MANAGEMENT BUY-OUT.

Medium-term note

A BOND with, as the name suggests, a medium life span, usually anything between nine months and 30 years. Medium-term notes became popular during the 1970s when companies were looking for an alternative form of financing to COMMERCIAL PAPER. Medium-term notes are usually sold as and when a company needs them (hence the term medium-note programme). They are therefore rarely underwritten by an INVESTMENT BANK, as happens with other forms of bond. So if they do not sell, the issuer does not get the money.

Merchant bank

A UK INVESTMENT BANK engaged in corporate finance, PORT-FOLIO management and a range of other activities for fees. Unlike a CLEARING BANK, a merchant bank is not heavily involved in taking DEPOSITS, running personal bank ACCOUNTS or in issuing and clearing CHEQUES. Many of these banks owe their origins to trading houses established during the 19th century by families such as the Hambros, Schroders, Rothschilds and Lazards. Hence the term merchant bank.

In the United States, a merchant bank is part of an investment bank that advises on MERGERS AND ACQUISITIONS, underwrites SECURITIES and takes positions on its own account in certain markets. It also covers banks that accept DEPOSITS from merchants stemming from CREDIT CARD or CHARGE CARD transactions.

I always said that mega-mergers were for megalomaniacs.
David Ogilvy

M

Mergers and acquisitions

Shorthand for mergers between companies and acquisitions of one company by another; also the name given to the department of an INVESTMENT BANK that advises on such things. The level of mergers and acquisitions (M&A) depends to a large extent on the buoyancy or otherwise of STOCKMARKETS, since most acquisitions by listed companies are paid for with the SHARES (or other SECURITIES) of the acquiring company. Thus the higher the value of the shares, the greater is a company's buying power. The boom in M&A during the 1990s, particularly among technology and telecoms companies, was therefore stoked by the investment boom that accompanied it, and vice versa.

M&A activity is more prevalent in Anglo-Saxon countries where there are developed CAPITAL MARKETS than in, say, parts of continental Europe. Japan is the exception; it has a developed capital market yet the level of M&A has traditionally been low. Fortunately for investment banks, the EQUITY and DEBT markets are rarely down and out at the same time.

Mezzanine

A layer of finance that falls between EQUITY and senior DEBT in terms of its priority in a payout or LIQUIDATION. Mezzanine finance is often used as part of a MANAGEMENT BUY-OUT where a company has difficulty borrowing money from a BANK, perhaps because it lacks tangible ASSETS against which the bank can have SECURITY or because its business is new. Mezzanine capital is usually made up in part or all of SUBOR-DINATED DEBT, CONVERTIBLE LOAN STOCK or PREFERENCE SHARES, all of which rank above straightforward equity if the company is ever broken up or liquidated.

Middle price

A price halfway between the buy price (which is higher) and sell price (which is lower) quoted for a SECURITY. When a newspaper or website quotes one price for a SHARE, it is usually the middle price (or mid price).

M

Mixed credit

Usually known by its French name, *crédit mixte*, this is a mixture of trade finance and development aid made available by governments and international agencies to pay for the export of goods or services to developing countries. The general agreement known as the CONSENSUS lays down that the aid portion of mixed credits must not be less than 20% of the total.

Monetary policy

A government's plans of how to regulate the MONEY SUPPLY in order to further economic policy on growth, employment, IN-FLATION and so on. In many developed countries (including the United States, the UK and the countries within the EURO zone), monetary policy is left to the CENTRAL BANK. This has

certain levers at its disposal (notably the ability to set the RATE
OF INTEREST, to buy and sell foreign currency in the exchange
markets and to set the level of RESERVES that banks must maintain) to influence the supply of money and CREDIT.

Changes in the bank rate (or, in the United States, the FED
FUNDS RATE) trigger a chain of events that affect SHORT-TERM
interest rates, FOREIGN-EXCHANGE rates, the money supply
and credit, which, in turn, affect employment, industrial output,
and the prices of goods and services on offer. Some central
banks and governments are better than others at getting the
balance right.

Money-center bank

A large BANK in the main FINANCIAL CENTRES of the United
States (New York, Chicago, Miami, Los Angeles and so on)
which acts as a CLEARING BANK for smaller banks in the
region. Money-center banks would rather lend to governments,
companies and other banks than to consumers. Because of their
bigger role, regulators worry more about the health of money-
center banks than they do about that of others.

Money laundering

The process of turning ill-gotten gains into seemingly legitimate
CASH. This usually involves passing dirty money through clean
places (such as Switzerland) in order to disguise where it came
from and to ensure that it avoids the gaze of the tax man. The
expression arose from the practice of one of the most infamous
launderers of the 20th century. Al Capone, who profited hugely
from dealing (among other things) in illicit alcohol during prohi-
bition in the United States, hit upon the idea of setting up legitimate laundries through which to channel his illegitimate cash.

These days, most of the cash generated from illicit businesses
is channelled through companies in places where their owners
can retain their anonymity. So easy is it to establish a company
that money can be whisked in and out of a FINANCIAL

CENTRE within a matter of hours. The Financial Action Task Force, an international body that tries to tackle money laundering, has come up with several ambitious plans to clamp down on it. The trouble is that most of these involve increasing corporate transparency and outlawing such things as BEARER SECURITIES, which most countries are reluctant to do.

If you want to know what God thinks of money,
just look at the people he gave it to.
Dorothy Parker

Money market

The market in which BANKS and other financial institutions buy and sell SHORT-TERM FINANCIAL INSTRUMENTS such as BILLS and COMMERCIAL PAPER. These days the market also includes an array of DERIVATIVES products based on the underlying SECURITIES, which are also short-term. (See also MONEY-MARKET FUND.)

M

Money is like a sixth sense without which
you cannot make full use of the other five.
W. Somerset Maugham

Money-market fund

A fund which gathers individuals' small savings and invests them in the MONEY MARKET. Money-market funds are particularly popular in the United States, where controls on INTEREST rates restrict the amount that banks can pay on such DEPOSITS. By investing in such funds, investors can get the benefit of investing in unregulated SHORT-TERM FINANCIAL INSTRUMENTS such as BILLS and COMMERCIAL PAPER. Securities held in a money-market fund typically mature within a month or so.

In the United States, money-market funds are big business, but the money deposited in them is not insured by the government. So the SEC, the main regulator of the country's financial markets, insists that most funds are rated by at least one recognised agency.

Money-purchase pension

A PENSION scheme in which the contributions are clearly defined and laid down but the benefits are not. The main difference between a defined-contribution scheme and a defined-benefit scheme is that, with the former, the investment RISK lies with the beneficiary. So if the value of a money-purchase pension plummets with the financial markets, there is no obligation on the part of the former employer to top it up. When the beneficiary of a money-purchase scheme retires, in many jurisdictions he or she must eventually use the lump sum to buy an ANNUITY.

Money remitter

Someone who transfers money, usually across borders, for people who do not have a bank ACCOUNT or access to a banking system. Money transfers are often used by immigrants as a means to send money home, usually from a rich country to a poorer one, to the family they have left behind.

Money supply

The amount of money circulating in an economy. In the United States, for example, the narrowest measure covers the most liquid forms of money in the hands of the public (NOTES and coins, traveller's cheques, DEPOSITS on demand and other accounts against which cheques can be written); M2 covers M1 plus savings accounts, certain time deposits and money-market MUTUAL FUNDS; M3 covers M1 and M2 plus big time deposits, institutional money funds, certain LIABILITIES of depositary institutions and EURODOLLARS held by US residents at the foreign BRANCHES of US banks. Most CENTRAL BANKS monitor the growth of the money supply carefully in the belief that it affects the level of prices and the speed with which an economy either grows or shrinks. How direct that link is deemed to be depends on the orthodoxy of the time.

Money talks ... but all mine ever says is goodbye.
Anon.

Moratorium

A period agreed between a borrower and a lender in which repayments of the PRINCIPAL sum owed by the borrower to the lender are allowed to lapse. However, a moratorium on INTEREST payments owed by the borrower to the lender is disliked by BANKS because it forces them to provide for the shortfall in their accounts.

Morgan Stanley Capital International Indices

M

A set of STOCKMARKET indices used by professional investment managers to measure their performance against the relevant BENCHMARK. Each day at the close of trading Morgan Stanley Capital International (MSCI) calculates by how much 11,000 or so indices (measuring everything from individual countries to industrial sectors) have gone up or down. This helps fund managers decide what WEIGHTING within their PORTFOLIO to give individual stocks and how well or badly their investments are fairing.

Mortgage

The transfer of an INTEREST in a property to somebody else as SECURITY for a LOAN. This transfer most commonly takes place between the buyer of a home and the financial institution (BANK, building society or other such lender) that is helping to finance the purchase. In many countries such institutions specialise in mortgages; in others, particularly continental Europe and Asia, the market is less developed because fewer people own their own homes. There are many different types of mortgages, from repayment (which are paid off bit by bit, month by month) to endowment (which are paid off in one go at the end of the period from an investment fund built up for the purpose). A risk with the latter is that the fund will fail to build up enough money to pay off the mortgage at the end of the period. If that happens, because of falling STOCKMARKETS, the borrower may be left with a shortfall. In sophisticated markets such as the UK, where a high proportion of people own their own homes, mortgages are competitive and big business for the banks and financial institutions that provide them.

MSB

See MUTUAL SAVINGS BANK.

MSCI

See MORGAN STANLEY CAPITAL INTERNATIONAL INDICES.

Municipal bond

A long-term BOND with a COUPON that is issued in the United States by a municipality, county or state in order to raise the money to build roads, schools, hospitals and so on. Like countries, banks and any other borrowers that are active in the markets, municipalities are often rated by agencies according to their financial standing.

Mutual

Something that is owned and run for the mutual benefit of a group of members. These "members" may be the investors in a fund (as in a MUTUAL FUND) or the depositors in a bank (see

MUTUAL SAVINGS BANK). The word has given rise to the term "demutualisation", which refers to the change of a mutual organisation into an incorporated one with shareholders. During the 1980s and 1990s, many of the UK's BUILDING SOCIETIES (mutual MORTGAGE lenders) and other mutual finance companies opted for incorporation.

Mutual fund

An open-ended investment fund that continually issues new units as it receives money from investors. Similarly, it redeems units as and when investors wish to sell. The money is invested in SECURITIES by professional managers who receive in return a management fee (usually between 0.5% and 2% of the value of the ASSETS invested).

Mutual funds are one of the easiest ways for private investors to benefit from the skill of a professional manager and to diversify the RISK of investing in the EQUITY or BOND markets. Mutual funds (called UNIT TRUSTS in the UK) often specialise in parts of the market (such as smaller companies in Asia), in the type of securities in which they invest (such as CORPORATE BONDS), or in INVESTMENT STYLE (such as GROWTH STOCKS that aim for CAPITAL appreciation).

Mutual savings bank

A group of financial institutions in the United States found mostly on the east coast. A mutual savings bank (MSB) is much like a SAVINGS AND LOAN ASSOCIATION (S&L) in that its prime purpose is the provision of a safe home for retail savings. MSBs differ from S&Ls in that they are treated like banks by regulators and that they are owned by their depositors. MSBs are usually run by boards, independent of the owners, who act as fiduciaries. These days, MSBs often issue CREDIT CARDS and offer current ACCOUNTS to their savers. Together, the MSBs and the S&Ls constitute the so-called THRIFT institutions.

Name

A backer of the LLOYD'S INSURANCE market who can demonstrate that he or she has a certain wealth which he or she is prepared to pledge to the market. Names are gathered together in SYNDICATES and each syndicate is managed by an AGENT. The syndicate uses the backing of its names to underwrite different insurance RISKS. The names' PROFIT (or loss) is based on the net PREMIUM income of the syndicate. The attraction to names is that they can use their CAPITAL twice: unencumbered ASSETS such as STOCKS and SHARES or property can be pledged to produce a second income.

Since the introduction of corporate capital to Lloyd's, the number of names has diminished, as has the number prepared to trade on the basis of unlimited LIABILITY. Today, Lloyd's underwrites increasingly specialist risks, both marine and non-marine, and the names that support the market are as likely to be shareholders of listed companies that manage a syndicate or group of syndicates as they are to be members of Lloyd's in their own right. They are thus able to limit their risk in ways they could not as individual names.

Narcodollars

Money used to finance the purchase of illegal drugs (dollars to buy narcotics). It is said that a remarkably high percentage of all the dollar bills in circulation today in the United States bear traces of narcotics.

Narrow market

A market in which there is only a small supply of goods or services available or being sold. The expression is applied particularly to financial markets (such as STOCKMARKETS) where there is a shortage, for example, of a particular company's SECURITIES on offer. If demand for the security outstrips supply, as in any market, this can have the effect of pushing up the price.

NASDAQ

Short for National Association of Securities Dealers' Automated Quotations, a computerised information system that provides brokers throughout the United States and in certain international markets with price quotations on a number of SECURITIES. It includes securities that are quoted on the NEW YORK STOCK EXCHANGE as well as some that are traded OVER THE COUNTER. NASDAQ became a byword for investors in high-growth companies during the technology boom of the late 1990s; it had big ambitions to expand internationally and set up offshoots in Japan and Europe (see next entry). When the technology bubble burst, NASDAQ was forced to scale back its plans, closing its Japanese offshoot. But it remains one of the main means of trading in SHARES over-the-counter.

NASDAQ Europe

A pan-European STOCK EXCHANGE, formerly called EASDAQ, designed for high-growth companies and modelled on NASDAQ in the United States which, since 2001, has owned a majority of it. NASDAQ Europe is based in Brussels and is independent of any national stock exchange in Europe. Much like NASDAQ in the United States, NASDAQ Europe provides the platform for a screen-based market in high-tech stocks. It began operations in 1996 and is part owned by a lot of financial intermediaries. Since the end of 2001, the exchange has also had links with the Berlin Stock Exchange, with which it shares a common trading system.

Nationalisation

The TAKEOVER and running of commercial companies by the state. Because of nationalist rivalries and a temptation to defend their champions from international competition, the financial sector frequently has a high degree of nationalisation. This is especially true of continental Europe. In France and Italy, for example, until recently a high proportion of COMMERCIAL BANKS and INSURANCE companies were in state hands. This has been reversed in recent years as governments realise that PRIVATISATION is a valuable source of funds and that such companies are usually more efficiently run as private enterprises. During the 1990s, Latin American countries also privatised many of their inefficient utilities (telephone, electricity companies and the like); many of them were bought by privately run utilities based in the United States and Europe.

NAV

See NET ASSET VALUE.

Nearby delivery

See DELIVERY.

N

Negative equity

The amount by which the market value of an ASSET falls short of the DEBT incurred to buy it. It applies in particular to the property market when the value of a house (perhaps bought at the top of the market) falls to the point where it is worth less than the value of the MORTGAGE taken out to purchase it. This happened to a number of homeowners in the UK during the recession of the early 1990s and is a spectre that hangs over every market during periods of strong rises in house prices.

Negative pledge

A condition that may be applied to a DEBT or SECURITY. The borrower pledges that no new debt can subsequently be issued which takes priority over it. Such pledges are usually made in the form of a COVENANT.

Negative yield curve

A situation in which the YIELDS on SHORT-TERM BONDS are higher than those on long-dated ones of the same or equal quality. The yields on short-term bonds are usually lower than those on long-dated ones because investors who commit their money for longer periods are taking on more RISK. However, if INTEREST rates climb sufficiently high, borrowers become increasingly reluctant to lock themselves into high rates for long periods, so they borrow for shorter periods instead.

Negotiable instrument

A FINANCIAL INSTRUMENT that can be handed from one owner to another without informing the original issuer; for example, a bank NOTE, a BEARER BOND or, indeed, a CHEQUE. A cheque may be made non-negotiable by writing the words "not negotiable" between the two lines across it.

N

Net

The amount remaining after making all the relevant deductions from the gross amount (such as the cost of sales in the case of PROFITS). In investment, this means the difference between the proceeds from the sale of a SECURITY and the cost of acquisition. Used as a verb, it has also come to mean the process of, say, NETTING losses against gains to arrive at a final taxable amount.

- **Net sales.** Total sales less amounts given as DISCOUNTS and amounts coming from goods returned.
- **Net profit.** Gross income less all costs (INTEREST payments, general expenses and tax).
- **Net worth.** Total ASSETS less outstanding LIABILITIES. A company with a negative net worth is technically insolvent, although it may still be able to carry on trading.

Net asset value

There are two main meanings.

1 The market value of a unit in a UNIT TRUST or MUTUAL FUND. Most funds calculate the net asset value (NAV) at the close of trading each day by adding the market value of all the SECURITIES owned, plus any other ASSETS (such as CASH on DEPOSIT), and dividing by the total number of units outstanding. Since open-ended unit trusts or mutual funds issue or redeem new units according to demand, this figure may vary from day to day. With unit trusts or mutual funds that carry no load (that is, charge no upfront fee), the NAV and offer price for each unit is usually the same.
2 The book value of a company's various classes of securities. (See also next entry.)

Net book value

The difference between the cost of an ASSET and its accumulated DEPRECIATION. The main purpose of depreciating an asset is to recover the cost of its purchase. So the book value of an asset may vary markedly from its market value. The former is usually calculated by taking the total value of all assets, less the value of any INTANGIBLE ASSETS (such as goodwill and patents), less all LIABILITIES (such as bank DEBT), less the value of SECURITIES with a prior claim (preferred stock), and dividing by the number of securities of that class in issue at the time.

Net present value

An estimation of the value today of a payment to be made (or received) tomorrow. The payment is discounted by an amount that takes into account the time between now and the day that the payment is due. This amount is calculated taking into account the expected level of INTEREST rates and the degree of RISK involved in the payment. The net present value of an investment project is the difference between the present value of the future revenue from the project, and the present value of the future costs.

Netting

A contract between banks or other financial institutions to offset their mutual obligations at their NET value. For example, if two banks owe each other $15m and $18m respectively, they might agree to value the mutual obligation at $3m, the net difference between the two. There are various ways of netting: bilaterally (the simplest); by involving a third party; or by novation, which is when a new agreement replaces the existing one. The increasing complexity of financial markets and the speed with which transactions take place has made netting an attractive proposition to many investors, particularly if they deal with each other regularly.

New York Board of Trade

The world's largest market for the trading of FUTURES in sugar, coffee, cocoa and orange juice, incorporating what used to be the New York Cotton Exchange. Although known chiefly as a market for agricultural products – sugar is its biggest single COMMODITY – the New York Board of Trade (NYBOT) also has a growing business in financial futures. Like other exchanges dealing with huge volumes of trading, it has invested heavily in new technology to speed up its trading and settlement systems.

New York Mercantile Exchange

The world's biggest recognised market in energy and precious metals. The New York Mercantile Exchange (Merc) began life as the Butter and Cheese Exchange of New York in 1872, but it no longer deals in agricultural products. In the late 1970s, it was the first exchange to launch trading in FUTURES contracts for heating oil. After merging with the Commodity Exchange in 1994, the Merc now boasts two divisions: the NYMEX, which specialises in futures and OPTIONS on energy (including oil), platinum and palladium; and the COMEX, which trades mainly in GOLD, silver and copper.

New York Stock Exchange

Still the world's biggest and most prestigious STOCK EXCHANGE. With few exceptions, the New York Stock Exchange (NYSE, also called the Big Board and The Exchange) quotes the shares of the cream of corporate America. Even today the market CAPITALISATION of a single company on the NYSE is as big, if not bigger, than the total value of all the companies quoted on a number of other (admittedly small) exchanges outside the United States. As well as STOCKS and SHARES, the NYSE trades in the BONDS, WARRANTS, OPTIONS and RIGHTS of companies listed on it.

The exchange was first constituted under an agreement between 24 STOCKBROKERS and merchants in 1792. Called the Buttonwood Agreement, it was signed under a buttonwood (sycamore) tree. Today its famous trading FLOOR is located at 11 Wall Street where DEALERS operate from octagon-shaped trading posts.

NIF

See NOTE ISSUANCE FACILITY.

Nikkei Stock Average

A leading INDEX of the TOKYO STOCK EXCHANGE (originally called the Nikkei-Dow Jones Stock Average until it was renamed in the 1980s). It is an average of the 225 biggest stocks by market CAPITALISATION quoted on the exchange.

Nil basis

A method of calculating EARNINGS PER SHARE which assumes there is no distribution of profit to shareholders, just the relevant payments of tax.

Nominal price

A quotation for a FUTURES contract during a period when no trading is actually taking place. A nominal exercise price can also refer to the balance owed on a BOND after deducting the price for which it can be bought.

Nominee

Someone whose name is used in place of somebody else's. This could be either a person or a firm (such as a BANK or BROKER) in whose name a SECURITY or other ASSET is held. Sometimes this is to avoid divulging the identity of the underlying owner; sometimes it is purely for convenience. To ensure greater SECRECY, some Swiss banks will allow depositors to hold money in the name of a nominee. The nominee passes on the INTEREST (minus his or her fee) to the ultimate beneficiary. Unsurprisingly, such accounts are unpopular with regulators trying to stamp out MONEY LAUNDERING and the use of legitimate banking services to hide illegal transactions.

Non-performing loan

A LOAN on which INTEREST payments are considerably overdue. US banks are required to consider loans to be non-performing when no interest has been paid for 90 days or more. When they pass the 90-day threshold, such loans have to be reported as non-performing in the banks' accounts.

Note

A written acknowledgement of a DEBT (due either on demand or at a date in the future), in two different forms.

- **Paper money.** As in a dollar or EURO note or "notes and coins".
- **A type of SECURITY.** As in FLOATING-RATE NOTE or PROMISSORY NOTE.

Note issuance facility

A bank GUARANTEE that funds will be available to the issuer of SHORT-TERM PROMISSORY NOTES in a period before the notes have actually been issued. The guarantee usually involves the guarantor in buying any notes left unsold from the ISSUE. Note issuance facilities (NIFS) are often rolled on from one issue of short-term notes to another.

N

Notional amount

With DERIVATIVES, the amount of the underlying ASSET to which the CONTRACT applies. For example, a FUTURES contract for 1,000 bushels of corn has a notional amount of 1,000. Most derivatives settled in CASH usually make payments according to some formula but also depend on the amount of the underlying asset being traded. So a CALL OPTION on 100,000 barrels of oil would be 100,000. Or the notional amount of a six-month dollar EURIBOR contract could be $10m, or whatever the amount of the underlying asset.

Numbered account

A Swiss invention designed to allow depositors to hide behind a veil of SECRECY. In practice, the veil is more transparent than they think. A numbered ACCOUNT in Switzerland differs from ordinary BANK accounts in the country only in the number of people who know the true identity of the holder, usually three or four senior executives within the bank. The rest of the staff know the account simply as a number.

NYBOT

See NEW YORK BOARD OF TRADE.

NYSE

See NEW YORK STOCK EXCHANGE.

OBU

See OFFSHORE BANKING UNIT.

Odd lot

A transaction in fewer SHARES than is normally permitted on a market. The minimum permitted amount is usually 100 shares. It costs more to trade in odd lots than in larger amounts because of the inconvenience for BROKERS who charge a COMMISSION for each transaction. The difference in price is called the odd-lot differential.

Off balance sheet

Any transaction by a financial institution that does not have to appear on its balance sheet, for example, a FIDUCIARY DEPOSIT. LEASING is usually off-balance-sheet business for the lessee, but not for the lessor. Such transactions are particularly attractive for BANKS, which have to pay an additional price (in the form of extra RESERVES) for every extra cent that appears on the balance sheet. In recent years, off-balance-sheet financing has also been used to great effect, and at great cost to shareholders, by companies such as Enron, an energy-trading firm that went spectacularly bust in 2001. By piling up DEBTS that did not appear on its balance sheet, Enron was able to hide its true financial position from regulators and its shareholders.

Offer for sale

The proposed sale under UK law of a parcel of SECURITIES at a quoted price to the general public. The sale is usually organised by a group of UNDERWRITERS who receive a fee for guaranteeing the minimum amount under the sale to the vendor and for taking the RISK that the offer might flop if the market goes against it.

Off-exchange

Dealing in SHARES that takes place between buyers and sellers outside a recognised STOCK EXCHANGE. INVESTMENT BANKS holding large amounts of a company's STOCK will occasionally deal directly to save costs and complete a deal quickly. Yet in most developed economies, the amount of off-exchange dealing in EQUITIES is remarkably low. This is because the growing use of screen-based trading (which allows DEALERS to buy and sell SECURITIES at the touch of a button) has reduced costs and speeded up transactions even for the majority of deals that pass through an exchange's hands.

Off-market

The transfer between two parties of a COMMODITY or FINAN-CIAL INSTRUMENT without recourse to an exchange or official marketplace. Such deals are often done at a DISCOUNT and therefore do not reflect market prices. For example, two BANKS may decide to enter into a SWAP agreement based on INTEREST payments below the market rate for instruments of a similar MATURITY. They then compensate for the difference with an extra payment at the beginning or the end of the deal. A government may choose to complete the PRIVATISATION of, say, an airline by issuing SHARES off-market to existing shareholders in proportion to those they already own. Any shares left over may then be sold as part of a wider offer to outside investors. The parties to an off-market transaction must generally consider whether, in doing such a deal, they are flouting tax rules or illegally shutting out other interested parties.

Offshore

Financial business denominated in foreign currencies and transacted between foreigners. Some jurisdictions tolerate legitimate FINANCIAL CENTRES (such as the Isle of Man or Gibraltar) where regulation is low and where non-residents may hold

ASSETS offshore. Such centres provide a relatively safe haven and lower taxes for people who spend a minimum amount of time out of the country of which they are a citizen. Yet for professional investors London, the home of the EURODOLLAR market, is by far the world's biggest offshore financial centre.

Offshore banking unit

A BRANCH set up in an international FINANCIAL CENTRE (such as London or Hong Kong) by a non-resident BANK. Offshore banking units (OBUS) may accept deposits from other OBUS and from foreign banks but not from domestic savers. Since the 1970s, OBUS have been established in a number of international centres, most of them to make loans in the EURO-MARKETS. Since the early 1980s, US banks have been allowed to set up international banking facilities in large US cities which conduct more or less the same kind of business.

Old Lady of Threadneedle Street

O

See BANK OF ENGLAND.

Ombudsman

An independent person appointed to hear and act upon citizens' complaints about government services. Invented in Sweden, the idea has been widely taken up by other developed countries. For example, groups of BANKS, MORTGAGE lenders and IN-SURANCE companies have appointed ombudsmen to attend to the complaints of their customers. Regulators will also often fill a similar role. In most cases, customers who approach an ombudsman but who fail to resolve their disagreement still have the right to pursue their case through the courts.

Open-end fund

See CLOSED-END FUND.

Open interest

The number of CONTRACTS in a FUTURES or OPTIONS market that are still open; that is, the number that have not been exercised, closed out or allowed to expire. It also refers to the number of contracts outstanding on an underlying FINANCIAL INSTRUMENT – for example, a futures contract to deliver so many barrels of oil in six months. The level of open interest is reported daily and so provides an idea of the popularity of a particular contract or market and its LIQUIDITY.

Open-market operations

Dealing in the money markets by a country's CENTRAL BANK in order to adjust the amount of money and CREDIT circulating in the economy. Central banks buy or sell government SECURITIES, which has the effect of contracting or expanding the MONEY SUPPLY. This, in turn, affects the level of banks' RESERVES, causing a knock-on effect on the supply of credit and therefore on economic activity generally. The difficulty for central banks, of course, is that there is a lag between what they do in the money markets and its effect on the economy generally. Open-market operations are only one of several tools at the disposal of an independent central bank in executing MONETARY POLICY.

Open outcry

A way of trading in COMMODITIES or SECURITIES in which traders stand on the FLOOR of an exchange and shout out their orders. Once they have attracted each other's attention, buyers and sellers then get together to finalise a deal. Such noisy and colourful scenes (traders often wear bright jackets to distinguish one firm of traders from another) are fast vanishing from the floors of FUTURES and OPTIONS exchanges. Most dealing in such instruments is now done via computer screens by traders seated at desks.

Money doesn't talk; it shouts.
Bob Dylan

Open position

A NET long or short position in a FINANCIAL INSTRUMENT. The situation that arises when an investor has a commitment to buy (or sell) more SHARES than he or she is committed to sell (or buy). The two obligations are balanced and effectively cancelled out when an investor closes his or her position.

Opportunity cost

There are two definitions, both employed by investors when assessing the relative RISKS and rewards of a proposition.

1 What investors will lose by not putting their money into the ASSETS with the highest YIELD available. For example, an investor might buy a SHARE yielding only 2% because it promises to show a greater CAPITAL GAIN even though a safer investment might yield 5%. The 3% difference between the two is the opportunity cost.
2 The maximum amount of PROFIT that could have been made if factors of production had been put to other uses. This assumes that the two courses of action carried roughly the same risk.

Option

The right to buy a specific number of SECURITIES at a specific price within a specified period of time (usually three, six or nine months). Such a right can be bought or sold, but it expires if it is not exercised within the specified period. The purchaser of the option then loses his or her money.

A CALL OPTION gives the purchaser the right to buy, say, 100 SHARES of an underlying security at a fixed price before a specified date in the future. For this right, the buyer of the call option pays the seller, called the WRITER, a fee, called a PREMIUM, which is forfeited if the buyer fails to exercise the right within the agreed period. The purchaser of a call option therefore bets that the price of the underlying security will rise within the specified period.

In contrast, a PUT OPTION gives the buyer the right to sell, say, 100 shares of an underlying security within a specified period. Buyers of put options therefore expect the price of the underlying security to fall within the period. An investor who thinks the price of ABC company will fall may buy, say, a six-month put option for 100 shares at $100 each. The premium might be $5. If the price of the shares falls to $80, the owner of the put option can exercise the option to sell the shares for $100 each. He or she will first buy the shares in the market for $80 each and then sell them on to the WRITER of the option, according to the terms of the deal, for $100 apiece. The owner of the put option thus makes a profit of $15 ($20 less the $5 cost of the original premium).

In practice, most call and put options expire before they are exercised. Investors make (or lose) their money by speculating on the rises and falls in the premiums paid for options traded on recognised exchanges throughout the world.

Ordinary share

The basic type of SHARE in a company, called common stock in the United States. Unless specified otherwise, such shares carry the right to vote (for instance, on the appointment of directors or auditors) and entitle the holder to a DIVIDEND as and when one is declared by the board of directors and approved by a majority of the shareholders. Ordinary shares are the riskiest of all forms of CAPITAL because they have no prior claims to any of a company's ASSETS if it goes into LIQUIDATION. However, they also stand to gain the most in value if the company's business prospers.

OTC

See OVER THE COUNTER.

Out of the money

A traded OPTION is said to be out of the money if the price of the underlying SECURITY moves against either the buyer or the seller. For example, a CALL OPTION to buy SHARES in ABC company in December for $50 each would be out of the money if the shares were selling for, say, $45 each because the owner of such an option is betting that the price will rise. Similarly, a PUT OPTION to sell a similar number of shares in December for $60 each would be out of the money if the price rose in value within the specified period of the CONTRACT to $65 a share. Contrast with IN THE MONEY.

Outsourcing

The handing over of responsibility, popular among financial services firms, for various specialist functions such as information technology, logistics and data processing. BANKS, FINANCIAL INSTITUTIONS and investment companies of various kinds find it cheaper to outsource tasks that may be important but not central to their business, so leaving them free to concentrate on what they do best. In return, the companies to which the task is being outsourced generate economies of scale and specialised skills from handling large volumes of data processing and so on. FUND MANAGERS even outsource the custody and settlement of their clients' investments to experts in the field.

Overdraft

A CREDIT facility that allows borrowers to draw upon it (up to a specified limit) as and when they need to. Borrowers pay only for what they use. Overdrafts are popular with companies and consumers alike because of their flexibility. By a quirk of history such facilities are peculiar to Europe, and are rarely found in Japan or the United States. The nearest equivalent in the United States is a LOAN facility, a LINE OF CREDIT for which borrowers must pay whether they use it in full or not.

Overfunding

There are two meanings.

1 A PENSION FUND is overfunded when, according to its ACTUARIES, it has received more in contributions than it is contractually obliged to pay out to future claimants. This may happen when STOCKMARKETS are buoyant and a fund's investments are rising strongly in value.

2 A government is said to be overfunded when it has issued more BONDS in a particular year than it needs to finance its DEBT. This may also occur during periods of strong economic growth when a government's tax revenues are high.

O

Oversubscribed

An ISSUE of SHARES or other SECURITIES is oversubscribed when the number of applications exceeds the number of shares on offer. For example, if there are 600 applications for 100 shares, then the issue is five times oversubscribed. During BULL markets, when shares rise strongly in value, issues can be 20 or even 50 times oversubscribed. The prices of new issues that are heavily oversubscribed often rise strongly both in the GREY MARKET, before trading officially begins, and when the shares are listed on a STOCK EXCHANGE. In the past, INVESTMENT BANKS which underwrite such issues have been criticised for underpricing the shares on offer and thus enabling preferential clients to benefit by later selling their shares in the market at a healthy premium.

Over the counter

Describes an open market for SECURITIES that are not listed on a regular STOCK EXCHANGE. Over-the-counter (OTC) markets have traditionally been favoured by smaller companies that need CAPITAL to grow but fail to meet the more onerous LISTING requirements of established exchanges. A full listing on a recognised exchange can also be expensive.

In the past, OTC markets such as NASDAQ differed from established exchanges in that all dealing was conducted not on an exchange FLOOR but by telephone and via computer screens. However, the drift towards computerised trading even for recognised exchanges has blurred the distinction. The fact that high-tech companies such as Microsoft have spurned established exchanges in favour of NASDAQ has also given OTC markets a boost.

Companies and financial institutions dealing directly in securities or DERIVATIVES of one sort or another are also said to be trading over the counter.

Overweight

An investment fund is said to be overweight in a particular SECURITY or ASSET if it holds a higher proportion than the BENCHMARK against which its performance is measured. So a MUTUAL FUND specialising in Asian EQUITIES would be overweight in Thailand if it owned a greater percentage of SHARES in that market than, say, the relevant MSCI INDEX that it was using as a benchmark. Similarly, a fund would be UNDERWEIGHT if it held too few shares in that market. TRACKER FUNDS, which mimic the composition of an index (by holding in proportion all the shares that make it up), should be neither overweight nor underweight.

Panel on Takeovers and Mergers

Commonly known as the Takeover Panel, a body in the UK that ensures fair play for shareholders in MERGERS AND ACQUISITIONS of companies whose SHARES are publicly traded. Although supported by statutory bodies such as the Competition Commission and the Office of Fair Trading, the Takeover Panel still operates under a voluntary code of conduct. The threat of action by government agencies or the STOCK EXCHANGE is enough to ensure that its word is as good as law.

The panel was first set up in 1968 after a spate of TAKEOVERS in which acquiring companies rode roughshod over the rights of ordinary shareholders. Since then it has presided over more than 7,000 bids and about half as many deals which, in the event, were never announced.

Par

The nominal or face value of a SECURITY. In the case of STOCKS and SHARES, this is almost always way below their market value. A security is at par when it is trading at its face value.

Parallel financing

When two aid donors commit themselves to financing different parts of the same project. The donors co-ordinate the financing between them in parallel.

Parallel market

A market in a particular FINANCIAL INSTRUMENT that develops outside the standard channels for such a market. An example is the market for AMERICAN DEPOSITARY RECEIPTS (ADRS) which developed as an easy way for US institutions to invest in the SHARES of overseas companies. Dollar-denominated ADRS trade in parallel (albeit sometimes in different time zones) with the underlying shares of the company. Sometimes there may even be scope for ARBITRAGE between the two.

Partly paid

Shares on which some of the capital is still uncalled; that is, shareholders have yet to be asked to pay all that is due from them. Partly paid shares are unpopular when they give the company the right to call for the unpaid part at its discretion, particularly if (as often happens) the partly paid shares are trading below the level at which they were first issued.

Pathfinder

A PROSPECTUS with a rough outline of a company's history and its prospects. A pathfinder is distributed to potential investors in advance of a full prospectus, mainly in the hope of arousing interest. Pathfinders are often used when privatising nationalised industries which have been extensively restructured or which need to educate investors about their prospects. In the United States, preliminary prospectuses are frequently issued in advance of a new ISSUE of SHARES to stimulate interest among investors. Such documents lack the final issue price and other details that may change in the run-up to the offer. Because the front page is usually printed in red ink to distinguish the document from the final version, it is popularly known as a RED HERRING.

Paying agent

A financial institution appointed by a borrower to be responsible for paying the INTEREST and PRINCIPAL on the borrowing instrument (a BOND or a SYNDICATED LOAN) as and when it is due.

Penny stock

A SHARE whose price is less than $1 or £1, depending on the market in which it is issued. Such shares are usually traded OVER THE COUNTER or on small STOCK EXCHANGES (such as Denver or Salt Lake City in the United States) which deal in speculative stocks. As a result, they are notoriously volatile, sometimes rising or falling by as much as 20% or more in a day. Unsurprisingly, penny stocks often carry warnings which the shares of established companies traded on recognised exchanges seldom require. One reason for their VOLATILITY is that a smaller proportion of the company's share CAPITAL is available in the market, thus making the price more susceptible to swings in sentiment. For example, a majority of General Electric's shares are publicly traded, whereas as little as 25% of the share capital of a newly floated company may be in public hands. This makes the market in the shares less liquid and therefore more volatile because a relatively small group of investors may influence the price.

Pension

A periodical payment made by a former employer (a company, government or similar body) in recognition of past services and/or payments. There are two main types of pensions, based on the different ways of paying for them.

1 The pay-as-you-go pension, in which the pensions of one generation are paid for out of the EARNINGS of the next one. This becomes expensive when, as is happening in many developed countries, the proportion of old people rises.
2 The funded pension, in which savings are accumulated over time for the specific purpose of providing pensions for the people whose savings were accumulated (see next entry). This is the model towards which most governments in the developed world are heading, some more quickly than others.

Pension fund

A fund set up by a company or other organisation to manage the savings of employees and to pay the PENSION benefits to which these savings or contractual obligations entitle them. Some pension funds, called DEFINED CONTRIBUTION PENSIONS, guarantee a minimum amount to former employees irrespective of the investment climate and the movement of STOCKMARKETS; others, called DEFINED BENEFIT PENSIONS, place the investment RISK squarely on the (former) employee. So if there is not enough in the pot, the beneficiary suffers.

Pension funds are among the largest investors in the world's stockmarkets but have traditionally kept a low profile in the affairs of the companies whose SHARES they own. Following the spate of scandals and corporate excess at the turn of the 21st century, pension funds are taking a closer interest in corporate GOVERNANCE.

PEP

Short for Personal Equity Plan, a scheme introduced by the UK government in 1987 to encourage individuals to accumulate savings and invest more in the STOCKMARKET. In 1999, PEPS were more or less replaced by ISAS (Individual Savings Accounts).

P/E ratio

See PRICE/EARNINGS RATIO.

Performance bond

A GUARANTEE from a BANK to an importer (often provided by the exporter's bank) that the exporter will fulfil a CONTRACT according to its terms and conditions. Performance bonds are often used in the construction industry when the buyer wants to ensure that a contractor completes a project on time and as promised. Failure to comply with the terms of the contract gives the buyer some degree of compensation for the delay and/or the failure to meet the specifications.

Perpetual

Something that goes on for ever. So a perpetual DEBENTURE is a BOND that never gets repaid.

Personal identification number

Commonly known as a PIN, the number needed by every plastic cardholder to access the details of their personal financial ACCOUNT(s) through an AUTOMATED TELLER MACHINE. For obvious reasons, individuals are advised not to write down their PIN and not to store it in the same place as their card.

Pfandbrief

DEBT instruments issued by German and other European banks. Although one of the largest of its kind, the *Pfandbrief* market is little known outside Europe. Most *Pfandbriefe* are backed by MORTGAGES and are issued by highly rated German banks. Compared with debt of a similar MATURITY in the United States, *Pfandbriefe* often offer a high RETURN for a comparatively low level of RISK.

P

PIN

See PERSONAL IDENTIFICATION NUMBER.

Pink sheet

A daily publication in the United States on which are listed brokerage firms that make markets in OVER-THE-COUNTER stocks and ADRS. Pink sheets are printed on pink paper and can be obtained from most brokerage offices.

Pit

The area on a trading FLOOR where specific types of FUTURES, OPTIONS or SECURITIES are bought and sold, usually through OPEN OUTCRY. Perversely, most pits are raised, not sunken. Although pits have been a feature of futures trading for decades, many are being phased out in favour of electronic, screen-based dealing.

Pitch

The place where MARKET MAKERS, or DEALERS, have their stalls on the FLOOR of a STOCK EXCHANGE.

P

Placement

A method of selling SHARES in which blocks of shares are placed with a small number of large financial institutions, often at a DISCOUNT to the market price. A placing is usually done in private, and because fewer people are involved it is cheaper than an OFFER FOR SALE. (See also PRIVATE PLACEMENT.)

Plain vanilla

A FINANCIAL INSTRUMENT in its most basic form, with no bells or whistles attached.

Poison pill

One of a number of techniques used to fend off a HOSTILE BID or unwanted TAKEOVER. In principle, a poison pill is something that turns nasty when swallowed – that is, a large financial penalty that is written into a company's articles and that is activated only by an unwelcome takeover, thus deterring suitors. The practice became widespread in the United States during the 1980s when predatory companies pursued their prey with the help of junk, or high-YIELD, financing. Poison pills are frowned upon by regulators in most Anglo-Saxon jurisdictions.

Ponzi scheme

A classic confidence trick that has been repeated many times both before and since Charles (Carlo) Ponzi gave it its name in the 1920s. The scheme begins with a crook setting up as a DEPOSIT-taking institution. The crook invites the public to place deposits, offering them a generous rate of INTEREST. The interest is then paid out of new depositors' money, while the crook lives well off the old deposits. The scheme collapses when there are not enough new deposits to cover the interest payments on the old ones. By that time, the architect of the scheme hopes to be living under an assumed name in a country with few extradition laws.

P

Portfolio

A collection of financial ASSETS belonging to a single owner – an individual or some kind of institution. A well-diversified portfolio will contain a mixture of assets, ranging from fixed ones such as property to more liquid ones such as bank DEPOSITS, BONDS, GOLD, and STOCKS and SHARES. Many financial institutions, including PRIVATE BANKS, offer services designed to preserve the CAPITAL and to maximise the investment income earned from it without taking on too much RISK. Others will become CUSTODIANS and take care of the settlement of any transactions carried out by the manager. This is known as portfolio management. For a fee, such institutions will collect the DIVIDENDS and claim any RIGHTS ISSUES or SCRIP ISSUES due.

Portfolio insurance

The use of DERIVATIVES to HEDGE the RISK in an investment PORTFOLIO. If the STOCKMARKET begins to decline, investment managers may sell FUTURES or OPTIONS based on a stockmarket INDEX. Any PROFITS they make by buying back the contracts at a lower (and therefore cheaper) price are used to offset losses incurred by the fall in the value of the SHARES in the actual portfolio.

As with most things to do with markets, this is fine in theory but does not always work in practice. On BLACK MONDAY in 1987, when stockmarkets around the world fell dramatically, exchanges were overwhelmed by the sheer volume of financial instruments traded. Hence many investment managers did not have time to take the precautionary steps they had planned to take. As a result, portfolio insurance lost its infallibility.

P

Portfolio management

See PORTFOLIO.

Position

The quantity of SECURITIES held (or not held) by a DEALER or investor. Investors who own more of a particular security than they owe are said to be LONG in the security; those who owe more than they own are said to be SHORT in it. (See also OPEN POSITION.)

Post-date

To add a future date to a FINANCIAL INSTRUMENT (such as a CHEQUE) so that the payee cannot obtain payment until that date. BANKS are obliged not to clear post-dated cheques until the date indicated.

Power of attorney

A legally binding document that empowers one person to act on behalf of another. A power of attorney may specify that the power is for a limited range of purposes or for a limited time; or it may be given unconditionally. Power of attorney is often given to guardians by minors or by old people to their advisers or heirs. Unsurprisingly, such powers can be open to abuse.

Pre-emption rights

The right to do something before others, as in the pre-emption right of existing shareholders in a company to buy a new ISSUE of the company's SHARES before they are offered to the public. Many agreements between companies merging or establishing joint ventures will contain pre-emption rights, giving each partner the right to buy out the other's share should one or other wish to terminate the arrangement.

Preference share

A SHARE carrying a fixed rate of DIVIDEND which has to be paid in full before ordinary shareholders can receive a cent; called a preferred stock in the United States. In the case of a winding up or LIQUIDATION, preference shareholders, as the name suggests, have a claim to the company's ASSETS ahead of ordinary shareholders. As a result, preference shares are regarded as an unexciting but relatively RISK-free form of investment. Such shares are often issued by INVESTMENT TRUSTS and other CLOSED-END FUNDS.

Preferential creditor

If a company is liquidated, some creditors are more equal than others and get paid first. Preferential creditors include the tax and customs authorities, as well as certain of the company's lower-paid workforce. Then follows the BANK and certain holders of the company's DEBT, followed by holders of any PREFERENCE SHARES. At the back of the queue are holders of the company's ORDINARY SHARES.

Preferred stock

US terminology for PREFERENCE SHARE.

Premium

There are a number of meanings.

- A regular payment to an insurer for providing INSURANCE cover.
- The amount paid by a purchaser (for example, to buy an historic car) over and above its quoted price.
- The amount by which a BOND sells above its face value. For example, a bond with a face value of $1,000 would sell for a premium of $200 if it cost $1,200.
- The amount by which the REDEMPTION PRICE of a bond exceeds the face value when the bond is called. (See also CALL PREMIUM.)
- The price that a buyer must pay to a seller for an OPTION contract.
- The price charged by a lender of a STOCK or SHARE to an investor who has borrowed stock to make delivery on

a short sale (that is, after selling stock in the market which he or she does not own).

◪ The amount by which a company's share price exceeds those with which it is comparable (that is, other companies in the same sector or industry). In such cases, the market assumes that the first company, for whatever reason, is likely to generate higher PROFITS.

Prepayment

The prepayment of a DEBT before it becomes due. Some LOAN contracts have a prepayment clause allowing them to be prepaid at any time without penalty (often the case with a MORTGAGE). With other loans, prepayment may entitle the lender to charge a fee, which is known as a prepayment penalty.

Price/book ratio

The market price of a SHARE divided by its BOOK VALUE per share. This measure is used by ANALYSTS and investors to judge a STOCK's relative value to the market. A high price/book ratio would suggest that the company's EARNINGS are likely to grow faster than the average; these GROWTH STOCKS appeal to investors mainly looking for a CAPITAL GAIN. If the stock is selling below its book value, then the company could be worth more broken up than as a going concern. Such a prospect may appeal to value investors, who seek out undervalued companies whose share prices fail to reflect their true worth.

Price/earnings ratio

The market price of a SHARE divided by its EARNINGS PER SHARE. When divided by its reported EARNINGS, it is known as the historic price/earnings (P/E) ratio; when divided by its anticipated earnings, it is known as the prospective P/E ratio. The ratios listed in newspapers and other such media are usually historic.

The P/E ratio is a measure of the number of years it will take for a share purchased now to repay its purchase price to an investor if all its earnings are paid out as DIVIDENDS. Although other measures drift in and out of favour according to the fashion of the time, most investors keep at least one eye on P/E ratios. That said, the average ratios for different markets vary widely. In Tokyo, where investors place great store on CAPITAL GAIN, P/E ratios are comparatively high; in Anglo-Saxon countries, where most investors expect to receive at least part of their reward in the form of dividends, P/E ratios are generally lower (although even there they have tended to rise because some big companies, such as, until recently, Microsoft, still shun dividends).

Primary dealer

The limited number of financial institutions that are authorised to buy newly issued government SECURITIES directly from the Treasury in the United States and the UK. These primary DEALERS are also secondary ones in that they make markets in old government securities as well. In most countries, governments offer new securities to the primary dealers through a form of auction.

Primary market

A market in which FINANCIAL INSTRUMENTS are sold when they are first issued; that is, a market in which the proceeds from the sale of the securities go directly to the issuer of the securities (be it a government issuing sovereign DEBT or a company issuing new SHARES). (See also SECONDARY MARKET.)

Principal

The face value of a financial ASSET, such as a BOND or a LOAN;

the amount that must be repaid when the asset (that is, the loan) matures. It also refers to the MARKET MAKER (or stock jobber) who acts as principal on his or her firm's account in trading SECURITIES. A BROKER (that is, AGENT) deals only on somebody else's behalf.

Principal-only bond

A BOND on which no payment of INTEREST IS due. The bond is issued at a DISCOUNT, and on MATURITY its full face value is repaid.

Private bank

Originally a BANK owned by a limited number of partners, each of whom bears unlimited LIABILITY for the business. Private banks of this sort were popular in Switzerland in the days when secrets were easier to keep. In recent years, the expression has come to mean any bank that caters for the needs of wealthy individuals, of whom there is an increasing number in Europe and Asia as family businesses are sold to large corporations. Most big international banks have private banking divisions, which aim to preserve their clients' CAPITAL and to generate a reasonable income without too much RISK. Some of these banks are still Swiss.

P

Private equity

The business once known simply as venture capital but now combined with other forms of financing. Private EQUITY is directed at three main targets:

- ◪ private companies (often in fast-growing, high-tech industries) that aim one day to issue SHARES to the public;
- ◪ middle-sized firms whose managers are planning buy-outs, joint ventures or some other form of reconstruction;

■ managers of (investment) funds which allocate dollops of CAPITAL to specialist advisers active in a particular market niche, such as life sciences.

Venture capital requires a higher than average RETURN for a higher than average degree of RISK. For most investors in private equity, the payoff comes when the company in which they have invested makes a public offer of its shares or is taken over.

Private placement

The sale of a large part of a new ISSUE of SHARES (or a chunk of existing ones) to a small group of investors, usually big institutions such as INSURANCE companies or PENSION FUNDS, which may already own the company's STOCK. The sale is private in the sense that it is not offered to the general public and is not sold through a recognised STOCK EXCHANGE.

Privatisation

The sale to the private sector, by a government, of businesses or agencies that may at one time have been bought by previous governments. The UK was one of the first countries in Europe (where a surprising number of businesses still remain in public hands) to realise the benefits to the enterprise and to the public purse of returning them to the private sector. Utilities providing telecoms, electricity, gas and water were among the first to be privatised; the railways were among the last, and controversy persists as much about the way it was done as about the beast it was done to.

Some of the biggest sales of public ASSETS took place in eastern Europe after the fall of the Soviet Union. Particularly notable was the work of Germany's Treuhandanstalt, which succeeded in privatising literally hundreds of businesses across the country.

Profit

To an economist, profit is what is left over in an enterprise after all its bills have been paid. Profit is the entrepreneur's reward for the RISKS he or she takes. To an accountant, profit is the difference between the revenue from sales and the total cost of producing those sales. NET profit before tax is what is left after all money costs have been deducted from sales revenue – that is, wages and salaries, rent, fuel, raw materials, INTEREST and DEPRECIATION. Gross profit is net profit before tax, and before interest and depreciation. (See also EARNINGS BEFORE INTEREST, TAX, DEPRECIATION AND AMORTISATION.)

A business that makes nothing but money is a poor kind of business.
Henry Ford

Profit-and-loss account

Every company is obliged to produce regularly a BALANCE SHEET and a profit-and-loss account (P&L account). The P&L account shows the PROFIT (or loss) made by the company during a particular period (usually a year but for some public companies three months). It records the company's total sales (or turnover) and the cost of those sales. From the NET sales figure is then subtracted the overhead costs to arrive at a figure for the company's net profit. In the United States, the profit and loss account is called the income statement.

P

Profit-sharing

A system that allows employees to participate in the profit of the organisation that they work for. Profit-sharing schemes are designed to motivate people without actually giving them a share in their company. An advantage of such schemes for employees and employers alike is that both benefit when the enterprise is successful. Piling up fixed costs in the form of high wages and salaries is rarely conducive to effort and entrepreneurship at any level of an organisation. Most companies try to link profit-sharing to achievable targets set for divisions or individual teams. Otherwise employees find it hard to relate their job to the overall profitability of the company.

Program trading

The use of computers to determine when to buy and when to sell blocks of STOCKS, FUTURES and OPTIONS. FUND MAN-AGERS still have the final say, but, in today's sophisticated markets, computer programs are used to spot opportunities to ARBITRAGE between different types of FINANCIAL INSTRU-MENTS in different markets. Program trading has frequently been blamed for the increasing VOLATILITY of markets, but the real culprits are the growing use of DERIVATIVES by banks and other financial institutions and the growing volume of trading in and out of certain SECURITIES. Computers merely help investors to monitor their PORTFOLIOS more closely and to react more quickly (admittedly sometimes en masse) when opportunities arise. The greatest strain is placed on markets during the third Friday of March, June, September and December when options, INDEX OPTIONS and futures contracts all expire at the same time. Known as TRIPLE WITCHING HOUR, this has often resulted in huge volumes of trading and volatility in international financial markets.

Project finance

A method of financing big CAPITAL projects, such as the building of a motorway or the digging of a mine, that depend for their COLLATERAL on the expected CASH FLOW of the completed project. It does not rely on guarantees from third parties (such as BANKS). In the United States, municipal authorities issue project notes, which are SHORT-TERM BONDS used to finance the building of public housing. When the project is completed, the notes are redeemed and the DEBT refinanced (more cheaply) over a longer period.

Promissory note

A legally binding promise between two parties that one will pay the other a stated amount at a prescribed future date, with or without INTEREST. Often referred to simply as a NOTE. Such notes are often also NEGOTIABLE INSTRUMENTS; that is, they can be sold to a third party.

Prospectus

A document containing a company's future plans, particularly in relation to the ISSUE of new SHARES to the public. In many countries the required contents of a prospectus are laid down by law. Individual STOCK EXCHANGES may have their own specific requirements. Such documents usually have to be filed with a regulator, such as the SEC. Some jurisdictions also require the issue of a PATHFINDER or preliminary prospectus (also called a RED HERRING in the United States) to give investors an idea of the proposed offering of new SECURITIES before the details are finalised.

Provisions

Money that a BANK sets aside out of its PROFIT to compensate for its doubtful DEBTS, that is, LOANS that it feels may never be repaid in full. Banks in different countries set aside more or less provisions depending on their prudence. For example, Japanese banks have more leeway than US or European ones. In general, there are two types of provisions.

- **Specific provisions**, which are set aside against specific identifiable borrowers who, for whatever reason, look unlikely to repay their debt in full.
- **General provisions**, which are not linked to individual borrowers but are based on the bank's hunch about what future market conditions might mean for borrowers in general. In other words, during difficult economic times, banks' general provisions usually rise.

Proxy

A vote delegated to somebody else (particularly at company meetings) by the person authorised to exercise it. Proxies are used by shareholders who are unable to attend a company's annual meeting. In this case, they sign a form delegating their right to vote (according to the number of SHARES they hold) to somebody else, usually a director of the company. Proxy fights break out when a group of shareholders tries to gain control of the votes of other shareholders in order to force their point of view on to the meeting, or to vote their own representatives on to the board of directors.

Put option

An OPTION that gives the right to sell a fixed number of SECURITIES at a specified price (the STRIKE PRICE) within a specified period of time. In return for this right, the buyer of a put option pays a PREMIUM. If the holder fails to exercise the option by the due date, it expires worthless. Buyers of put options generally hope that the price of the underlying security will drop in price. They will then be able to sell the security to the seller, or WRITER, of the put option for the agreed price and then pocket the difference between this price and what it costs to buy. Contrast with CALL OPTION.

P

Qualitative analysis

An analysis that concentrates on the touchy-feely aspects of a company's track record and reputation, such as the calibre and experience of the chief executive or the breadth of the board's vision. Usually combined with, but to be distinguished from, QUANTITATIVE ANALYSIS, to form a rounded judgment.

Quant

Shorthand for an ANALYST with above-average mathematical and computer skills who crunches numbers to test investment hypotheses.

Quantitative analysis

An analysis that concentrates on measurable things such as the cost of a company's CAPITAL, its projected sales and likely PROFITS. Usually combined with, but to be distinguished from, QUALITATIVE ANALYSIS, to arrive at a rounded judgment.

Quotation

What a company gets when its SHARES become quoted on a recognised STOCK EXCHANGE. To get a quotation it has to meet certain standards laid down by the exchange. It has to maintain prescribed levels of disclosure to its shareholders and the public in general. In return, the exchange helps to make the company's shares marketable by providing a price and a means through which buyers and sellers can get together.

Ramp

To push up the price of a SHARE artificially.

Random walk

A forecasting theory based on the premise that the past never repeats itself. The hypothesis is that all TECHNICAL ANALYSIS and predictions of future price movements based on past behaviour are worthless. The random walk theory was first developed in 1900 by Louis Bachelier, a French mathematician, and was popularised in the 1960s. Its most ardent supporters claim that future movements in markets are no more predictable than the random walk of a drunken man.

Rate of interest

The cost of money over time. The difference between the cost of interest paid by banks to their depositors and the rate of interest that borrowers pay to BANKS for their LOANS is called the banks' TURN. Rates of interest are influenced by three main factors.

1 The rate of INFLATION, which acts as a floor. Only in exceptional circumstances will a key interest rate fall below a country's rate of inflation.
2 The degree of RISK run by the lender. A BLUE-CHIP company will be charged a much lower rate than a high-tech start-up with no track record.
3 The demand for money. If the demand for money increases because of faster economic growth, a CENTRAL BANK can dampen demand by putting up interest rates (thus increasing the cost of money).

Each country's financial markets have their own key rate (or rates) of interest. In the United States, the PRIME RATE, the rate at which commercial banks lend to their most creditworthy customers, is the central rate. This, in turn, is influenced by the FEDERAL RESERVE, the US central bank, which acts to raise or lower SHORT-TERM interest rates.

Rate of return

A yardstick by which investors judge the merits of a SECURITY. In the case of an ORDINARY SHARE, the rate of return is the annual DIVIDEND YIELD divided by the purchase price of the share. For the total rate of return, include the CAPITAL GAIN (or loss) since the share was purchased. For most FIXED-INCOME securities, the rate of return is the COUPON (or published RATE OF INTEREST) divided by the purchase price.

Rating

A classification of the quality of different FINANCIAL INSTRU-MENTS and of the companies or organisations that issue them; an assessment of the CREDIT RISK attached to the instrument – that is, the chances that the INTEREST and PRINCIPAL will not be repaid as and when due. The international business of awarding ratings is dominated by three big agencies: Standard & Poor's, Moody's Investors Services and Fitch. Each has a slightly different method for assessing the creditworthiness of the organisations they rate, but all split ratings between INVESTMENT GRADE and non-investment grade (or junk). The higher the rating the cheaper it is, by and large, for an issuer to raise money by issuing BONDS in the financial markets. Rating agencies have considerable clout. By downgrading a company's creditworthiness, an agency can not only increase the cost of its CAPITAL but also, in some cases, determine whether a troubled company survives or goes bust.

R

Rating agency

An agency engaged in rating the creditworthiness of issuers of FINANCIAL INSTRUMENTS (see previous entry).

Receivables

Money that is owing to a company but has yet to be received. This is a figure that is watched closely by AUDITORS, bankers and STOCKMARKET ANALYSTS because it can determine a company's financial strength (or otherwise).

Reciprocity

The granting by A of certain privileges to B on condition that B also grants them to A. Reciprocity is a principle that has been widely applied in international finance. For example, one country's financial regulator will let another's set up on its turf if the favour is reciprocated. Countries negotiate reciprocal treaties under which companies operating in both are taxed only in the country in which they are based. Attempts to crack down on MONEY LAUNDERING and the illicit movement of money from drug dealing have increased governments' desire to scratch each other's backs. As always, trust is the key.

Recycling

A specific reference to the role of BANKS in taking surplus funds from OPEC's oil-producing members in 1973–74 and moving the money to places where it could be profitably absorbed. In many cases, this effectively meant that the banks were lending the money to other countries so that they could buy more oil from OPEC.

Red clause

A clause typed in red on a LETTER OF CREDIT permitting an exporter to receive all the amount due on the letter of credit in advance of the goods being shipped. Red clauses originated in the Australian wool trade.

Red herring

See PATHFINDER.

Redemption date

The date on which a SECURITY can be redeemed (that is, when the PRINCIPAL can be repaid). This is not necessarily the same as the MATURITY date. The security may have a fixed maturity but also contain an OPTION to call for repayment earlier.

Redemption yield

The total YIELD on a FIXED-INCOME SECURITY which includes the flat yield (the declared rate of INTEREST) plus the discounted present value of the future CAPITAL GAIN on the security. So a government BOND with a COUPON of 3%, a face value of $100, a market price of $50 and three years to MATURITY has a current yield of 6%. Its REDEMPTION YIELD is 6% plus the discounted present value of $50 that is to be gained in three years' time.

Red lining

The allegedly once common practice by banks of putting a red line around certain neighbourhoods or ghettos, and refusing to lend to any borrower within that area. Red lining based on race or racial mix is now illegal in most countries.

R

Refinancing

Paying off an existing DEBT with a new LOAN (which is cheaper, bigger or has a longer MATURITY). As the RATE OF INTEREST falls, borrowers want to refinance debt taken out at a FIXED RATE. When some sorts of projects are completed (such as a housing development or a major road), the existing debt can be refinanced at keener rates because the RISK of the project not being completed on time has been lifted. In some cases, banks impose penalties on the early repayment of debt. (See also PREPAYMENT.)

Registered representative

A person in the United States registered with the SEC to give advice on what SECURITIES to buy and sell. Registered representatives pass on a client's orders to a BROKER (which may also employ them) to be executed. In return, the registered representative receives a percentage of the brokerage COMMISSION.

Registered security

A SECURITY whose owner has to be registered with its issuer. When the security changes hands, the new owner has to inform the issuer of the change. In most developed countries, every company is obliged to keep a register of the owners of its shares. In it are recorded the owners' names and addresses (or of the appointed NOMINEES), the day they became shareholders and the day they ceased to be. The place where this register is kept (and where it is open to the public) is the registered office of the company (or that of its designated registrar). (See also BEARER SECURITY.)

Regulation Fair Disclosure

A set of rules in the United States designed to put private investors on the same footing as big institutional ones. Issued by the SECURITIES AND EXCHANGE COMMISSION in 2000, Reg FD, as it is known, prohibits the selective disclosure of material information to professionals in the securities industry (ANALYSTS, FUND MANAGERS and the like) by public companies. Until the rules were introduced, companies often gave professionals titbits in advance of the general public because they were keen to keep big investors on their side. Despite expected arguments over the definition of "material", the rules have done much to level the playing field between private and professional investors. To many, though, Reg FD was a small victory compared with the damage done to shareholders by companies such as Enron and WorldCom, which for years misled investors by declaring PROFITS that did not exist.

Reinsurance

An INSURANCE company's insurance; the practice among insurers of spreading the RISK that they take on. An insurer will reduce its LIABILITY – for example, of a satellite not reaching its required orbit – by laying off part of the risk with a reinsurance company. The reinsurer may accept only a layer of the potential liability – for example, of a payout between $10m and $20m – should the ultimate client claim. Reinsurance, like the insurance industry as a whole, is highly cyclical. As PREMIUMS rise, more capital is sucked into the industry until supply exceeds demand, and premiums start to drop again. During such times both insurers and reinsurers hope to make up from investment RETURNS what they lose from accepting unprofitable business.

Remittance

R

The EARNINGS that migrant workers send from their place of work to their families in their country of origin. For countries such as Turkey or the Philippines, these earnings are a significant source of FOREIGN EXCHANGE. "Remittance basis" is the term used to describe the principle used in taxing overseas income. The income is taxed as and when it is remitted to the jurisdiction of the receiving country.

Renunciation

The decision by shareholders not to take up their rights to a new ISSUE of SECURITIES (usually issued pro rata according to their existing holdings of SHARES). If shareholders renounce their rights, the rights shares can be sold on to somebody else. (See RIGHTS ISSUE.)

Repackaging

The splitting of a SECURITY into separate bits (the separate entitlements of repayments of INTEREST and PRINCIPAL, for instance). These are then sold as separate FINANCIAL INSTRUMENTS, often to different types of investors looking for different things. (See also STRIPS.)

Replacement cost

The cost of replacing any ASSET that is wasting over time. To ensure that they have enough CAPITAL to replace old plant and machinery, wise companies set aside some of their PROFIT every year. In the United States, replacement cost is also called current cost and replacement value, but it amounts to the same thing. Under replacement cost accounting, companies are allowed to depreciate part of the difference between the original cost of plant and the current cost of replacing it. (See also DEPRECIATION.)

Repo

See next entry.

Repurchase agreement

An agreement between a BROKER and a company with surplus

cash. The company buys SECURITIES (usually government BONDS) from the broker and agrees to sell them back again on a future date at an agreed price. By the time the securities return to the broker, it hopes to have found a (longer-term) investor to buy them.

Repurchase agreements (repos) are common in the United States. They are attractive to companies with surplus cash because they are flexible and can be negotiated for as long or as short a time as the company likes. The FEDERAL RESERVE, the US CENTRAL BANK, also makes use of repos when tinkering with the MONEY SUPPLY. To boost the supply of money in the banking system, the Fed buys securities from DEALERS which, in turn, deposit the proceeds with their commercial banks, thus increasing the money supply. (See also REVERSE REPURCHASE AGREEMENT.)

Rescheduling

The creation of a new payment schedule for a DEBT, done with the agreement of both the borrower and the lender; that is, formally putting off until tomorrow what you cannot pay today. Rescheduling is done by both large debtors (such as Latin American countries which have borrowed from international lenders) and small ones (such as impecunious consumers of public utilities). Rescheduling is easiest when there are few debtors involved. The widespread use of the international CAPITAL MARKETS even by relatively small countries or by agencies within those countries has made it harder to agree on deals to reschedule debt. It takes only one disgruntled lender to scupper a deal.

R

Reserves

Surplus funds that are stored away by organisations to meet future expenditure. A company's CAPITAL and reserves belong to its shareholders. They are an amalgamation of the original capital put up by the shareholders and the reserves that have been set aside out of the company's EARNINGS. Financial institutions such as BANKS have to maintain reserves at a level ordained by their supervisors and regulators because they are the first line of defence against a RUN on a bank. Countries hold reserves (of GOLD and foreign currency), which are held by the CENTRAL BANK, to meet future expenditure in trading or to support their currency's exchange rate. Currencies in which countries prefer to denominate their reserves (usually the dollar) are called reserve currencies.

Restructuring

A rearrangement of an organisation's financial or CAPITAL structure. A company will often restructure itself when its business becomes uncompetitive and the strain on its finances intensifies. In this case, a company may bring in an INVESTMENT BANK to advise it on its options (which may include selling a subsidiary, a merger or a joint venture). The crucial distinction between a restructuring and a RESCHEDULING is that most of the time the former is voluntary, whereas the latter is usually done at the instigation of the lender (or lenders).

Retail bank

R   A BANK whose main business is the provision of services (essentially LOANS and money transmission) to individuals and corporations. To be distinguished from wholesale banks (which deal mainly in financial markets) and INVESTMENT BANKS. The business of retail banking has changed radically from the days when banks simply took a TURN on the money they received from depositors and the money they lent to borrowers, not least because of the increasing pace of technological change.

Retire

There are two meanings.

1 To retire from work; that is, to stop working permanently, generally on reaching an age at which a PENSION can be received.
2 To retire a debt; that is, to remove the obligation associated with the debt by repaying it (or by some other arrangement which amounts to the same thing).

Retirement fund

Money set aside by an organisation to pay the PENSIONS that it has promised its employees (see also PENSION FUND).

Return

A measure of the reward flowing from a business during a specified period, usually the reward as measured by the PROFIT generated. For investors, RETURN (or, more particularly, TOTAL RETURN) is used to refer to the sum of the profit (that is, the flow of income) together with the CAPITAL GAIN to have accrued from an investment over a specified period. A return in the abstract has little meaning, so it is usually expressed as a ratio by relating it to something else, as follows.

- **Return on equity** (ROE). This has become an important measure of the performance of companies in general and of BANKS in particular. It relates return to the amount of shareholders' EQUITY used to obtain that return. Companies that pay too little attention to maximising their ROE do so at their peril, particularly in Anglo-Saxon economies.
- **Return on assets** (ROA). This relates return to the total ASSETS being employed to obtain that return. Since the assets in question are the sort that are valued in BALANCE SHEETS (fixed assets not human ones), ROA is not as useful in comparing one company with another. For example, a service business (such as a designer of semiconductors) will have fewer assets than a ship-owner. So the former's ROA will be far higher than the latter's.

R

🗹 **Return on sales** (ROS). This is a measure of how much of each unit of sales ends up as reward to the providers of CAPITAL. It may well be that increasing sales reduces the ROS. This could lead to a CONFLICT OF INTEREST between a company's shareholders and its sales force, which is paid (partly at least) on COMMISSION.

Reverse repo

See next entry.

Reverse repurchase agreement

The opposite of a REPURCHASE AGREEMENT, in this case between an investor and a BROKER. To ensure that it has the desired quantity of SECURITIES available at the right time, a BROKER may buy what it lacks from an investor on the understanding that it will buy them back at a future date at an agreed price. As with repos, reverse repos usually involve government BONDS.

Revolving credit

A LOAN with a particular condition: as soon as one bit of it is repaid, it can immediately be borrowed again. A revolving credit has an upper limit on the amount that can be borrowed, but no limit on the number of times the limit can be reached. As well as INTEREST on the loan, the lender will charge a fee for making the funds available. In the CAPITAL MARKETS, a revolving credit facility is known as a revolver.

Revolving underwriting facility

Commonly called a RUF, a GUARANTEE given by a group of BANKS that funds will be made available to a borrower which is raising money through an ISSUE of SECURITIES to the public. (See also NOTE ISSUANCE FACILITY and REVOLVING CREDIT.)

Rights issue

An ISSUE of SHARES that gives existing shareholders (normally pro rata according to the number of shares they already hold) to buy additional shares at a DISCOUNT to the prevailing market price and to the price at which they may later be offered to the wider public. Such an issue (called an offering in the United States) is arranged by an INVESTMENT BANK or BROKER, which usually makes a commitment to take up on its own books any rights that are not sold as part of the issue.

Ring

There are two meanings.

1 The spot on the FLOOR of an EXCHANGE where trades are finalised. Not to be confused with the PIT where traders first attract each other's attention.
2 A group of investors or DEALERS acting (illegally) in concert. Their aim is usually to manipulate prices to their advantage. A notorious (and ultimately unsuccessful) ring at the end of the 20th century was created by the Hunt family of Texas. Their aim was to corner the silver market.

R

Rising star

A company whose CREDIT RATING has been raised from non-investment grade (or junk) to INVESTMENT GRADE. This is good news for a company that wants to borrow in the CAPITAL MARKETS because, in general, the higher its credit rating, the lower is the cost of its money. The opposite of a FALLEN ANGEL.

Risk

The chance of making a loss. Investors are rewarded for taking risks; in general, the higher the risk, the greater is the reward. Investors who play safe (only buying US government BONDS, for example) are said to be risk-averse. In financial markets, risk takes several forms.

- **Exchange-rate risk.** The danger of borrowing in one currency and lending in another, or of having receipts denominated in one currency and payments in another.
- **Interest-rate risk.** The danger from, say, taking DEPOSITS at a fixed RATE OF INTEREST and making LOANS at a FLOATING RATE. It also refers to the danger that a FIXED-INCOME SECURITY will fall in value because of a rise in interest rates.
- **MATURITY risk.** The danger that arises when payments are due in seven days and receipts are not coming in for eight or more.
- **CREDIT RISK.** The danger that an outstanding bond or other form of DEBT will not be repaid as and when it is due. CREDIT RATINGS awarded to borrowers by independent agencies (such as Standard & Poor's or Moody's Investors Services) aim to assess this risk.
- **Market risk.** The danger that the market will move against a borrower or a company planning an ISSUE of SECURITIES, so foiling its plans.
- **Underwriting risk.** The danger that a new issue of securities will not be taken up by investors and that the INVESTMENT BANK or BROKER underwriting the deal will be left with the unwanted securities.
- **Political risk.** The danger of a change of government in the country of the borrower. The change may compel the borrower to renege on the debt or somehow to reduce its value.

To be alive at all involves some risk.
Harold Macmillan

Risk capital

The sort of "high-risk" CAPITAL put up by PRIVATE EQUITY and venture-capital firms. Because it goes to start-ups (often in the form of "seed" capital) and other young companies, such investment is riskier than average and so requires a higher return. Most risk capital is gathered from wealthy individuals or in small amounts from larger financial institutions. It is usually parcelled out to deserving cases by small firms running investment funds that specialise in such things.

Risk management

The sophisticated business of assessing and managing the many different types of RISK taken on by a company or by an investor. The process involves identifying and analysing the risks and then deciding whether or not to reduce them. HEDGE FUNDS and other professional investors have computer programs to do this for them. There are three main ways of reducing risk: by INSURANCE, by HEDGING and by reducing an investor's or a company's exposure to that type of business.

Rocket scientist

A name given to the highly qualified mathematicians and computer boffins employed by INVESTMENT BANKS and financial institutions. As markets have become more complex, so has the job of the experts charged with the task of seeking out new opportunities and then of assessing the RISKS of those investments. (See also QUANT and QUANTITATIVE ANALYSIS.)

R

Roll-over

The extension of a LOAN beyond its original final payment date. So-called SHORT-TERM loans can be rolled over so many times that eventually they become long-term loans.

Round lot

The minimum number of SHARES that can be offered to make a trade on a STOCK EXCHANGE, normally 100 shares or $1,000-worth or the equivalent for BONDS. The minimum is usually lower for thinly traded shares and higher for most orders placed by institutions.

Roundtripping

The process whereby BLUE-CHIP companies borrow money from BANKS using their OVERDRAFT and then place that money in the money markets for a PROFIT. This assumes that the company's cost of borrowing is low and that it can find relatively RISK-free places to park the money. It also refers to the practice in the United States of making SHORT-TERM trades in FINANCIAL INSTRUMENTS. Investors who do this can usually negotiate lower rates of COMMISSION with their BROKERS. Too much roundtripping of other people's investments by a professional investor can become churning (see CHURN).

RUF

See REVOLVING UNDERWRITING FACILITY.

R

Run

As in a "run on a BANK" or a "run on the peso". The nightmare of all financial institutions is the sight of depositors queuing round the block to get their money out of a bank, or out of a particular currency. In both cases, the run is caused by fear: either that the bank is about to go bust, or that the currency may be devalued (thus reducing the value of any DEPOSITS denominated in it). In both cases, the fear may become self-fulfilling: either the bank will go bust if all depositors want their money at the same time, or a currency will be devalued if too many people want to sell it. CENTRAL BANKS or governments can sometimes play for time (for instance, by freezing deposits in one currency or by closing the banks), but sooner or later the pressures become too great to withstand unless confidence in the currency or the bank is restored.

S&L

See SAVINGS AND LOAN ASSOCIATION.

Samurai bond

A yen-denominated BOND issued in Japan by a non-Japanese borrower; the Japanese version of a YANKEE BOND or a BULLDOG BOND. Samurai bonds are attractive to Japanese investors partly because they are free of withholding tax.

Sarbanes-Oxley Act

A tough SECURITIES law introduced in the wake of the corporate scandals that rocked the financial markets in the United States at the beginning of the 21st century. Among other things, it established a Public Company Accounting Oversight Board to supervise the auditing standards of large companies; required CEOs and chief financial officers to sign off personally on their companies' accounts; banned auditors from selling some consulting services to the same client; gave the audit committees of big companies the power to hire and fire auditing firms; made it a crime not to disclose material transactions that take place off companies' balance sheets; and increased the penalties for white-collar crime. Draconian in its scope, the act was regarded by many as too much, too late. It gave the SECURITIES AND EXCHANGE COMMISSION the job of fine-tuning the new legislation.

Satellite banking

A way of organising a BANK'S BRANCH network so that it is clustered around larger branches. Smaller branches provide a limited range of services; big, complicated business is referred to the larger branches.

Savings and loan association

A main provider of MORTGAGES to home owners in the United States. The savings and loan associations (S&LS), often called thrifts, lend long-term and often at a fixed RATE OF INTEREST. Their borrowing (that is, their DEPOSITS) became more SHORT-TERM in the 1980s as US financial markets were deregulated. In return for being allowed to enter markets previously reserved for BANKS, S&LS had to give up some of the advantages they enjoyed over mortgages. Having to base their business on floating RATES OF INTEREST caused great difficulty for many S&LS. Poor management and corruption were also to blame. Hundreds of thrifts up and down the country became insolvent and were forced to close their doors. The Federal Savings and Loans Insurance Corporation, a government agency, was unable to cover the claims of savers and also failed. The government was left with no alternative but to step in with billions of dollars in new money. These days, S&LS offer their customers retail products and services like any other bank and remain a potent force in the country's financial system.

Savings bank

A BANK whose raison d'etre is (or at least was) the gathering of DEPOSITS from small savers. Such banks limit the withdrawal of deposits on demand. Traditionally, savings banks have had little or nothing to do with businesses, and provide no money transmission services. In many countries savings banks have strong local roots, either as national banks with a regional structure or as separate regional institutions. Indeed, in parts of Europe many still enjoy benefits because of their regional clout. On both sides of the Atlantic, savings banks are often set up as mutual institutions (and are therefore owned by their depositors) and not as limited companies. In return for greater access to the CAPITAL MARKETS, savings banks have become more like their commercial cousins in recent years.

Scrip issue

A handout of SHARES to a company's existing shareholders in proportion to their stake in the company; also known as a bonus issue. A scrip issue is little more than an accounting device; it does nothing to increase the value of a company. After it has taken place, the shareholders' EQUITY is worth the same. It has simply been divided into smaller bits. For this reason, scrip issues are often used to make a company's shares more marketable, since small investors are often daunted by a company whose individual shares are worth, say, hundreds of dollars each. Companies also make scrip issues instead of paying a DIVIDEND; shareholders are offered new shares instead of CASH.

SDR

See SPECIAL DRAWING RIGHT.

SEAQ

See STOCK EXCHANGE AUTOMATED QUOTATIONS.

Seat

S

The membership of a STOCK EXCHANGE or COMMODITIES exchange, bought and sold (like the FINANCIAL INSTRUMENTS traded within its doors) for prices that are determined by supply and demand. So when DEALERS are making lots of money the prices of their seats usually rise, and when they are not the reverse happens. A seat gives the holder the right to use the facilities of the exchange and to participate in its business.

SEC

See SECURITIES AND EXCHANGE COMMISSION.

Secondary market

A market in second-hand FINANCIAL INSTRUMENTS. When first issued, STOCKS, BONDS, CERTIFICATES OF DEPOSIT and other such instruments are sold in the PRIMARY MARKET, and the proceeds from these sales go to the companies or organisations that issued them. One of the attractions of the secondary market is the LIQUIDITY provided by the exchanges, which subsequently make markets in those same securities.

Secrecy

It is a fundamental duty of financial AGENTS that they do not disclose details of their clients' affairs against their clients' wishes. This duty is in direct conflict with the desire of governments and law-enforcement offices to track down the proceeds of drug traffickers, criminal gangs, money launderers and the like. Even jurisdictions such as Switzerland, which has traded on its reputation for neutrality and banking secrecy, have bowed in recent years to the demands for more information to be shared among governments. While the threat of terrorism remains, such conflicts are likely to increase, not diminish.

S

Secured loan

A LOAN which provides a lender with the right to take over certain prescribed ASSETS of a borrower should the borrower fail to repay. The assets given as security for the loan may be physical (such as property or goods) or they may be legal agreements entitling the lender to certain payments. As a result of their secured lending, BANKS have ended up owning all sorts of strange things, from domestic appliances to car factories.

Securities

See SECURITY.

Securities and Exchange Commission

A US government department that regulates and polices the
ISSUE and trading of most aspects of the SECURITIES industry.
Based in Washington and established in 1934, the main weapon
of the Securities and Exchange Commission (SEC) is disclosure.
The SEC forces issuers of securities to divulge much more than
similar agencies in other countries. Indeed, it is something of a
shock to the directors of foreign companies seeking a LISTING
on a US exchange or issuing securities there to find out how
stringent the country's securities laws are.

The SEC is made up of five commissioners who are appointed on five-year, rolling terms. To ensure that the body
remains independent of the administration of the day, no more
than three members may be from the same political party, yet
the chairmanship is in the gift of the US president. The scandals
over corporate excess and wrongdoing in the United States at
the start of the 21st century showed how important it is to have
strong leadership at the heart of the financial markets, something which, curiously, the SEC of the time was unable to
deliver.

Securities lending

The practice of lending SECURITIES to investors (or their
BROKERS) who are planning to SHORT the market (that is, sell
shares that they do not already own). The securities are supplied when and if they must be delivered to the buyer's broker.
No PREMIUM is usually paid. In the United States, the SEC does,
however, insist that brokerage clients give permission (as part of
a standard agreement) for their securities to be lent in this way.

Securitisation

The use by corporations of the SECURITIES markets as a source of external finance, instead of BANKS and other financial intermediaries. All sorts of things can be securitised, from car LOANS to MORTGAGES and CREDIT-CARD RECEIVABLES. By aggregating existing DEBT of this kind in pools, and then issuing new securities backed by the COLLATERAL provided by the pool, securitisation does two main things:

- it gives other investors the opportunity to share in the PROFITS;
- it enables the originating banks and financial institutions to spread their RISK without having to sacrifice a share of the profit.

(See also ASSET-BACKED SECURITIES.)

Security

There are two main meanings.

1 Something of value given to a lender by a borrower to support his or her intention to repay. In the case of a MORTGAGE, the security is the property that the loan is being used to purchase. (See also COLLATERAL.)
2 Evidence (on paper or otherwise) that its owner is entitled to a share of the EQUITY of a company. The term (usually used in the plural) applies to common and preferred STOCK, WARRANTS and RIGHTS, as well as BONDS (both INTEREST-bearing and those CONVERTIBLE into stock).

S

Seller's market

A market in which the seller has the upper hand; where demand for SECURITIES outstrips supply; and where as a consequence prices are expected to rise.

Many people believe in cutting losses at a set limit, but I never do this personally unless I find that the "story" (what attracted me to the share in the first place) has definitely changed for the worse.
Jim Slater

Separate trading of registered interest and principal of securities

See STRIPS.

Serious Fraud Office

A special body set up in the UK at the end of the 1980s to investigate large and serious cases of suspected fraud. The squad is an independent government department run by the attorney-general, who heads the country's criminal justice system. There were three main reasons for setting up the Serious Fraud Office (SFO):

- concern that deregulated markets had made crookery easier;
- the complicated nature of large cases of financial fraud, and the need for an investigative team with specialist (that is, accounting) skills;
- the ability of fraudsters to play off one government department against another; the SFO was designed to make it easier for crime-fighting teams to co-operate with each other.

So far, the SFO has spent a lot of public money on investigations but successfully prosecuted few alleged fraudsters.

SET

Short for Secure Electronic Transaction, a standard protocol that is designed to do two things:

- to ensure the security of electronic transactions, particularly transactions over the internet;
- to convince consumers that remote electronic transactions can be made secure.

After a slow start when the internet bubble burst, together with a reluctance among consumers to divulge details of their CREDIT CARDS online, remote transactions have picked up. Shoppers, particularly those short of time in the run-up to holidays such as Christmas, are realising that online transactions can be made securely and with the minimum of fuss.

Settlement date

The date by which deals for the buying and selling of SECURITIES must be settled; that is, the securities must be paid for by the buyer and delivered by the seller. With the growth in electronic trading, settlement dates have crept closer and closer to the date of the agreed transaction. Many exchanges now aspire to T + 1 (settlement one day after the transaction has taken place).

SFO

See SERIOUS FRAUD OFFICE.

S

Shadow accounting

A form of accounting used for internal purposes when a company is unable to ascribe something accurately, for example, the CREDIT for a particular sale. If, say, two AGENTS are equally involved in the sale of an INSURANCE contract to a customer, then the insurance company may add the full value of the contract to each agent's account. For the purposes of the PROFIT-AND-LOSS ACCOUNT, of course, this would be double counting.

Share

A word used interchangeably with STOCK to denote part ownership of a company. Shares are granted in exchange for CAPITAL and can be traded on a STOCK EXCHANGE or sometimes OVER THE COUNTER. Those who own shares are said to have EQUITY in a company. Together with BONDS and other forms of DEBT, shares form a company's capital.

Shareholder value

The idea that all business activity (at least that of quoted companies) should be directed towards maximising the value of shareholders' EQUITY in a company. It is an idea that arouses strong support and equally strong antagonism. The notion of shareholder value took on greater meaning when the practice of granting SHARE OPTIONS to managers became widespread, particularly in the United States. Institutional shareholders had sympathy with the view, espoused by managers, that it was in everybody's interest to maximise the share price and thus shareholder value. What was good for one must be good for the other. It soon became apparent, however, that the interests of shareholders and managers did not always coincide. As the corporate scandals at the start of the 21st century showed, managers were prepared to go to extraordinary lengths (sometimes even as far as FRAUD) to maintain the share price so that their options were worth more. When the fraud was discovered, the pack of cards collapsed and everybody lost out.

Share option

Part of a remuneration package designed to motivate managers and to encourage senior employees to stay with their company. Share options give employees an opportunity to buy shares in the company they work for at some future date. The price at which they can buy the shares is fixed when the option is granted and is favourable at the time. But there is no guarantee that it will remain that way. Indeed, the system is open to abuse in that many boards of directors, seeing the value of their options vanish as the share price falls, simply re-price them at more favourable rates.

Share premium

The amount by which the proceeds of an ISSUE of SECURITIES exceeds the nominal value of the issue. In the issuer's accounts the amount appears in the share premium reserve.

Shelf registration

A system in the United States that allows companies to file in advance with the SEC details of the SECURITIES they intend to issue to investors over the next two years. So, instead of having to wait while their plans are cleared, a company can pull issues off the shelf as and when it needs them. With a minimum amount of updating from quarter to quarter, companies have much of the flexibility they need. The SEC established the practice in the 1980s under Rule 415, and such issues are sometimes called Rule 415 issues.

Short

Usually called shorting or selling short. Investors agree to sell SECURITIES that they do not already own. They are betting that the price of the securities will fall by the time they have to be delivered. If they do, the sellers make a profit on the deal. If they do not, the sellers must buy them at a PREMIUM and therefore lose money on the deal. Short sellers often borrow stock from other investors to fulfil their end of the bargain. (See also SECURITIES LENDING.)

S

Shorts

GILT-EDGED SECURITIES issued by the UK government that are due to be repaid within five years. (See also GILTS.)

Short sale

See SHORT.

Short-term

A LOAN with an original MATURITY of less than 12 months is generally considered to be short-term, although the term is used quite loosely.

Short-termism is the name given to the recognised inability of financial institutions in the Anglo-Saxon world to make genuinely long-term investments. More than their counterparts elsewhere, particularly in continental Europe, they are under pressure to show returns by the time of the next (quarterly) report to shareholders.

Shunter

A BROKER who deals on two different exchanges in a SECURITY that is quoted on both.

Sight deposit

A BANK DEPOSIT that can be withdrawn immediately.

Single capacity

The separation (once strictly observed in the UK) of market-making in SECURITIES (the job of the JOBBER) and dealing in securities (the job of the BROKER). It was rather like the distinction between wholesaling and retailing. Single capacity was effectively abolished by the City of London's BIG BANG.

Sinking fund

An ACCOUNT into which money is paid at regular intervals to meet a large payment that is expected at some future date.

Smart card

A plastic CREDIT CARD or DEBIT CARD that contains information about the balance (or lack of it) available on the card.

Smurfing

The transfer of lots of small amounts of money from many different BANK ACCOUNTS into a single account, often OFF-SHORE. Commonly used as a means for those engaged in MONEY LAUNDERING to disguise the sources and uses of their ill-gotten gains.

Socially responsible investing

See ETHICAL INVESTING.

S

Solvency

The condition of an organisation whose ASSETS are worth more than its LIABILITIES. Being solvent is not enough on its own to ensure the financial health or indeed viability of an organisation. LIQUIDITY is also important.

Sources of funds

Where borrowers get their money from. In the case of corporations there are two sources: internal (the cash they generate from their businesses) and external (the funds they procure from the CAPITAL MARKETS). Governments also have two sources: taxation and borrowing.

South Sea Bubble

The inflation and subsequent collapse in 1720 of the SHARES of the South Sea Company. These had been subjected to an extraordinary amount of ramping, SPECULATION and manipulation before, like a bubble, they burst. The bubble began to inflate when the company, which said it planned to trade in South America, offered to swap all the British government's debt for its shares. Hyped by the company's confidence and speculators' greed, the shares rose from £100 to more than £1,000 each before crashing. All subsequent STOCKMARKET regulation and SECURITIES legislation have been influenced by the events of 1720.

Special drawing right

A pseudo-currency invented by the INTERNATIONAL MONETARY FUND in 1967 and designed to provide countries with an alternative reserve currency to GOLD and dollars. The special drawing right (SDR) was an esoteric oddity until it was simplified into a basket of main currencies: the D-mark and French franc (both since replaced by the EURO), the dollar, the yen and the pound. The simplification resulted in wider use of the SDR; for example, a few commercial BANKS began to offer LOANS and DEPOSIT facilities denominated in SDRs. In recent years, however, the SDR has again assumed a narrower role. As such, it cannot claim to be a currency, simply a claim on the currencies of the countries whose currencies make it up.

Specialist

A member of a STOCK EXCHANGE who makes and maintains a market in the SHARES of a number of companies by buying all such shares that are offered and selling all that are requested. In the United States, specialists are expected to buy and sell within a narrow price range in order to maintain orderly markets. In certain circumstances, therefore, specialists can buy and sell on their own account to preserve LIQUIDITY in the market.

Special-purpose vehicle

Companies or legal entities set up specifically to hold ASSETS and (where permitted by regulators) to isolate the LIABILITIES associated with them. Such companies are often used by insurers to protect part of their CASH surpluses from claims in the event of a catastrophe or natural disaster. BANKS set them up to hold pools of financial assets, such as financial LEASES or RECEIVABLES from consumer CREDIT, which in turn support BONDS or other forms of ASSET-BACKED SECURITIES.

The special-purpose vehicle (SPV) buys the LOANS to be securitised and then issues new securities to investors, whose income and CAPITAL are repaid out of the proceeds of the loans. So the SPV has on its BALANCE SHEET securities as assets and loans as liabilities. Banks can therefore use SPVs to help them reduce the burden on their balance sheets. This gives them more leeway with regulators when they have to meet rules on CAPITAL ADEQUACY. SPVs are also employed by the trust and private-banking arms of banks to hold and ring-fence investments in low-tax jurisdictions such as the Cayman Islands.

Since the collapse in 2002 of Enron, an energy-services firm in the United States, regulators have become concerned about the way some companies have used SPVs to distance themselves from potential liabilities.

Speculation

The purchase of a financial ASSET (or the right to it) with the aim of making a PROFIT. Although it has a bad name, speculation is essential to the proper functioning of a financial market. Speculators will assume a certain amount of RISK in anticipation of making a gain, but, unlike most gamblers, they will take steps to reduce the chances of a loss. They HEDGE their losses by selling SHORT, taking out STOP ORDERS and trading in FUTURES and OPTIONS. In its purest form, speculation assumes that a proposition can be analysed and measured; it differs from investment mainly in the degree of risk that a speculator is prepared to take on.

Spin off

The hiving off of a subsidiary by a parent corporation, traditionally by giving SHARES in the subsidiary to shareholders of the parent in proportion to their existing holdings. Often this is done through a special DIVIDEND. Parent companies can also spin off a subsidiary by selling it to its managers (through a buyout) or as part of some other form of share-ownership plan for employees. Many subsidiaries that are spun off later become listed companies in their own right.

S   Split-capital investment trust

An INVESTMENT TRUST (known in the United States as a CLOSED-END FUND) with a predetermined life whose EQUITY is divided into two or more main classes of SHARE. Holders of income shares receive all or most of the income earned by the company during its lifetime, as well as a predetermined proportion of the CAPITAL value when the company is wound up. Holders of capital shares receive no income but are entitled to the ASSETS remaining after the income shares have been paid off. ZERO-COUPON PREFERENCE SHARES, as the name suggests, pay no income but rank higher than either income or capital shares if a trust is liquidated. Splits, as they are known, suit investors looking either for income or for capital growth, but rarely both at the same time.

Splits have got into trouble in the past by investing in each other's shares, which is fine when markets are rising but can be disastrous when they are not. This is because some splits borrow money from BANKS as well as investing their shareholders' funds. As markets fall, the HURDLE RATE rises – that is, the rate at which a trust must generate enough income to preserve the value of its original investment while paying INTEREST on the money it has borrowed. Three consecutive years of declining STOCKMARKETS until the end of 2002 caused some splits to fail, spelling disaster for shareholders. Many had invested in splits in the belief that they were safer than ORDINARY SHARES, only to find that they were not.

Spot market

A market where things are quoted at their SPOT PRICE.

Spot price

The price quoted for a transaction that is to be made on the spot; that is, the price for something that is to be delivered now and paid for in CASH now.

S

Spread

In general, the difference between one item and another, most frequently related to the difference between a buying price and a selling price. For example, a spread is:

- the difference between the rate paid for DEPOSITS and the rate received for LOANS;
- the difference between the YIELD on BONDS of the same MATURITY but different quality;

- the difference between the price at which a SHARE is sold and the price at which it can be bought;
- in underwriting, the difference between the total cost of an ISSUE to the UNDERWRITER and the proceeds from successfully selling the issue to the public;
- the variety that a company enjoys in its borrowings or its business, or a BANK has in its loans. A good spread of maturities, for example, helps to provide a smooth CASH FLOW.

Spread betting

A way of betting on the outcome of movements in the financial markets. Like bookmakers at the races, specialist firms accept bets on the movement up or down over a period of a STOCK INDEX or an individual SHARE. The profit or loss is calculated on the basis of the number of "points" between the price at the outcome and what it was when the punter made the original bet.

Take XYZ company, which is quoted at a spread of, say, 863–870 pence. If you think the price is going to fall, you would take out a "down" bet for, say, £15 at 863 pence, the lower of the two prices quoted, over a period of, say, two weeks. If at the end of the period the spread quoted has fallen to 830–837 pence, you would buy back your original down bet at 837 pence, making a PROFIT of £390 (863 − 837 = 26, then 26 × £15 = £390). Conversely, if the spread quoted had risen to 880–893 pence, you would lose a corresponding amount (863 − 880 = −17, then −17 × £15 = −£255).

Spread betting is risky because, unless you cap your LIABILITY by taking out an equal and opposite bet or otherwise minimise your exposure, you are liable for the full extent of your losses should the price fall. Although spread betting in financial markets began only in the 1970s, it has long been popular with followers of sport. Today it is possible to gamble in the same way on the outcome of, say, a cricket match by taking an up or down bet on the number of runs a particular side will score. A boon for UK residents is that profits from all such transactions are free of CAPITAL GAINS tax and stamp duty.

Spreadsheet

A series of rows and columns of numbers – for example, of a financial intermediary's sales and the COMMISSION due on each deal. Because of their complexity and the fact that changing one number invariably has a knock-on effect elsewhere, spreadsheets were early candidates for computerisation. These days sophisticated models of a company's financial profile can be generated at the touch of a button. ANALYSTS use fancy software to assess the impact of changes in a company's borrowing costs or its trading margins on its expected PROFIT.

SPV

See SPECIAL-PURPOSE VEHICLE.

Stag

Somebody who speculates that an ISSUE of SECURITIES will be OVERSUBSCRIBED. Stags order more securities than they can afford, knowing that if the offer is oversubscribed they will get fewer shares than they requested and, more importantly, that an oversubscribed issue is almost certain to sell at a PREMIUM to the offer price as soon as trading starts in the SECONDARY MARKET. The stag thus hopes to make a handsome PROFIT, a practice known (if successful) as stagging an issue. In the United States, the term is used generally to apply to somebody who aims to make a quick profit by buying a security and then selling it on.

Standing order

An instruction from a customer to a BANK to make a regular (often monthly) payment of a fixed amount to a named creditor or recipient.

Stock

For almost all intents and purposes the same as a SHARE. Stock refers to the stock of CAPITAL belonging to a company, its common stock, preferred stock and so on. Shareholders are people (or institutions) with a share in this stock.

Stockbroker

A member of a STOCK EXCHANGE who is authorised to deal in SECURITIES. Stockbrokers charge a COMMISSION, usually related to the size of the deal and the frequency with which the customer trades, for their services. So when STOCKMARKETS are rising and trading volumes are high, brokers generally do well. A stockbroker acts as an AGENT on behalf of a client, usually an investor. Contrast with a MARKET MAKER, who stands ready to buy and sell (that is, to make a market in) certain types of securities and is somebody with whom a broker deals. (See also REGISTERED REPRESENTATIVE.)

Stock dividend

The payment of STOCK in lieu of a CASH DIVIDEND. With a 5% stock dividend, shareholders receive five new shares for every 100 that they already own. If these are newly issued shares, then the shareholders are getting less than some might expect. In this case, it is more akin to a SCRIP ISSUE, which simply divides the same amount of EQUITY into smaller chunks.

Stock exchange

Traditionally, the physical place where securities were bought and sold. Stock exchanges are often found in grand 19th-century buildings in the centre of capital cities. Nowadays, more and more dealing is done by BROKERS sitting in their offices and communicating via a computer screen and a telephone. Exchanges themselves are also investing increasing amounts in technology that allows them to display prices and match bargains not just across borders but in a variety of DERIVATIVES as well as in PLAIN VANILLA SECURITIES. Indeed, most exchanges are owned by companies that are themselves quoted on an exchange; exchanges therefore have their own shareholders to satisfy.

Stock Exchange Automated Quotations

Introduced by the LONDON STOCK EXCHANGE in 1986, SEAQ, as it is commonly known, is a trading system that carries the MARKET MAKERS' BID and offer quotations for UK SECURITIES. Members of the exchange not only have access to a continuously updated database of prices and volumes; they are also able to deal in securities via their computer screens. SEAQ International is based on the same system and has done much to reinforce London's position as the world's leading centre for international SHARE trading.

Stock index

A measure of the change in value of a representative group of STOCKS. Strictly speaking, an index is an average expressed in relation to an earlier, established value. Confusingly, some published stock averages are actually indices, and vice versa. Indices can be broadly based (representing an overall market, like the S&P 500) or they can be narrow (concentrating, for example, on a particular industry or sector). Stock indices are used as the base for a variety of DERIVATIVES (such as stock index FUTURES, INDEX OPTIONS and options on index futures). Most such products are used to HEDGE an investor's exposure to movements in a particular market or as a way of spreading RISK.

Stockmarket

An organised market in SECURITIES, whether on an official STOCK EXCHANGE or OVER THE COUNTER. In recent decades, there has been a huge growth in the volume of securities traded on exchanges around the world. Volumes generally rise most strongly during BULL markets (periods when SHARE prices are rising strongly).

> *Emotions are your worst enemy in the stockmarket.*
> Don Hays

Stockmarket sector

A particular group of STOCKS usually found in one industry (such as airlines, chemicals, media or support services). ANALYSTS generally cover industries or STOCKMARKET sectors, so investors interested in the SHARES of a certain type of company can usually find information that will help them decide what to buy. Some UNIT TRUSTS (MUTUAL FUNDS) also specialise in sectors of the market. By investing in EXCHANGE TRADED FUNDS, investors are able to buy the equivalent of a diversified PORTFOLIO of companies in a particular sector.

> *Investing is simple, but not easy.*
> Warren Buffett

S

Stock split

The issuing of free extra SHARES to existing shareholders according to some fixed proportion; two for three, for example. This does nothing to add to the value of the existing EQUITY; it merely makes a greater number of shares represent the same stake in the company. What was represented by three shares is, after the split, represented by five. (See also SCRIP ISSUE.)

Stop order

An order to a STOCKBROKER to sell (or buy) SHARES in the future when they reach a particular specified price, called the stop price. Such an order is given by a client either to protect a PROFIT or to limit a loss. Suppose an investor buys shares at $1 each and they rise to $5. Everybody says sell, but the owner thinks they might rise higher. The owner hangs on to them but gives a stop order to the BROKER to sell should they fall to $4, so protecting a profit of $3 a share. A snag with stop orders is that, in volatile markets, they can sometimes trigger a sale too early.

Straddle

The purchase by a speculator of an equal number of PUT OPTIONS and CALL OPTIONS on the same underlying STOCK, STOCK INDEX or COMMODITY FUTURE. Although each contract may be taken out separately, in theory they should all have the same MATURITY date. If speculators can get a perfect (or near perfect) match, then they cancel out their RISK (and in the process cease to be speculators).

Street name

The registration of SHARES in the name of a BROKER without the real owner taking delivery of them. The use of a street name makes it easier subsequently to sell the shares if the real owner intends to sell them quickly. Another advantage is that the shares (or proof of their ownership) do not have to be shipped back and forth after each deal.

Strike price

The price, in contracts for PUT OPTIONS and CALL OPTIONS, at which the option to buy or sell the underlying SECURITY can be exercised. Also called the exercise or basis price. (See also IN THE MONEY.)

Strips

Shorthand for SEPARATE TRADING OF REGISTERED INTEREST AND PRINCIPAL OF SECURITIES, the practice of separating a BOND into its CAPITAL element (the corpus) and its COUPONS (the bits that bear the INTEREST). The capital is then sold as a ZERO-COUPON BOND and the coupons as an interest-only security. In this case, the acronym (Strip) preceded the full name. Investment bankers hit upon the idea and started trading in the stripped securities before the US Treasury actually legitimised the practice. Indeed, the idea took off so well that now the Treasury issues pre-stripped obligations to certain types of Treasury bonds so that they can be traded as Strips. The term also refers to certain combinations of PUT OPTIONS and CALL OPTIONS and to SHARES stripped of their entitlement to DIVIDENDS.

Subordinated

A LOAN or SECURITY with an inferior (or more junior) claim to repayment compared with other loans or securities. In the pecking order of securities, a junior subordinated DEBENTURE therefore ranks below a subordinated debenture. But the latter may still be downgraded if the issuer agrees to demote it by means of a subordination letter. The chance for one type of security to throw its weight around at the expense of others only really occurs if the company issuing them is liquidated.

Sub-prime lending

Lending to people who find it difficult to borrow from traditional sources, such as BANKS, because they are perceived to be a bad RISK. Sub-prime loans carry a high RATE OF INTEREST to compensate the lender for the higher chance of DEFAULT. In the

United States, sub-prime lending is big business; some large financial institutions do little else. In most other countries, when a bank says "no", a borrower has few other options.

Supplier credit

A LOAN to an importer guaranteed by the EXPORT-CREDIT agency of the country of the exporter.

Surrender value

What the holder receives when a fixed-term investment (such as a life INSURANCE policy) is cashed in before the end of the term. If they need the CASH, most holders are better off selling the policy in the SECONDARY MARKET than surrendering it.

Suspense account

A sort of dustbin ACCOUNT into which payments are shunted temporarily while in transit from one financial institution to another, or when there is doubt about their rightful destination.

Swap

A transaction in which two parties exchange ASSETS or entitlements to income. The two most common types of swaps are as follows.

S

- **Currency swaps**, which originated as a way of avoiding EXCHANGE CONTROLS in different countries but have since developed into yet another way for financial institutions to borrow in different markets. Institutions simply sell each other amounts in different currencies and re-exchange the PRINCIPAL when the LOANS mature.

◪ **Interest-rate swaps,** where counterparties agree to exchange periodic INTEREST payments on loans or BONDS. This enables them artificially to extend or shorten the duration of their investment (that is, the relationship of a bond's price to its YIELD). This, in turn, helps to balance the RISK to which the institution may be exposed.

Swaption

An OPTION to SWAP. A payer swaption gives the buyer the right, but not the obligation, to enter into an INTEREST-rate swap at a predetermined rate on a future date. The buyer pays the seller a PREMIUM for this right. A receiver swaption gives the buyer the right to receive certain fixed payments. The seller agrees to provide the swap if called upon to do so, thus giving the buyer a form of INSURANCE.

Syndicate

A group of institutions or individuals that get together to do something that each could neither afford to do on their own nor contemplate individually because of the RISK. So a syndicate of INVESTMENT BANKS might get together to underwrite a new ISSUE of SECURITIES; or a syndicate of BANKS might get together to make a multimillion-dollar LOAN to a developing country (a SYNDICATED LOAN); or a group of LLOYD'S names might join forces as part of a syndicate to underwrite INSURANCE risks. In all cases, the legal agreements that bind them together and set out what happens if it everything goes wrong are both voluminous and onerous.

Syndicated loan

A single LOAN that is shared among a large number of lenders, usually because it is too big for any one of them to take on by itself. Much of the international lending in the EUROMARKETS is syndicated.

Synthetic asset

The artificial creation of an ASSET by combining different forms of DERIVATIVES. For example, by purchasing a CALL OPTION and selling a PUT OPTION on the same STOCK, an investor can create a synthetic asset with the same potential for gain as the underlying SECURITY. Similarly, by putting together two INTEREST-rate SWAPS with offsetting interest payments, an investor can create, say, a FLOATING-RATE NOTE pegged to LIBOR which also pays a PREMIUM twice a year.

Takeover

A change in the controlling interest of a listed company. A takeover may be friendly and sought by the existing directors. Or it may be contested (see HOSTILE BID). Either way, it requires the consent of a majority of shareholders who will be asked to vote on the acquirer's proposals. Takeovers can be paid for with CASH (so much per SHARE), or the shares of the acquiring company, or a combination of both. In developed markets, takeovers are strictly regulated in the interests of shareholders. The directors of acquirers and those whose company is being taken over traditionally seek the advice of INVESTMENT BANKS in valuing BIDS, friendly or otherwise. (See also PANEL ON TAKEOVERS AND MERGERS.)

Tap stock

An issue of UK government BONDS which is sold bit by bit, not all at once.

Tax loss

Any loss which a company can legitimately transfer to another accounting period and set off against its PROFIT for tax purposes. The ability to carry such losses forward (and backwards against the profits of previous accounting periods) varies from country to country.

---

*The avoidance of taxes is the only intellectual pursuit
that still carries any reward.*
John Maynard Keynes

Tax shelter

An activity that allows a taxpayer the opportunity to shelter otherwise taxable income from liability to tax. Governments are usually quick to plug loopholes that are abused or overused (such as the tax benefits enjoyed by limited partnerships in the United States until the 1980s). Most developed countries allow savers to shelter from tax any money put into legitimate retirement accounts (for example, INDIVIDUAL SAVINGS ACCOUNTS in the UK and INDIVIDUAL RETIREMENT ACCOUNTS and Keogh Plans in the United States). Wealthy individuals also get tax breaks if they establish foundations for charitable purposes. These not only save the donor tax but also increase the flow of CASH into bona fide charities.

> *The difference between tax avoidance and tax evasion*
> *is the thickness of a prison wall.*
> Denis Healey

Technical analysis

The art of predicting future price movements of STOCKS, SECURITIES or markets by looking at past price movements. Not to be confused with fundamental analysis, which is concerned with the financial position of a company and therefore the relative value of its SHARES. Technical analysis, also called CHARTISM, involves looking for recurring patterns in price movements (such as HEAD AND SHOULDERS), which provide clues as to whether the underlying demand for a STOCK may be about to change. Most technical ANALYSTS concentrate on the short to medium term but some believe that long-term patterns can also signal turning points in financial markets. When they do, such analysts issue "buy" or "sell" recommendations to their clients.

T

Technical rally

A surge in SHARE (or COMMODITY) prices for technical reasons. This may be because ANALYSTS have spotted, for example, that a certain market INDEX has reached a natural plateau. Or it may have something to do with the way the market itself operates; for example, some markets move errati-cally in the run-up to SETTLEMENT DATE. (See also WITCHING HOUR.)

Many of the core technologies of computing – processing power, storage capacity, graphics capabilities and network connectivity – are all continuing to advance at a pace that matches or even exceeds Moore's law (which famously, and correctly, predicted that the number of transistors on a computer chip would double every two years).
Bill Gates, *The World in 2003*

Technology, media and telecommunications

A STOCKMARKET SECTOR which enjoyed the biggest rise during the dotcom boom that began in the late 1990s and suf-fered the brunt of the bust that followed. In the belief that de-veloped economies had entered a new paradigm, in which technology would propel productivity for evermore, investors pushed up the prices of technology, media and telecommunica-tions (TMT) STOCKS to unsustainable levels. This led to huge amounts of overinvestment as companies rushed to satisfy a seemingly insatiable demand for new technology. Easy to say in retrospect, but of course it could not last. Demand outstripped supply, PROFITS wilted and share prices crumbled. Many TMT companies are still living with the consequences of the huge amounts of DEBT they built up during the boom years.

When your business depends on technology – whether it's aerospace, computer and electronics firms in the 1960s or internet, telecom and networking companies in the 1990s – volatility is a fact of life.
Michael Milken

T

Tender offer

A method of selling SECURITIES developed by the UK govern-ment and now used all over the world. The seller sets a price (the tender price) at which it is prepared to sell the securities. Offers are invited, and the applicants state what price they are prepared to pay; nothing below the tender price is acceptable. Should not enough bids above the tender price be received, the offer lapses. The whole ISSUE can then be withdrawn.

Several European governments used the technique to great effect to sell licences to operate 3G (third-generation) mobile telephones. They raised billions from international companies. When the technology bubble burst, many of these companies wished they had paid less for the right to operate technology that may be slow to catch on.

Terminal bonus

An extra discretionary amount that may be paid by an INSURANCE company when a with-profits insurance policy expires, or when the policyholder dies. The holder of a with-profits policy is entitled to share in any surplus shown in a valuation of the relevant fund. These with-profits policies are supposed to help policyholders smooth out the ups and downs of the STOCKMARKET. In reality, insurance companies are often tempted to pay out too much during good times in order to attract new customers, only to find that there is too little in the kitty during bad times.

Term loan

A LOAN granted for a predetermined length of time, typically between two and ten years. A four-year loan is a term loan; an OVERDRAFT is not.

Thrift

An institution whose primary purpose is the encouragement of thrift. A general expression used in the United States to cover organisations such as SAVINGS AND LOAN ASSOCIATIONS and MUTUAL SAVINGS BANKS.

Tick

The smallest incremental movement in a SECURITY's price that a market will allow. It could, for example, be one BASIS POINT. Also used to describe a group of STOCKS whose last movement was up or down.

Time deposit

See DEPOSIT.

Tip sheet

A publication or internet site designed for private individual investors which gives advice on hot STOCKS. The more influential tip sheets can noticeably move share prices and sometimes even markets.

TMT

See TECHNOLOGY, MEDIA AND TELECOMMUNICATIONS.

Tokyo Stock Exchange

The main market for the buying and selling of Japanese SHARES. STOCKS and shares have a rather different role in Japan's financial affairs than they do in either the United States or parts of Europe. Companies are not so dependent on them for CAPITAL; their bankers have traditionally been a more important source of funds. And shareholders are not fed with generous DIVIDENDS; they have to rely for their reward on CAPITAL GAIN (of which there has been precious little during the past few years while the economy has been in recession, or close to it).

The Tokyo stock Exchange is divided into two sections: the

First Section and the Second Section. All major Japanese compa-nies are listed on the First Section. The requirements for compa-nies to obtain a LISTING on the First Section are more onerous than the requirements for the Second Section.

Tombstone

An advertisement placed in a financial newspaper or magazine to announce the completion of a SYNDICATED LOAN or a new ISSUE of SECURITIES. It is called a tombstone because it consists of little more than a list of names and numbers. The names are those of the borrower who pays for the tombstone and of the fi-nancial institutions which participated in the deal. They are ordered in strict seniority, the size of the typeface indicating their importance in the deal.

Tom/next

Short for tomorrow/next day, referring to the practice among FOREIGN-EXCHANGE traders of swapping currencies for short periods to maximise the holders' return on their money. For example, a trader may switch from the Australian dollar to the US dollar overnight and then buy back Australian dollars the following day in time to settle an earlier transaction. (See also SWAP.)

Tontine

See ANNUITY.

T

Total return

A measure of investment return that calculates not just any CAPITAL GAIN (or loss) but the income or DIVIDEND YIELD too. Suppose an investor bought $10,000 of stock and sold it for

$12,500 and in the meantime had received dividends worth $150. The total return would therefore be $12,650 ($12,500 + $150). Notional returns of this kind are widely used in the SWAPS and FUTURES markets, particularly where investors are trying to HEDGE their RISK or balance their RETURN from another investment. (See next entry.)

Total return swap

A SWAP in which one side of the transaction is based on the TOTAL RETURN of an EQUITY or FIXED-INCOME SECURITY with a life longer than the swap itself. Total return swaps are most common in equity or COMMODITY markets, but they are also used in fixed-income markets if one of the counterparties to the deal is subject to WITHHOLDING TAX. This can sometimes be avoided if the domestic investor pays the foreign one by way of a total return swap.

Tracker fund

A UNIT TRUST (or MUTUAL FUND) that mirrors a particular market or STOCKMARKET SECTOR, usually as measured by an INDEX or other BENCHMARK. To do this, the fund has to buy the SECURITIES that make up the index, purchasing others from time to time as they are promoted to the index and selling others as they drop out of it. Many investors like to be invested in the stockmarket but have little faith in a professional manager's (or their own) ability to beat it over the long run. So they invest in tracker funds. An advantage of tracker funds is that it is cheaper to own units in them than in a fund whose manager is trying to beat the market.

Tracking stock

A class of SHARE that pays a DIVIDEND based on the perform-ance of a particular division or subsidiary of a larger company;

also sometimes known as targeted stock or letter stock (because they often carry the name of the parent company, for example, General Motors H). A tracking stock is usually issued by a large conglomerate when it feels that the value of a small offspring is not being fully appreciated by the market. The offspring may be a high-tech subsidiary in a different but complementary business. Shareholders of most tracking stocks have little or no claim to the ASSETS of the parent company, should it be liquidated or wound up.

Tranche

Part of a LOAN doled out by the lender bit by bit to the borrower. Tranche most commonly refers to the chunks in which the INTERNATIONAL MONETARY FUND hands out its loans to member countries. Release of an IMF tranche usually depends on a borrower making pre-ordained changes to its economy.

Transferable credit

A trade credit in which an importer opens a LETTER OF CREDIT in favour of an AGENT (or middleman) who then has it transferred to the exporter. This allows the agent to be the importer without putting up the CAPITAL necessary to fund the deal. It also enables the agent to keep the identities of the importer and exporter hidden from each other.

T

Transfer agent

A body which transfers SECURITIES from one owner to another on behalf of the company that has issued them. In the United States, a transfer agent also keeps a record of a company's shareholders.

Traveller's cheque

A clever method of payment for travellers invented towards the end of the 19th century. It relies on a double signature for security: the owner signs once when he or she buys the CHEQUE at home, and again when it is cashed abroad. The recipient only has to check that the signatures match. The traveller's cheque has also proved useful in countries that have a poor banking system (as in parts of Africa, for example), or that are too large to have a single, nationwide payments system (like the United States).

The issuers of traveller's cheques make a small charge per cheque for their services. Most of the benefit to the issuer, however, comes from the fact that cheques are often bought and held for some months before they are cashed. During that time the issuer has the use of the chequeholder's money, at no extra cost.

Treasury bill

A SHORT-TERM DEBT instrument issued by a government, usually with a MATURITY of three months but sometimes for up to two years. Treasury bills are traditionally sold at a DISCOUNT to their face value, and their YIELD is a leading indicator of INTEREST-rate trends. In the UK, BANKS are the biggest holders of Treasury bills. In the United States, Treasury bills are more widely held. Because of their safety, LIQUIDITY and the fact that there is an active SECONDARY MARKET in them, Treasury bills are popular with corporate treasurers as well as banks and other government agencies. The FEDERAL RESERVE buys and sells Treasury bills to help it shape MONETARY POLICY. OPTIONS and FUTURES on Treasury bills are also actively traded.

Triple witching hour

The time when the expiry dates of three types of US FINANCIAL INSTRUMENTS coincide:

◪ STOCK INDEX FUTURES;
◪ OPTIONS on these contracts;
◪ options on individual stocks in the index.

Such simultaneity can, and has, moved markets, sometimes dramatically. To relieve the pressure on the financial system, exchanges that trade in DERIVATIVES have spread the time when the contracts expire. Instead of all coming to an end at the same hour on the same day, some now change at the beginning of the trading session and some at the end. (See also WITCHING HOUR.)

Trust

There are two main meanings.

1 A combination of companies that act to create a MONOPOLY in restraint of competition and free trade. The practice was outlawed at the beginning of the 20th century, hence the term trust busters. Starting with the Sherman Anti-Trust Act of 1890, the US Congress has taken repeated steps since then to stamp out monopolies, price fixing and other forms of restraint of trade. Other countries have largely taken their lead from the United States.
2 A fiduciary relationship in which somebody called a TRUSTEE holds title to ASSETS for the benefit of another person, called the beneficiary.

T

Trustee

A person who is entrusted with property belonging to somebody else. The purest form of trustee, one who has absolutely no beneficial interest in the property, is called a naked trustee. A trustee can act in many different roles:

◪ as the person charged with disposing of a dead person's property according to a will;

- as the person charged with looking after the interests of a minor until he or she comes of age, or an adult;
- as the person charged with looking after money donated to a charity;
- even, as in the case of *The Economist*, a person charged with looking after the editorial integrity and independence of a newspaper or magazine.

Turn

The difference between the cost of funds to a financial institution and the RETURN it can get from using those funds. For a BANK, this is the difference between the average RATE OF INTEREST on its DEPOSITS and the average rate of interest on its LOANS.

Two-way market

A market which is as free for buyers as it is for sellers. With SECURITIES, a two-way market is one in which brokers are as willing to sell a security at its quoted selling price as they are to buy it at its quoted buying price.

UCITS

Short for Undertakings for Collective Investments in Transferable Securities, Euro-speak for MUTUAL FUNDS. The European Commission passed a special law authorising the sale of UCITS through the European Union, believing that it is the product most likely to become pan-European.

Underweight

The degree to which a FUND MANAGER may hold fewer SHARES in its fund than that STOCK'S WEIGHTING in a particular INDEX or other BENCHMARK; the opposite of OVERWEIGHT. A manager may also be underweight (or overweight) in a particular sector, market or type of SECURITY. The fund manager may have decided to remain underweight on investment grounds or may sometimes be unable for some reason to buy enough stock to bring the fund up to its weighting.

Underwriter

Most commonly, an institution that commits itself (usually as part of a group or SYNDICATE of other institutions), for a fee, to buying up the whole of a new ISSUE of SECURITIES to the public. The difference between the price that the underwriters pay for the issue and the price at which they sell it to the public is their PROFIT, known as the underwriting SPREAD. If the public spurns the issue (or the market moves against it), then the underwriters are stuck with the issue and may make a big loss unless they can subsequently sell it.

The term has its origin in the 17th century when underwriters wrote their names at the bottom of INSURANCE policies, thus guaranteeing to provide COVER according to the terms of the policy. LLOYD'S insurance market still works with a similar system of underwriters, who accept RISK on behalf of syndicates.

Unfunded

Something for which no money has been expressly set aside. An unfunded PENSION plan is therefore one that is funded out of current income as and when funds are needed by retired people or other beneficiaries. Most German companies have unfunded pension schemes, simply providing for the cost of a pension each year as it is incurred.

Unitary tax

A system of taxing institutions based on a calculation of the proportion of the company's business that is done in the tax authority's jurisdiction rather than on the (more normal) basis of the PROFIT earned in the jurisdiction. The most notable proponent of unitary tax is California.

Unit trust

The name for a MUTUAL FUND in the UK and in a number of other English-speaking countries.

Universal bank

A bank that is able to carry out almost any type of financial business, from underwriting an ISSUE of SECURITIES to straight lending and DEPOSIT-taking. Universal banks have historically been strong in Switzerland and Germany, but banks in most countries are becoming more and more universal.

Unsecured

Without SECURITY against a borrower's ASSETS. Such lenders have to wait until all secured creditors have been paid before they can get anything back from a debtor's LIQUIDATION.

Use of funds

An accounting statement of the flow of funds in and out of a company during the year. In some countries such statements are legally required; in others they are voluntary. (See also SOURCES OF FUNDS.)

Usury

The charging of an exorbitant RATE OF INTEREST. Nowadays all developed countries have laws to protect borrowers from usury.

- Most US states have laws limiting the amount of interest that borrowers can be charged. The limits vary according to the type of lender and the type of LOAN. Some federal laws allow the limits to be broken under special circumstances.
- In the UK anti-usury laws can be traced back to King Henry VII. At one stage in the 19th century anything over 48% prima facie was considered to be usurious.
- In continental Europe, the concept is also embodied in law.

(See also ZAKAT.)

Value added

The amount by which the value of something is increased by a specific process or service. Commonly used as the yardstick to justify a new business activity, as in "Where's the value added?".

Value-added tax

A form of consumption tax much favoured by countries in the European Union. With few exceptions, in countries where it is applied the tax is levied on a product or service at each stage of its manufacture. Opponents claim that value-added tax (VAT) is regressive and is levied on those least able to pay it. Proponents argue the opposite: that sales taxes are fairest because they are aimed at those who actually use the product or service.

Value at risk

A method of establishing the RISK to which an investment PORTFOLIO may be exposed from day to day and thus of avoiding unnecessary losses. The huge losses suffered from trading in DERIVATIVES by Barings, Orange County and others in recent years have encouraged the search for systems that will warn of impending disaster. Some methods aim to quantify risk by measuring the standard deviation of a portfolio's return; others use a sampling technique based on history. None, so far at least, has proved itself foolproof.

Value date

The date on which a transaction in the FOREIGN-EXCHANGE market is settled. For deals done in dollars, it is usually one business day after the CONTRACT matures; for most other currencies it is two business days.

Value investing

An approach to investing best summed up by Benjamin Graham, a veteran American investor, who urged others to seek a "Margin of Safety"; the opposite of GROWTH INVESTING. Value investors ferret out the STOCKS of companies (that is, VALUE STOCKS) which have solid businesses and BALANCE SHEETS but which, for one reason or another, are out of favour with the market. Such investors aim to buy low and sell high. Their techniques vary. Warren Buffett, one of the most successful investors of all time, values companies on the basis of the present value of their future CASH FLOWS. Others look for companies whose PRICE/EARNINGS RATIOS are below the average for the market as a whole. Most take a long-term view of investment. A UNIT TRUST or a MUTUAL FUND that uses such an approach is called a value fund.

Value stock

A SHARE in a company whose price appears cheap compared with the value of its ASSETS or the size of its EARNINGS and with the averages for the STOCKMARKET as a whole. Value stocks are often in mature or low-growth industries that have fallen out of favour with investors. The DIVIDENDS they pay are high in relation to their share prices, giving their shares a high YIELD but low PRICE/EARNINGS RATIO. A value fund, therefore, is a UNIT TRUST (MUTUAL FUND) which seeks out such shares in the hope that they will eventually rise in value.

Variable rate

A RATE OF INTEREST that varies in line with some BENCHMARK. (See also FLOATING RATE.)

V

Venture capital

See PRIVATE EQUITY.

Virtual enterprise

An enterprise that is hard to kick, one with few tangible ASSETS. A company that transacts most of its business electronically and which subcontracts (see OUTSOURCING) almost anything that requires the use of fixed assets. The virtual company creates the semblance of a huge enterprise yet has control over few resources. Although this helps to keep costs down, it does not necessarily lead to PROFITS. The most successful virtual enterprises are those whose chief assets are their intellectual property (for example, a designer of semiconductor chips).

Volatility

Large and frequent fluctuations in the price of a SECURITY, COMMODITY, average or INDEX, sometimes caused by a thin or narrow market or a lack of LIQUIDITY. One way to measure volatility is to study something called a BETA coefficient. This shows how volatile a FINANCIAL INSTRUMENT is compared with its respective baseline – for example, the S&P 500 STOCK INDEX. The index itself has a beta coefficient of one, so anything greater than that is more volatile than the market as a whole.

Wall Street Journal

The most successful US business newspaper; a daily that is owned by the Dow Jones Company, which also gave its name to the main INDEX of the NEW YORK STOCK EXCHANGE. The *Wall Street Journal* is one of the few US newspapers to be truly national. In recent years, it has also spread its wings internationally, launching the *Asian Wall Street Journal* and the *Wall Street Journal Europe*. Like most of its competitors, it also offers readers an online service.

Warehousing

Disguising the purchase of SHARES in a company by using NOMINEES to buy them. The purpose may be to enable the nominees to act in concert and make a surprise TAKEOVER bid for the company. Many countries try to reduce the chances of this happening by regulating the behaviour of CONCERT PARTIES and by insisting that all shareholdings above a certain limit (often 5%) are made public. (See also HOSTILE BID.)

Warrant

A certificate authorising the holder to buy a specified number of SHARES in a company at a named price and within a specified period of time. This is similar to shares issued as part of a RIGHTS ISSUE, except that the period of time in which a warrant can be exercised is much longer. A warrant is also a written instruction that makes legal a payment that would otherwise be illegal.

Weighting

The multiplication of an average by factors that affect it in order to take account of their importance. Thus investors talk of a bond's weighted average term to MATURITY as a measure of its remaining life. The term also refers to the proportion of a SE-CURITY or ASSET that an investment fund may hold in relation to the BENCHMARK against which its performance is measured. So, for example, a fund specialising in Asian markets might be OVERWEIGHT in Thailand if it held a greater share of securities listed in that market than the MSCI index it was using as a benchmark. (See also UNDERWEIGHT.)

White knight

An investor who appears out of the blue to rescue a company that is about to fall into the hands of a hostile suitor. In practice, white knights rarely charge out of the blue and never without an incentive. They are usually persuaded by a company that is subject to a hostile bid (or its INVESTMENT BANK) to come to its rescue.

Window dressing

The process of dressing up a company's accounts to make them look as attractive as possible. (See BALANCE SHEET and PROFIT-AND-LOSS ACCOUNT.) By sleight of hand and prac-tised eye, accountants can enhance accounts by concealing and revealing, just as in a shop window. It also refers to the practice among FUND MANAGERS and professional investors of dress-ing up their figures at the end of the year to show them to best advantage. This can boost STOCKMARKET turnover at certain times of the year.

Witching hour

W   The time when an event occurs that affects the whole of a SE-CURITIES market; for example, the last hour before a widely traded stock INDEX OPTION expires. Such events can cause considerable VOLATILITY in market prices, exacerbated by traders who try to anticipate the witching hour by hedging against it. (See also TRIPLE WITCHING HOUR.)

Withholding tax

A tax that is withheld at source; that is, before the taxpayer has touched the income or CAPITAL to which the tax applies. Withholding taxes are often imposed on BOND INTEREST and DIVIDENDS, and sometimes on BANK interest too. They are attractive to governments because they reduce the potential for tax evasion. A DOUBLE-TAXATION AGREEMENT between countries usually goes to some lengths to ensure that taxpayers are not charged twice on income for which the tax has been withheld.

With recourse

A BANK that discounts a BILL OF EXCHANGE for a customer may do so with recourse; that is, the bank retains the right to claim the amount for the bill from the customer if it is not honoured at MATURITY.

Working capital

What is left over from a company's paid-up CAPITAL and RESERVES after all its fixed ASSETS have been paid for; that is, what is left for the day-to-day running of the business. Working capital bridges the gap between the time when a company decides to produce a product or a service, and the time that payment is received for the first sale.

Workout loans

An umbrella term for LOANS made by a financial institution which are not being repaid strictly to the terms of their CONTRACT. Workout loans include NON-PERFORMING LOANS, which give rise to certain regulatory requirements. They also include loans which are overdue (or are not being repaid strictly according to the terms of the contract) but are still considered to be current (that is, not non-performing).

W

World Bank

The common name for the International Bank for Reconstruction and Development (IBRD), a sibling of the INTERNATIONAL MONETARY FUND. It has its headquarters across the street from the IMF, on Washington's H Street. The World Bank was established in 1944 as part of the BRETTON WOODS AGREEMENT to help countries rebuild their economies after the second world war. It provides long-term loans (usually for 15–20 years) to governments and government organisations. To fund its lending, the bank borrows in the international CAPITAL MARKETS.

The World Bank itself has two specialist siblings: the International Development Association (IDA) and the International Finance Corporation (IFC).

Writer

A person who issues an OPTION, who at the end of the day has to buy or sell (depending on whether it is a PUT OPTION or a CALL OPTION) the ASSET on which the option is written, should the person who holds the option wish to exercise it.

Xetra

An international platform for trading in EQUITIES and WAR-RANTS. Set up by the Deutsche Börse, it covers SECURITIES quoted on the Frankfurt Stock Exchange. A boon for investors is that they can continue to trade in securities on Xetra after Wall Street has opened for business in the morning.

Yankee bond

A BOND issued in the US CAPITAL MARKETS by a non-US borrower.

Yearling

A one-year BOND issued by a local authority in the UK.

Yellow sheet

A daily list published in the United States by the National Association of Securities Dealers that is to BONDS what the PINK SHEET is to STOCKS: a list of prices and of firms that are in the market for OVER-THE-COUNTER CORPORATE BONDS.

Yield

The annual income in DIVIDENDS or INTEREST from a SECURITY, expressed as a percentage of the market price of the security. Thus a BOND with a face value of $100, a COUPON of 10% and a market price of $50, has a yield of 20%.

- EARNINGS yield is the RATE OF RETURN to shareholders if all their company's earnings are distributed as dividends.
- The yield gap is the difference between the yield on a reputable INDEX of EQUITIES and the yield on bonds, as measured by a standard gilt-edged government bond. This is usually positive since equities are riskier than bonds (and therefore higher-yielding). On occasions, however, the yield on bonds is higher than that on equities, and there is then said to be a reverse yield gap.

(See also INVERSE YIELD CURVE and REDEMPTION YIELD.)

Yield curve

The shape of a graph plotted to show the structure of INTEREST rates. Since the rate for long-term FINANCIAL INSTRUMENTS is higher than for SHORT-TERM ones, the curve usually slopes upwards from the bottom left-hand corner to the top right-hand corner (assuming that rates are on the vertical axis and MATURITY is on the horizontal axis). However, in circumstances where the market expects that a currently high rate of INFLATION will soon fall rapidly, the curve can slope the other way. (See INVERSE YIELD CURVE.)

Yield to maturity

The same as REDEMPTION YIELD, the yield that takes into account the PREMIUM or DISCOUNT in the purchase price of a FIXED-INTEREST SECURITY.

Zakat

The practice among Muslims of making an annual donation to charity or to the community at large. The word *zakat* literally means "purification" and "growth". Donors are allowed to deduct expenses and what they owe in taxes. They may also set aside the equivalent of 85g of GOLD; on the remaining balance they are obliged to pay a levy equal to at least 2.5% of their wealth.

Zero-coupon bond

A SECURITY bought and sold in the SECONDARY MARKET at a deep DISCOUNT to its face value because it carries no COUPON; that is, it pays no INTEREST to the bondholder. Purchasers get their PROFIT from the gradual increase in the market price as the price closes the gap with the bond's face value, that is, the amount repayable when it reaches MATURITY.

Zero-coupon preference share

A SHARE issued in the UK by a split-CAPITAL INVESTMENT TRUST (CLOSED-END FUND) and carrying no DIVIDEND. As with ZERO-COUPON BONDS, the shares are usually issued at a DISCOUNT and appreciate in value as they reach MATURITY. Zeroes rank higher than ORDINARY SHARES and are entitled to a certain proportion of the trust's accumulated capital when it is wound up. For this reason, they are often used by investors who know when they will need the money (for example, when a child goes to university or when the holder retires).